RIGHT
ON THE
MONEY

RIGHT ON THE MONEY

Taking Control of Your Personal Finances

Chris Farrell

VILLARD
NEW YORK

VILLARD BOOKS is a registered trademark of
Random House, Inc. Colophon is a trademark of
Random House, Inc.

Library of Congress Cataloging-in-Publication Data
Farrell, Chris.
Right on the money: taking control of your personal finances/
Chris Farrell.
p.   cm.
Includes bibliographical references.
ISBN 0-375-50369-2 (acid-free paper)
1. Finance, Personal.   I. Title.

HG179 .F365   2000
332.024—dc21   00-35910

Villard Books website address: www.villard.com
Printed in the United States of America on acid-free paper
24689753
First Edition

To Maria, Peter, and Connor

ACKNOWLEDGMENTS

Television is a collaborative enterprise. While putting together this book, I was struck by how many people contributed their talents, ideas, and insights to create each episode of *Right on the Money*. I'd like to thank the families and individuals who invited us into their homes and talked openly about their personal finance issues; the experts who shared their knowledge and commonsense solutions; and the television professionals who pulled it all together into compelling stories and useful information.

However, I'd like to single out several individuals because their contributions are so vital to the show's success. *Right on the Money* wouldn't exist without Gerry Richman, who is technically our executive in charge but in reality our maestro. Executive producer Joe Garbarino is the show's tireless advocate, and executive producer Catherine Allan keeps our standards high. It's a pleasure to work with videographer Robert Hutchings, a true artist, and audio man Bernie Beaudry, a genuine professional. I don't know how they manage to pull together episodes week after week, but I've been lucky to collaborate with and learn from such creative individuals as producers Jim Leinfelder, Leslie Grisanti, and Nancy Esslinger, as well as freelance producers Laurie Stern, Barbara Weiner, and Julie Johnson. The series has also benefited from the talents of associate producers Rebecca Richards and Maggie Tacheny, production coordinator Natasha Chuk, production assistants Chris Coley and Erin Halden, and production managers Karen Arnold and Vic Miller. Offline editor Kay Dimarco makes us all look good. Val Mondor and Mitch Griffin have polished our look and sound in postproduction. The late Bradley Chamberlin got it all started.

A special thanks and debt of gratitude to series producer Margaret Brower. For the past two years, she has been the creative force driving the enterprise forward. She's handled a difficult task with intelligence, warmth, and humor.

In recent years, I've come to rely on the knowledge of certain individuals expert in personal finance, and I'd like to thank Ruth Hayden, Ross Levin, Ed Slott, Eric Tyson, Paula Kennedy, Julie Garton-Good, and Robin Leonard. ReliaStar underwrites *Right on the Money*, and its support has been terrific.

Of course, this is a book, and it came into existence only because of the superb efforts of my agent Jonathan Lazear. Dennis Cass is an astute editor who managed to bolster my spirits with his wry humor. His high expectations pushed me to write a better book. Bruce Tracy, my editor at Villard, made sure this book happened.

Over my past two decades in journalism, I've worked with many wonderful people, especially my colleagues at *Business Week*. I'd particularly like to thank Bill Wolman, Seymour Zucker, Michael Mandel, Karen Pennar, and Robert Barker for their friendship, their passion for ideas, and everything they have taught me. At Minnesota Public Radio, *Sound Money* producer Karen Tofte is both a colleague and a friend. Stephen Smith and Bill Buzenberg are two colleagues who demand a lot—and give more.

And, finally, to Maria, my friend and soul mate, and to Peter and Connor, my children and love, I owe too much to put into words. All I can say is that I should be around a lot more now that the book is done.

CONTENTS

INTRODUCTION

The *Right on the Money* staff gathers every Friday for an editorial meeting. We talk about what we've done so far, exchange ideas about the programs we're currently creating, and discuss possible personal finance topics for future shows. These meetings are lively. We all draw on our own money experiences and issues, as well as viewer e-mails, economic trends, and the news. Conversations similar to the ones we have about saving for retirement, getting rid of credit card debt, paying off student loans, investing in the stock market, and all the other pressing money issues of today are going on at the workplace and in homes all around the country.

I broke into finance and economics journalism two decades ago, and since then I've witnessed a remarkable transformation in how money is dealt with in American society. Personal finance has evolved from being a tributary of our culture to being an everyday mainstream concern. Managing money is a growing worry for good reason. Our anxiety is the result of the financial upheavals caused by soaring inflation in the 1970s, the extensive layoffs of the 1980s, and the spread of self-directed retirement savings plans in the 1990s. Many of the things we associate with the good life, such as a home, a college education, and a decent standard of living in our old age, have become increasingly costly. What's more, we've moved at a quicksilver pace from a limited world of passbook savings accounts, 30-year mortgages, and whole-life policies to a cosmos of almost infinite financial choice. And the rapid growth of the Internet suggests you ain't seen nothing yet when it comes to financial innovation.

Still, the democratization of finance is an extraordinary force that has been mostly for the good, as finance for the elite turns into finance for the masses. But better money choices come with a steep price. It sometimes seems that managing our hard-earned dollars threatens to become a full-time occupation. We worry about the choices we're making, and it's clear that many people are unsure about their decisions. How much of my retirement portfolio should go into stocks? Should I invest in technology stocks? Why do I keep slipping back into credit card debt? How will I ever afford to send my kids to college, save for my retirement, and still pay my monthly bills and daily expenses?

Right on the Money is designed to bring order to the confusion. We keep things simple. Our guiding idea is that you can manage your money and control your financial risks intelligently with good information, a thoughtful focus on your values and goals, and a commonsense appreciation of economic trade-offs. And we believe that that approach leaves you the time to do the things that matter much more than deciding whether to buy a growth or value equity mutual fund.

Every episode of *Right on the Money* starts with a family or an individual confronting a personal finance problem. Their stories are both intensely personal and very typical. We take their questions to several leading financial experts for their knowledge and insight. Then we give the family the expert advice and return for a follow-up interview. For me, this is the best part of the show. I get to sit down with the family and find out what they learned, what information works for them, and, sometimes, what advice doesn't. After all, the experts may tell them which ten things they should do, but guests' individual lifestyles, values, and competing demands on available time may dictate that only three of those ten remedies make sense. It's their choice. Their decision. And that's how it should be.

Just like our guests, you can benefit from the *Right on the Money* approach through this book. We deal with a number of different money topics, but underlying them all are some common principles. You're every bit as smart as the money elite and you know your circumstances better than any Wall Street mandarin. So take control of your finances. That's what the *Right on the Money* television show and this book are all about.

RIGHT ON THE MONEY

1

Personal Finance 101

Money is better than poverty, if only for financial reasons.
—Woody Allen

If you've opened this book, you're probably concerned about your finances. Maybe you're carrying credit card debt, worrying about paying for your children's college education, or wondering whether you're investing wisely in your retirement savings plan at work. I'm also betting that you're feeling a bit overwhelmed about your cash flow and expenses. Maybe the word "chaos" rather than "control" best describes your finances.

Little wonder, too: Managing our finances is daunting at times, and all of us make money mistakes. Many of us share deep insecurities about our ability to handle our finances. When we were growing up, the money and job issues that occupied our parents were distant and somewhat mysterious, late-night conversations for adults only. Schools didn't teach financial literacy, and they still largely ignore the subject today. The cash we earned at teenage jobs was quickly spent on high-tech gadgets and movies in most cases; sometimes we put it into a savings account for a bigger purchase such as a first car or maybe for college. But investing in the stock market, saving for retirement, handling credit cards, balancing a checkbook, comparing insurance policies, and other staples of personal finance today? They weren't on my radar screen, and probably not on yours, either.

The first time many of us start dealing with finance is when we get an employee benefits form at our first job and turn for help to our older coworkers. Do I need life insurance? Should I pay for disability coverage? How do I invest in the retirement savings plan? Take Danielle Grimes. She works as a page-one layout artist for the *Saint Paul Pioneer Press,* a major daily newspaper in Minnesota. Her job is creative and demanding, with tight deadlines, hordes of impatient editors, and late nights. The pressure is intense, but Danielle, a smart, savvy 30-year-old, clearly loves what she's doing. And like a lot of busy people, Danielle has little time for or background in finance. I met with Danielle one morning for *Right on the Money* to look at her investment portfolio, which was mostly in tax-deferred retirement savings plans. She had invested everything in the stock market.

"You really like the stock market?" I asked Danielle.

"I guess so, apparently," she said. "But I don't know. I mean, I have no idea if what I'm doing is right. I didn't even know the money was in equities. I don't know these things. I'm not a financial whiz."

"Why did you put everything into equities?"

"I don't know how that happened," she said.

"You just had to make a choice?"

"Right. Exactly."

Now, it turns out that Danielle had created a good long-term portfolio, and at most she needed to make a few minor changes to add some diversification to her investment strategy. But her investing acumen was mostly happenstance, the equivalent of choosing equities by throwing darts from across the room at a newspaper's stock tables. We often don't realize just how ignorant we are about money until we suddenly have financial responsibilities for others, such as taking care of aging parents, finding a life partner, and, above all, raising children. Suddenly, our family, our peers, our neighbors, and our society expect us to be smart and in control when it comes to our finances, and, no surprise, we often don't feel up to the task.

What's more, the personal finance industry, from Wall Street behemoths to independent planners, is masterful at manipulating our insecurities when it comes to our saving and spending decisions. On the one hand, it seems that we are assailed almost daily with commentary about how spendthrift Americans aren't saving enough money, especially the profligate baby-boom generation. Brokers, mutual fund marketers, and financial planners love to trot out figures documenting the nation's anemic savings rate and to highlight doleful studies showing that people are saving a fraction of what they need to maintain their current living standard during their twilight years. The visions grow darker with the foreboding jeremiads issued by modern-day Calvinists. Their stern and unforgiving message combines the admonition "It's your own fault you're not rich" with Franklin's hoary "A penny saved is a penny earned." Taken altogether, personal finance is truly serious stuff. You'd better turn your money over to the professionals now—and even then, it may be too late.

On the other hand, there are the get-rich-quick schemes of the feel-good peddlers. A classic example is the infomercial on television promoting a no-money-down real estate deal or some other surefire, no-risk big-money opportunity. Many people still fall for the lies told by shady boiler-room operators making dinnertime cold calls. "Have I got a stock for you! It's called cybertreesgrowtothesky.com. No one else knows about it—I'm telling you first—but this company is making a fortune. Got to get in early. Research? Don't have time for research. So shall I put you down for five thousand shares?" How about the giant marketing campaigns by mutual fund companies bragging about their market-beating performance and the online trading firms with their alluring pitch that a fortune is only a click away? You too can become a millionaire (billionaire?) by investing in a hot mutual fund or trading on the Internet. We know it's hype, but the lure of a quick buck taps into a deep strand of the American psyche, from the schemes of the hustler Rizzo in *Midnight Cowboy* to the humorous moneymaking designs of Fred Flintstone. It's like playing the lottery at your neighborhood deli. You know the odds of winning are millions to one—or worse—but when the reward hits the stratosphere you cross your fingers, stand in line, and make your bet.

Okay, what are you supposed to do? Let's face it: Managing money isn't enjoyable for most people. Eating out with friends, browsing through a bookstore, watching your child ride a bike for the first time, getting a promotion at work—all these things are fun. But going over a prospectus, comparing insurance policies, filling out employee benefit forms, and paying down credit card bills isn't fun. Yet for most people, personal finance isn't all that difficult, and you can do surprisingly well on your own. As you'll see, mostly all you need is some commonsense insight into your particular circumstances and an understanding of money basics to figure out the financial side of your everyday life. What's more, our financial task is easier than ever because over the past half century, finance economists have revolutionized our understanding of money and finance, and their approach and insights are tailor-made for individual finances. With a little thought, education, and discipline you'll steer clear of both the doom-and-gloom crowd and the siren song of the get-rich-quick promoters.

Full disclosure: *Right on the Money* is a guide to personal finance, but it won't make you rich or the life of the party regaling your peers with tales of your stock-picking savvy. I wouldn't know how to give such advice, and I wouldn't believe anyone who does give it. I'll never forget the time I was asked by a father with two babies to list for him 12 stocks with a guaranteed annual return of 18% over the next 18 years so he could afford their college tuition bill. I passed.

No, my goal is much more modest. When you are managing money, you are always trying to balance your home and work life with your savings and investment decisions. The intent of this book is to get you thinking, to encourage you to reflect about your values, and to offer some practical financial knowledge that will help you achieve your goals. This book should help you intelligently take control of your finances, without turning managing your money into a second job. I also include at the end of each chapter suggestions of books and web resources for further reading and research. My idea is not to swamp you with references—just to share some books I've learned from and web sites I enjoy using. One of my favorite quotes comes from *Enthusiasms,* by Bernard Levin, the British writer: "We are made and shaped by people, by events and experiences, by love and hate, by heredity, by what we eat and whether we hunger, by the things we understand, by pain and joy, by accident and design, by whatever it is that gives us a life and the duty to make what we can of it. But we are also shaped by what we read." You can manage your own finances better than any professional. You're every bit as smart, and the knowledge you need is readily available.

VALUES AND FINANCE

When it comes to personal finance, values come before budgets, before calculations, and before investment products. To be sure, personal finance ends with you managing your money well; but it begins with thinking about values and desires. Personal finance is putting money behind the question "What really matters to me?" For instance, exploring what you want to do during your retirement years is as important as funding a retirement savings plan. Do you want to consult part-time? Go back to school? Start your own business? Play golf? Personal finance is an evolving process, an ongoing dialogue about how you want to live your life. You have to establish priorities, and then fund those goals.

Just ask the hot-dog man. I was in downtown Boulder, Colorado, with a crew taping the closing lines for our show on starting your own business. The episode had been built around Robbie Oliver and Allene Ross, two Native Americans who ran Minneapolis-based At Your Finger Tips Office Supply, a fledgling virtual office supply company. While we were figuring out how to do the stand-up, a somewhat rakish, rather striking white-haired man selling hot dogs behind a cart caught our attention. Actually, he was impossible to miss, since he was yelling out in a driving cadence, "Hot dog, hot dog, hot dog, Pepsi, Pepsi, chips, chips," and greeting customers by name. He was doing a great business and clearly enjoying himself. He agreed to serve me a hot dog as part of my stand-up, which opened with the line "No matter what your small business aspirations— something as basic as your own hot-dog stand or something as innovative and high-concept as Allene and Robbie's virtual office supply company—start a small business because it's something you have a passion for and it's consistent with your values." I think it was when he was handing me my fourth or fifth hot dog (yes, it took me several takes) that he said, "You're right about passion and values, you know."

Turns out, Eddie Ermoian was born and raised in Chicago, about a one-mile walk from Wrigley Field, the Chicago Cubs' ballpark. His folks would let him go to day games by himself from about the time he was eight. "And there were two old hot-dog guys, one on the corner of Addison and Sheffield, and one on the corner of Wayland Avenue and Clark Street, which are the four corners that take care of Wrigley Field. And these guys were old Armenian guys, which is what my national heritage is,"

Eddie told me. "They were friends of my grandfather's, and they had the two hot-dog stands. And I'd go there and I'd get hot dogs all the time. I'd look at them, put that lower lip out. And they'd say, 'You want a hot dog?' I'd say, 'Yeah.' And they'd give me a hot dog. I'd run like hell to the other side. I'd do that three, four, five times a game. And I always, always wanted to have a hot-dog stand. My mother used to say when other kids wanted to be firemen or cowboys or policemen or whatever, I wanted to have a hot-dog stand."

He worked for Anheuser-Busch for about 40 years, and he owned a piece of a beer distributorship. At age 57, after retiring from the beer business, he took some of his savings, bought a hot-dog stand, and opened for business. "Everybody always has a hot-dog stand in the back of their mind," he says. And he loves what he does.

Peter Brown told me this story when we were chatting after a *Right on the Money* interview for an episode on living the life of a freelancer without subsisting on a diet of noodles three nights a week. He is an independent business consultant based in St. Paul, Minnesota. Thoughtful and soft-spoken, Peter has helped many individuals navigate the treacherous transition from employee to entrepreneur, from the corporate job track to selling know-how on their own. He and his wife went to the Grand Canyon for a vacation when they were in their mid-40s. One evening while gazing over the magnificent gorge, they talked about what they would like to do before they got too old. It's not unusual to have a conversation like that, especially on vacation, away from our everyday pressures, looking out over a vista or an ocean, or perhaps staring into the flames of a camp-fire. Peter and his wife hit upon living in the Tuscany region of Italy. What is unusual is that after some five years of planning, Peter and his wife did rent a villa in Tuscany for a year.

Personal finance starts with thinking about how you want to live your life. This approach informs every *Right on the Money* show, and it is an idea that is reinforced every time I delve deeply into a family's or individual's money issues, or question the experts about a possible range of solutions. It's also been my experience that I'm often discussing values as well as the financial basics during years of answering listener questions on *Sound Money*, a nationally syndicated one-hour weekly personal finance program on public radio I cohost. I've also found that as you home in on values and goals, the money questions become clearer and the answers easier to research. For instance, it's important to both my wife and me that our children be free to attend the college of their choice, and that's one reason we are saving. Of course, that opens up all the questions about what's the best way to invest the money for a goal like college— but at least we know what we are doing, why we are doing it, and the amount of time we have to work with.

A dialogue over what constitutes a good life for you and your family leads toward the savings, investing, and life insurance regime to maintain that standard of living. Each feeds off of, and depends on, the other. What matters to you is not an easy question to answer, and the answers will change over time. Your core values may remain the same, but the dreams of a 20-something single will differ from the desires of a 40-something parent or a 60-something employee about to say good-bye to her workmates for the last time. And on the finance side of the equation, economic theory suggests that households try to maintain a certain quality of life, a constant standard of living throughout their life. That's why young people typically borrow lots of money to buy a house and a car when they start out their work lives, middle-aged folks with higher incomes and more goods tend to save and invest more, and the elderly tap into savings to make up for lost income after they retire.

By the way, don't fall into the trap of trying to keep up with the Joneses and the Smiths. A lot of spending mistakes can be traced back to a yearning for more—or at least for what our neighbors and peers own. I think all of us at some point have the suspicion that everyone we know is doing better than we are. Other people own bigger houses, nicer furniture, and newer cars. They started investing in their 401(k) years before we even thought of saving for retirement, and they can tell fascinating stories about the dot-com stock they bought that tripled in value in less than a week. But the investments that went bad are conveniently ignored. It's easy to write and not always easy to do, but you will be way ahead in the finance game if you stick with your values and goals and don't try to match the Joneses and the Smiths.

Of course, it's tough to think about values as we get caught up in the blur of work and home life. After a hard day at work, then making dinner and cleaning up, then going over homework with the kids, few people are eager to discuss the meaning of life. I know I'm not. It's hard enough to take the dog out for a walk during a Minnesota ice-age winter. Time is a precious commodity, and all of us feel we don't have enough of it. Still, try to work your questions and issues into the fabric of the conversations you have with your partner, family, or friends. This is a dialogue, not a onetime summit meeting or New Year's resolution. While flights of fancy are always fun and dreams of the good life worth striving for, keep your discussion of goals in the realm of reason. I'd love to play basketball like Michael Jordan or run like Maurice Green, the world's fastest human, but I'm never going to play in the NBA or run in the Olympics. If you think ahead, focus on what's important, and build financial planning into your everyday habits, you'll be better prepared to cope with the inevitable stresses and disappointments that will come your way.

Indeed, many of the financial decisions we make aren't voluntary. Instead, bad things happen to good people. On a minor note, it always seems that my aging car needs some expensive repairs just about the time the savings plan my wife and I have crafted is starting to work. On a much more serious level, people get laid off because of a corporate merger, or they are in low-paying jobs with few prospects. Divorce tears apart many families, and women especially end up suffering financially. Elderly parents fall ill, and they need emotional support and financial aid. Good personal finance habits won't eliminate the anxieties and traumas of life, but it will give you far greater control and room to maneuver when trouble strikes.

THE SIGNIFICANCE OF TRADE-OFFS

You can't avoid making trade-offs with your personal finances. For one thing, goals and values can conflict. It's hardly surprising—nor is it necessarily bad. Sir Isaiah Berlin, the late British philosopher, noted that justice is an absolute value for some people, but it is not always compatible with their other deeply held values, like mercy and compassion. Democratic societies are always debating the proper balance between liberty and equality. Many parents struggle between the wish to do their job well and the desire to spend more time with their children. "These collisions of value are of the essence of what they are and what we are," says Berlin.

For another, there is never enough money. Economists are fond of saying, "There is no free lunch." Mick Jagger of the Rolling Stones, a graduate of the London School of Economics, captured the same idea with his lyric "You can't always get what you want." So often what we call money troubles reflect an unwillingness to actively confront our trade-offs and establish some priorities. If ever there was a misleading expression it's the phrase "cold, hard cash." Personal finance is anything but cold and hard. Our finances are intimately tied to our emotions, our sense of self, and our place in society, and that's why our judgment is often clouded. The stakes are high.

For instance, many couples face a difficult trade-off when they start having children. Should one of them step off the career path and stay at home with the kids? If yes, whose career should be put on hold? What budget sacrifices will they need to make? Take the experience of Mike and Brenda Polis. Brenda had stopped working full-time to spend more time at home with their two daughters. Mike, an accountant, was now the family's sole breadwinner. It was a lifestyle choice both of them believed was best for their children. But money was tight, and the financial squeeze exposed a deep split when it came to managing the household finances. They had very different approaches to handling money. Mike was frugal and wanted to know where every penny went, while Brenda misplaced receipts and was much looser with money. At one point during the course of a long, frank conversation, I asked Brenda how she would like to change Mike's approach to money: "I guess it would be more *carpe diem,* seize the day, not to worry about money so much." I put the same question to Mike about Brenda. "Being more conscientious about our money and maybe being more frugal." You get the picture.

Mike and Brenda are different. Boy, are they different. Yet once you get past the obvious clash in their money management styles and focus on their shared values, their fundamental agreement over the importance of her staying home with the children at this stage of their family life is obvious. Once they recognized their shared value again, both Mike and Brenda started making some realistic compromises and creating priorities.

David and Gulgun Yanko, parents of four-and-a-half-year-old Korai and two four-month-old twin girls, Yahim and Ezmay, also dealt with a similar change in lifestyle. A delightful, literate couple with broad interests and compatible philosophies, the Yankos had decided that Gulgun would leave her job as a museum administrator. Although she would continue to direct at an experimental theater, she was essentially becoming a stay-at-home mom and they were going to live off David's salary as a computer specialist. "I fear for our standard of living," said

David. "We have a very solid financial situation currently, but we don't have a great track record of cutting back when we need to."

The pressures aren't only financial; there is a significant psychological element at work, too, especially for the stay-at-home spouse. Without a paycheck and a market-based identity, many stay-at-home moms and dads feel much less independent than before. But the choice is working for the Yankos. "I grew up seeing my mother at home and thinking, no, I'm going to be someone who has a career, who has another identity, because that is what I'm going to be enriched by," said Gulgun. "But being at home is incredibly enriching. And seeing it as a very positive choice, rather than a negative, which some people do, is important. We find that it is right for us, and after a lot of thought and discussion we figured out how we could make it work without really damaging our long-term goals for our personal achievement. And we have done so in such a way that we really feel comfortable that our kids are getting enough of us, and that we're getting enough of them."

When we talk and think about values, we may discover what we want. But then we are confronted with the question of how much risk we are willing to take to achieve our goals. There is no right or wrong answer. People are more comfortable with one set of risks over another. Some people recoil from the stock market's stomach-churning gyrations, while others are barely fazed by the market's vagaries. The idea of changing jobs paralyzes some, while many more eagerly seek out a new employer or even change careers. For instance, freelancing is a great example of something that is risky but can be rewarding. Two years ago, Danny Siepp quit a good job with a regular paycheck and benefits to pursue a love of photography. Like many fledgling freelancers', Danny Siepp's enthusiasm is infectious. "I found myself losing my creative spirit," he said. "I knew deep down in my heart that photography was what I would love to make my living at, what I would love to have my blood and sweat go to." He's struggling, however. His wife, Kathy, a teacher, also doubles as his assistant. Their apartment is his studio, too, and Danny uses the same tripod and 35-millimeter camera he picked up ten years ago. While we talked about money, everything stemmed from his deliberate choice, against the odds, to become a professional photographer.

RISK AND REWARD

As Danny had learned, one of the most important trade-offs in personal finance is between risk and return. The trade-off lies at the core of any financial decision. The only way to create an opportunity for your money to grow is to take greater financial risks. In essence, risk is the flip side of opportunity. No one should take on any more risk than he or she can stand. I've always liked this story for putting risk into perspective. J. P. Morgan ranked among the great financiers at the turn of the previous century. The tale goes that a man was in a panic after putting all his money into the stock market. He wanted to be rich, but if the stock market crashed he was financially ruined. He couldn't sleep. One day, seeing the imposing figure of J. P. Morgan walk down Wall Street, he summoned up his courage and asked Morgan, "Mr. Morgan, I've invested all my money in the stock market and I can't sleep. I'm a wreck. What should I do?" Morgan coldly replied, "Sell down to the sleeping point."

More recently, a colleague of mine put a few thousand dollars into a Pacific Rim emerging market mutual fund. It was in the early 1990s, and investing in emerging markets was hot. Just weeks later, his investment was worth several hundred dollars less. The plunge unnerved him. He got out of that investment fast, which was the right thing for him to do. Investing overseas might be a good idea in general or for the average person, but individuals aren't average. He couldn't take that kind of volatility. The critical question is, what risks will you embrace, which risks will you avoid, and which risks are inevitable? What is your sleeping point?

You can't hide from risk. It's a constant companion to all our decisions, from the big ones, such as getting married or getting a job, to the small ones, like picking out a bottle of wine or choosing a link to the Internet. We care about risk because it affects our choices, and thinking about risk helps us make better decisions. Parents are always struggling to balance the desire to keep their children secure and the necessity of letting them take the risks they need to grow. Should you allow your youngster to walk to a friend's house all by himself? Should you hand over the car keys to your daughter so she can go on a date?

Don't get me wrong. Risk is not bad. The U.S. economy has long relied on immigrants, mavericks, and risk takers to generate the innovations and new ways of doing business that drive the economy forward. These days, more and more young people, lured by the inspiring achievements of Bill Gates, Steve Jobs, Jim Clark, and other entrepreneurs, are eager to make their mark by starting their own business. "The word 'risk' derives from the early Italian *risicare,* which means 'to dare,' " writes Peter L. Bernstein in *Against the Gods: A History of Risk.* "In this sense, risk is a choice rather than a fate. The actions we dare to take, which depend on how free we are to make choices, are what the story of risk is all about."

Steve Anderson certainly took a risk. He was just beginning his career as an intern architect, with all the struggles and doubts that plague anyone early in a career. Yet it was Steve's debt burden that was overwhelming him, especially since architecture is a low-paying profession in the early years. It had taken him nine years of school and $35,000 in student loans to get where he was today. I talked with Steve for our show that focused on managing student loan debt while maintaining at least the semblance of a sane life. Yet my main memory of my conversations with Steve is his love of architecture and his passion about his chosen field, especially when we shared tales about trips we'd taken to Italy and he showed me some of his projects and sketches. During one discussion, appropriately carried on in the philosophy section of the Hungry Mind, an independent bookstore, Steve took great satisfaction in concluding that he was right to have taken on $35,000 in debt. The debt had made it possible for him to become an architect. The issue now was how to deal better with his debt burden (and he did have options). But the risk he had embraced by taking on all that debt to pursue a dream was well worth it.

Similarly, millions of average Americans risked some of their hard-earned money in the stock market for the first time in the 1990s. The stock market is volatile. Stocks fluctuate violently as companies go bankrupt, managements stumble, and investor enthusiasms spiral out of control. Yet the stock market has shown an inflation-adjusted average annual return of 7% since 1802, according to data compiled by finance professor Jeremy Siegel of the Wharton School at the University of Pennsylvania. In sharp contrast, the real return on short-term fixed-income government securities has been 2.9%. Short-term U.S. government debt, with payments backed by the full faith and credit of the federal government, is probably the world's safest investment security. Individuals could put all their money into Treasury bills. They are essentially risk-free, but that doesn't mean your portfolio is risk-free. With their low return (the trade-off for scant investment risk), Treasury bills may not generate enough income to provide adequately for your long-term needs and wants, such as maintaining your current standard of living in retirement. Many workers have decided that the risk of living through fluctuations in the stock and bond market is less than the risk of not having enough money accumulated for their retirement.

The risk-and-reward relationship is easiest to see in the stock market, but it runs throughout finance. Speculators, whether they call Wall Street, Main Street, or dot com home, are out to make big bucks. And they're willing to risk losing a bundle, perhaps everything, in pursuit of the large payoff. Now, contrast that approach with that of your neighbors—and coworkers— who invest in the stock market. I bet most of them—including you?—are periodically putting some of their earnings into the stock market through a tax-deferred retirement savings plan, such as a 401(k) or 403(b). They may be putting additional savings into an equity mutual fund, a state-sponsored college savings plan, or Series EE savings bonds to help pay for their children's college education. In essence, what they are doing is taking out an insurance policy against the risk of a lower standard of living in retirement, or to limit how much their children will have to borrow to attend college. The insurance buyer's goal is to limit the downside—or to maintain a certain standard of living throughout life—rather than to reach for untold riches.

The idea is to find the right balance between risk and safety for you. For instance, take two women earning the exact same income. But one is a tenured university professor with a stable income, and the other makes her money off commissions and therefore has an income that fluctuates from month to month. The tenured university professor can afford to take considerable risk with her savings. But the saleswomen may want to be more conservative with her savings so that she has a financial cushion during those months her commission earnings decline.

Of course, your risk tolerance is not a constant. You learn about your ability to absorb risk with experience and education. I remember the first time I rappelled down a cliff. It was while I was attending Outward Bound in England's Lake District during my senior year in high school. It was incredibly frightening to lean back and walk down the precipice the first time. Yet with practice I grew comfortable rappelling down modest cliffs. Changing jobs is nerve-racking, especially the first time. But many people find that the career and job satisfaction opportunities of switching employers outweigh all the upheaval.

I joined up with Julia Chivers at the Eldora Ski Area outside Boulder for our show on women and investing. She skied well and with abandon; I sort of tagged along, often on my backside. A single parent, Julia had put herself through college and gotten an MBA, and was raising her two daughters on her own. She had worked her way up the corporate ladder, and when I met her she held a high-powered position as a benefits consultant at a prestigious firm. Smart, bold, and self-reliant, Julia had beaten the odds again and again. Yet she was concerned when it came to investing in the markets. Yet Julia's "problem" turned out to be simple: She was asking for investing and perfection to go together. They don't. The key for her was to get out there, start experimenting, and improve her money management acumen over time. And I have no doubt that she will master her financial life the way she mastered the ski slopes and the business world.

KEEP IT SIMPLE

The rest of this chapter suggests some guiding principles to help you realize your financial goals and face the inevitable money trade-offs. The first principle is to keep your personal finances simple. Simplicity is an underappreciated virtue in the world of money. Too many professionals seem to have a financial stake in selling complexity. Whether it's an insurance policy loaded up with all kinds of bells and whistles, an investment strategy that only a tenured mathematician can grasp, or a clever estate plan that dazzles the legal fraternity, the pros are making lush profits making things more complex than they really are, and people always get into trouble buying products they don't understand. The more complicated people make their finances, the more time they waste and the less money they make. A simple strategy, coupled with plain-vanilla, low-cost products, are what you want. There is no substitute for marrying common sense and financial simplicity.

PLAN

You need a plan to start funding your goals. Few of us like the idea of setting up a plan, which inevitably includes a budget. Still, a plan is the strategy, the approach that translates your goals into action. The plan puts you in control. Thanks to the Internet, it's easier than ever to fill in the number blanks in your plan, since there are many good web sites that will let you run some calculations and check out some "what if" scenarios. Any entrepreneur will tell you that a well-thought-out business plan is critical to success, even in our quicksilver Internet Age. But that same entrepreneur will also tell you that much of the business plan gets tossed out as experience proves some ideas wrong and as circumstances change. No plan is ever complete or carved into stone. For example, John Puckett and his wife, Kim, turned two coffee shops into a $70-million-a-year, and growing, chain of 130 specialty coffee bars in several states. "I think the best thing to do is be very disciplined and create a plan where you set down what your vision is," says John Puckett. "But your strategies will change as your business conditions change."

Remember, you know your circumstances better than anyone else. What works for some people may not be suited to your temperament or lifestyle. The best "expert" advice on any topic may give you a long list of things to do. Yet only a few of the suggestions may make any sense at all for you. For instance, several friends of mine avidly track their day-to-day spending habits using sophisticated software. But I don't have the time or the inclination to plug the data into my computer. I much prefer paper, pen, and calculator. By the way, the experts never do all the things they recommend you do, either. You can't—unless you want managing money to dominate your life.

Don't underestimate the importance of time in your financial planning. First of all, be patient when it comes to getting your financial house in order. How often have you made big, life-changing New Year's resolutions, only to fall short of your grand ambitions in a couple of months? (I speak from experience.) Start out with small, easily attainable goals when you are trying to build up some more savings or cut back on debt. You build on your progress over time. Personal finance is a marathon, not a sprint. Another advantage of getting going now is that time allows for mistakes. The financial penalty from a bad investment for a 30-year-old with at least three more decades of earnings ahead of her is much less than for a 60-year-old. Finally, time lets your savings and investments compound over the long haul. Here's what I mean. If you put $10,000 a year into a tax-deferred retirement savings plan at work and it earns 8% a year, at the end of ten years you'll have $156,455. Another ten years at 8% and your account will swell to $494,229, and at the 30-year mark, when you are thinking about retiring, your tax-deferred savings plan will be worth $1,233,459.

MANAGE DEBT

Debt can be dangerous. Let's say you had a $10,000 credit card bill at an 18% rate of interest, and you made only the minimum 2% payment. It would take you nearly eight years and an interest bill of $9,000 to discharge the debt. Sure, that may be an unrealistic example, but it makes the point: Far too many people are trapped by onerous debt burdens, especially credit card bills. In today's economy, personal finance often means getting out of debt and back to square one. I can't say it often enough: Don't run up credit card bills. No matter how tempting—and the lure can be strong—credit cards shouldn't be used to spend more than you make. The bill should be paid off monthly. Now, most of us do end up with credit card debt at some point. And despite all the horror tales you hear about people buying all kinds of luxury goods with plastic and falling far behind on their payments, most of us get into debt trouble for some good reason. We lose our job. There is an illness in the family. We need to make frequent visits to a dying parent. And sometimes we just get carried away during the holiday season. Unfortunately, once you have debt there is no magic formula for getting rid of it overnight. Usually it takes time to create a big debt burden, and it also takes time to work it down. When that happens, put the credit card away and focus your money energies on paying it down.

Now, it seems whenever the discussion turns to debt the tone quickly becomes condemnatory. Borrowing is synonymous with being a spendthrift, being profligate or irresponsible. Yet debt is not all bad. Far from it. Over the past half century, the increasing availability of credit has created vast opportunities, new wealth, and lots of pleasure for many Americans. Most of us can't afford to buy a home without taking out a mortgage, and owning a home is a good long-term investment. Shortly after accepting their hard-earned diplomas, most college graduates get another document signifying their four years of college—a student loan payment book. But on average the return on a college education is high measured by income and employment in our high-tech economy. The American middle class has been built on hard work and debt. A powerful theme of the movie classic *It's a Wonderful Life* is how George Bailey opens up homeownership through his savings and loan to immigrants and others shunned by the wealthy establishment.

The message isn't "Don't borrow"; it's "Borrow wisely."

INVEST

A basic, fundamental adage of personal finance is not to spend more than you earn. It's true, even if people groan at the statement. But you also want your money to grow, and it's critical to save for the long haul. Don't keep all your money in a checking account and a savings account at a bank or credit union. Among the most important long-term investments are stocks and bonds, especially through a tax-deferred retirement savings plan, such as 401(k)s for the private sector, 403(b)s for nonprofits, 457s for state and local government employees, Keoghs, SEP-IRAs, and SIMPLE IRAs for the self-employed, and IRAs and Roth IRAs for those who qualify. By investing regularly in the markets you will improve your margin of safety against adversity and increase your financial flexibility. Everyone should participate in a tax-deferred retirement savings account.

Now, the stock market has broken all kinds of records over the past decade. These days it's almost impossible to get away from the markets. For instance, when I travel, I usually watch the various morning business and finance television programs. These shows have many strengths: solid information, plenty of market and economic numbers, an increasingly international perspective, and some decent interviews with chief executive officers, high-level government officials, and other newsmakers. Still, I find them troubling with their incessant hyperventilating over the latest rumors, market gossip, and fast-buck trading schemes—not to mention their obsession with finding the next winning stock. It's as if everyone watching were a Wall Street trader wannabe. Well, most of us aren't traders, and imagining that you can beat the market is a huge mistake. The idea is to manage your overall household finances so that you achieve the lifestyle you want, not to chase after a false goal, such as beating the market.

Still, smart long-term investing is built on an equity base. If you can envision the U.S. economy remaining a leader among major industrial nations, full of dynamic companies and bold entrepreneurs, you'll want to own stocks. If you believe the global economy will continue to expand—despite stomach-churning fits and starts—you'll want a slice of international equities, too.

One caveat: The U.S. stock market has put on a remarkable, perhaps a once-in-a-lifetime, performance from 1982 to 2000. The stock market has posted average annual returns of 16%, after adjusting for inflation. Yet the stock market's long-term inflation-adjusted return is around 7%. The odds are that returns over the next 18 years or so will be markedly less than those over the past 18 years. So keep your investment return expectations realistic.

ESTABLISH A MARGIN OF SAFETY

Don Quixote de la Mancha was right when he said, "'Tis the part of a wise man to keep himself today for tomorrow, and not venture all his eggs in one basket." Even a cursory glance at history tells us that the road to prosperity is hazardous, full of sound and fury, of unexpected risks and debilitating setbacks. As Orson Welles, playing Harry Lime in the movie *The Third Man,* said: "In Italy for 30 years under the Borgias they had warfare, terror, murder, bloodshed—but they produced Michelangelo, Leonardo da Vinci, and the Renaissance. In Switzerland they had brotherly love, 500 years of democracy and peace, and what did that produce? The cuckoo clock."

The essence of investing and financial planning is uncertainty. No one knows what tax rates, inflation rates, stock returns, and economic growth will be 30 years from now. A classic example of uncertainty is when Western Union was offered the chance to buy Alexander Graham Bell's 1876 telephone patent for $100,000. Western Union's management declined because the telephone had "too many shortcomings to be seriously considered as a means of communication." Instead, Western Union offered to withdraw from the telephone business in 1879 in return for Bell's promise not to compete with it in the telegraph business. In the 1940s, Thomas Watson, Sr., president of IBM, then one of the world's leading adding machine companies, confidently predicted that "there is a market for maybe five computers." Forecasting is a hazardous business.

What's more, investment risk doesn't disappear with time. Take inflation. It's currently running at around a 2% annual pace. It's a reasonable guess that inflation will range somewhere between 1% and 3% next year. But what will be the rate of inflation in 2010? Want to hazard a guess? How certain are you in your forecast? With the collapse of communism and the embrace of freer markets by much of the developing world, U.S. investors are pouring money into emerging stock markets these days. Yet which countries will enjoy political stability and the rule of law two decades from now and which ones will have descended into chaos and banditry? China? Malaysia? Brazil? Venezuela? "You have a pretty good idea of what is going to happen a minute from now, the rest of today, tomorrow, and possibly the rest of the week," says Peter Bernstein, economist, investment adviser, and philosopher of risk. "As the time horizon expands, uncertainty increases because the range of possible outcomes widens as we look further and further into the future."

For the long-run investor, it's critical to create a portfolio with a margin of safety by including different assets—and not just stocks, bonds, and cash. Diversification includes owning your own home. After all, the American Dream is almost synonymous with homeownership, and a home has been a decent long-term investment.

In our high-tech, global economy, brains, skill, and energy—what economists call human capital—are also increasingly valuable. The returns of education show up in higher wages and greater job security. Economists estimate that the lifetime rate of return from investing in a four-year college education is between 10% and 15% annually. That's more than competitive with the average return on stocks. The returns on education show up not only in higher wages, but also in greater job security and a higher employment rate. It's not just college. Training, industry seminars, and other lifelong learning programs also pay off. So learning new skills and keeping current with advances in your profession, especially as people stay active longer, are other ways of reducing risk through diversification.

PURSUE FINANCIAL LITERACY

Learning the financial basics is key when it comes to managing your money well over a lifetime. I don't mean you should become a finance economist or a calculus wizard. But personal finance broadly defined is a lifelong learning experience, and financial literacy will help you make more informed choices.

Hopefully, learning about finance starts early in life. These days, many parents are trying to achieve the right balance between money and values with their kids. For example, Wayne Lomax had left a large inner-city ministry in Miami to open his own church in Timber Pines, Florida, in 1996. Imagine, on the outskirts of Fort Lauderdale he gave his first service in a rented classroom at ten o'clock one Sunday morning without knowing if anyone would show up. A mere handful did, and when I met him two years later his congregation numbered about 500. His wife, Teresa Lomax, is a head nurse at Jackson Memorial Hospital, Miami's giant teaching hospital. Their two children, Christopher and Marcus, are ages 15 and 11, respectively. The Lomaxes are easy to be around, and we touched on many topics the first evening we got together, from starting a church to playing basketball. Still, we had gotten together because the Lomaxes wanted to learn more about teaching their children about money. Wayne and Teresa raised all the classic questions, such as how to handle an allowance and when to open a checking account. What can parents do to encourage a sense of responsibility and thoughtfulness in their children? "We are trying to instill in them the principles of saving, budgeting, and prioritizing," said Wayne. Adults share the same goal, although the sums we're dealing with are much bigger and the consequences of a mistake hold greater repercussions.

A benefit of investing in your financial education is that it will enable you to answer a question for yourself that I get asked all the time: "Do I need a professional adviser?" I'm convinced that most working- and middle-class folks don't. But if it is necessary to hire outside help, being a knowledgeable, educated consumer will pay off for both you and your adviser.

Another reason I want to stress the importance of financial literacy is more personal: Finance is fascinating. To be sure, most of us would choose a mystery novel over a prospectus for late-night reading any day. I would. But the capital markets are a dazzling social and economic institution for communicating all kinds of information and knowledge through price changes. The stock market is the world's biggest chat room, where economists, investors, journalists, traders, money managers, professors, and just about anyone else remotely connected to money exchange data, gossip, rumor, and research. The markets tell stories. As the literary critic Peter Brook says, "Our lives are ceaselessly intertwined with narrative, with the stories we tell and hear told." The storytelling in the financial markets may not rival that of a Jane Austen or even a Michael Crichton. Nonetheless, the key to understanding the movement of markets lies in literature. When the stock market is open for trading, investors buy and sell equities for many reasons. At the end of the day or the end of the week, no one really knows why the stock market went up or down. But everyone involved in the market talks about the market's movements all the time. Eventually a dominant story emerges "that gives shape and meaning to all the contradictory information that swirls throughout the market," says Deidre McCloskey, an economic historian at the University of Iowa. This story line becomes a popular model for understanding our economy—until the evidence becomes overwhelming that the narrative is wrong or that circumstances have changed.

You should also educate yourself about the Internet. It is a revolutionary communications technology that is transforming the world of finance. Of course, mention the words "Internet" and "finance" and most people immediately think of online trading. I'm sure you've seen the television ads extolling the virtues of buying and selling stocks in cyberspace. I'm a card-carrying skeptic on the financial rewards of active trading, whether it's through a broker or an online account. Market history and current experience tell us that most people are wasting their time and money when they trade. No, the more important impact of the Internet lies elsewhere. The Internet is driving down the cost of financial transactions, from taking out a mortgage to doing business with a bank or a broker. The competitive pressure on financial institutions to bring down their fees and costs is relentless, and consumers will be able to comparison shop with increasing ease. But the real power of the Internet for personal finance is in the realm of education and knowledge. The Internet is making available to average consumers unprecedented amounts of information and analytical tools at little or no cost. Financial literacy and Internet literacy reinforce each other.

HAVE FUN

Above all, don't forget why you embarked on this personal finance journey in the first place. America may be the land of mass consumer capitalism, but it's also a country where we are constantly admonished to lead a more upright life by eating better, exercising more, turning away from material pleasures, and so on. Now, a part of this improvement ethos is attractive. We do believe we can lead a better, more fulfilling life if only we can try harder. All of us can nip and tuck our spending, and if we save the money, the payoff over time will be substantial. Take that $2.50 you spend daily on a cappuccino and invest it instead. You'll pocket more than $138,000 in 30 years, assuming your money compounds at a 9% annual rate. But sometimes the advice industry crosses the line. That two-week vacation you take with your family costs a bundle, say, $3,600 a year. If you invested that money instead of whiling away time at the beach with your wife and kids, you'd have more than $553,000 when you retire. Still want time off? Well, pack a lunch and take a day trip or maybe a long weekend.

Hold on. It is vital that we all set aside some of today's earnings as savings, especially for our later years. We should take on debt only for significant long-term investments, such as buying a home or paying for a college education. But let's be sensible. Don't transform the smart idea of saving for tomorrow into a rigid ideology of denial that dominates your life.

Put it this way. A while back, I came across an academic paper with the improbable title "The DJIA Crossed 554,428 (in 1997)." Since the Dow was around 10,000 when I saw it, you can see why I quickly—and skeptically—gave it a read. It turned out to be a serious research paper into how equity values are measured. Yet the authors, Meir Statman, a finance economist at Santa Clara University, and Roger Clarke, an international money manager, also made an important observation about personal finance. The article noted that the Dow Jones Industrial Average, the most famous measure of the stock market, started out with a value of $40.96 in 1896. That year, an 18-year-old with that sum in his wallet could have had a terrific evening on the town with some friends. Or he could have invested the $40.96 in the stocks that made up the Dow Jones Industrial Average and reinvested all the dividend income. By 1997—at the creaking old age of 122—he would have accumulated a nest egg of $540,294. Of course, all the money would then go to paying his medical bills. On the other hand, he could have spent the dividend income and still have $7,908 left over. "These are just three of the infinite number of ways you could be rich if you had $40.94 in 1896," say Statman and Clarke.

Saving to save is just as bad as spending to spend. Money pales when measured against family and friends, passions and enthusiasms. Time still flies, even though we are healthier and living longer. Take that vacation with your family or friends.

A GUIDE

Right on the Money is a show that tries to help people take control of their personal finances. My assumption is that you're doing better than you think, and with education and better finance habits you can do even better. Orton Tofte, a good friend of mine, makes beautiful furniture. He works out of a small garage in the evening, even during the harsh Minnesota winters, thanks to a woodstove. Now, I'm hopeless when it comes to building anything with tools, but his enthusiasm is infectious. I can spend hours listening about his art, learning the special characteristics of different woods, handling his collection of tools, and, of course, marveling at his latest creations. Once he told me that around the New Year he makes a cabinet. I gather that because it's hard, the first couple of years of cabinetmaking were frustrating. But now, having had time to gain experience and skill, he finds creating a new cabinet to be peaceful, relaxing, and a satisfying tradition. Personal finance is no different.

2

Budget

Annual income twenty pounds, annual expenditure
nineteen nineteen and six, result happiness. Annual
income twenty pounds, annual expenditure twenty
pounds ought and six, result misery.

—Charles Dickens, *David Copperfield*

Five frogs are sitting on a log, and three of them decide to
jump. How many frogs are left on the log?

Five.

Budgeting is like that. It's something we promise ourselves
we'll do around the end of the month when funds are short and
we can't figure out where all the money went. But something always comes up the Friday or Saturday night you set aside for creating a budget. Perhaps it's dinner with friends followed by a
movie, or maybe you're just too tired after a marathon week at
work. In the back of your mind, you're afraid the message from
looking at your income and spending is that you don't make
nearly as much as you think you do, and that you spend way
more than you should. You have champagne tastes on a beer
budget. Besides, you forgot to keep most of your receipts, and
what good is trying to figure out a budget without numbers? We
sit on the log.

I wish I could write that budgeting is fun. But I can't. It is stressful. The reason we budget is that our finances are out of control. We're spending more than we are earning, and that credit card debt has added up fast. We know we're wasting money, but we're not sure on what. Our incomes are good, but money always seems to be tight. It's never easy to change our spending behavior.

But the pain of creating and sticking to a budget is worth it. I can emphatically state that within a relatively short period of time the result of fashioning a budget is genuinely liberating rather than constraining. For one thing, a household budget is the starting point for taking control of your finances. It's the baseline for all your saving, investing, spending, and giving decisions. Without a budget you can't control risk. Instead, you are vulnerable to a sudden setback, such as car breakdown, job loss, or illness.

For another, a budget is really where values are transformed into reality. It's one thing to talk about values, to list them, and to prioritize them. But now you have to start adjusting your spending. The reward? You spend your money where you want it to go and save for what you would like to do with your earnings.

You don't need to spend enormous amounts of time tracking data. After a while, ballpark figures and estimates suffice for most people. But for a relatively small investment in time and effort up front, a budget will become a lifetime of good financial habits.

A BUSY LIFE

I first met Aaron and Melody Hill and their son, Jaalam, on a warm Kentucky afternoon. The Hills are easy to talk to and fun to be with. Aaron is part owner and president of a video duplication business, where he does everything from making dubs to doing deals. Melody works for the Louisville Community Development Bank. The bank lends to individuals and businesses in Louisville's inner city.

Next to their one-year-old son, church is a defining activity in the Hills' life. The Canaan Baptist Church in Louisville has a large, devoted congregation. Every Sunday, Aaron directs the TV production of the service, while Melody sings from the pews. "I have one ministry that I'm in that gets me there once a week just for a couple of hours, and then the Bible study," says Melody. But Aaron, with his television work at church, "could live there," she adds. Aaron agrees. "I could pop a tent there," he says. "I'm there, let's see, Sunday, Monday, skip Tuesday, Wednesday, sometimes Thursday, sometimes Friday, and I'm there Saturday."

The Hills own a handyman special they bought about two and a half years ago. When they first bought their home, they lived in the basement while the contractor finished up some basic work upstairs. They'd come up to eat and then go back downstairs. Luckily, those days are behind them, but the house still needs a lot of work. "It's not quite what we want it to be simply because we don't have the time," says Aaron.

Oh yes, the Hills love to travel. When we got together, Aaron and Melody had just come back from a weekend in New Orleans. They showed me pictures from other places they've been, such as Jamaica, Toronto, and Niagara Falls.

The Hills are a typical two-income couple, and, as is true of many others with similarly busy lifestyles, their finances are a mess. Now, let me be clear. They pay their bills on time. There are no debt issues. Their only debts are a mortgage and some outstanding student loans. They are both funding retirement accounts at work, and there are some emergency savings. They carry adequate insurance for their family.

No, with their full schedules, the money from their paychecks comes in but seems to pour out as quickly. Eating out and take-out dinners. Late-night runs for formula. Grocery shopping when they need something that evening. "Well, it seems like the whole time we are running out at the last minute and having to pick up this and get that," says Aaron.

And now they have another child on the way. No wonder the Hills feel a pressing need to bring order to their finances before they become a family of four. They worry that without a budget, they will become seriously strapped for cash. "We are really getting serious about needing a budget, because here comes another baby," says Melody. "And more formula. And Jaalam won't be out of Pampers. So that's double Pampers and less time."

Their desire for a budget goes beyond cash-flow concerns, though. They need more time. More time to relax. More time to get their house fixed up the way they would like. More time for conversation. They also want to save more. To save for their children's college education. To save for their retirement. They'd also like to change where their money is going. For instance, both Aaron and Melody want to spend less on take-out food and more on travel. "If there is some way the budget could keep things in order so we wouldn't have to run out and get this and run out and get that," says Aaron, "some more structure so we could actually have time to do the things we want."

Of course, the Hills have an idea what a budget looks like. Most of us do. But now, with another child on the way, they have a reason to act. How should they—or you—begin crafting a budget? Better yet, how do you stick to a budget after the initial impetus of good intentions has faded, and the lure of resorting to prior habits beckons?

LET'S GET STARTED

The legendary oil tycoon J. Paul Getty owned and controlled some 100 companies and amassed a world-renowned art collection, and his wealth totaled well over $1 billion. Yet he was probably best known for his miserliness. For example, Getty installed a pay phone for his guests in his stately English manor. Okay, he's an extreme. But the message from the recent obsession with absorbing lessons from millionaires all around the country is that the road to wealth lies in wearing old clothes, avoiding haircuts, driving the same car for twenty years, and eating out at the local all-you-can-eat buffet. "Budget" and "cheap" are synonymous.

Let's begin our budget from a very different mind-set. Before you go over a single receipt or even talk about cash, the first step is to ask yourself the basic questions about your core values and aspirations, and then hold them up to the reality of how you're investing your time. At this point in the budget process, there is no right or wrong, good or bad. The list you are creating is very personal. Perhaps you have been married for several years, and you and your spouse feel it's time to buy a house. Or maybe you feel dual-income living isn't giving you enough time with your children, since they are getting older faster than you thought possible. Maybe you just want to exchange the clutter of day-to-day existence for more freedom.

What goes on your list of priorities often depends on your stage in life and circumstances. For a single person new to the job market, building a wardrobe and entertainment typically loom large. The Hills have very young children, and their kids are the center of their universe right now. The costs associated with feeding, caring for, and educating their kids are a big priority. Travel, the theater, and long dinners out rank high with many empty nesters.

Unfortunately, the stress that typically accompanies creating a budget is painfully accentuated following a recent divorce or the death of a spouse. The same goes for couples battered financially and emotionally by a huge debt burden that has accumulated over time. It doesn't take a rocket scientist to figure out that they have to keep better track of how much money is coming in and where it is going, and cut back to pay down their debt. Still, the core budget issue even for people with debt is figuring out priorities. Where do you want to be five years from now? If you didn't have any debts, what would you spend your money on? "Budgeting is the most simple activity we have," says financial educator Ruth Hayden. "We either have to increase our income or we have to decrease our expenses. Where we decrease our expenses is not mine to tell you. You spend the money where you believe you have a life that works."

One reason to focus on values is that your dreams, your ideas of where you want to go, are a positive force offsetting the difficult process of setting up a budget. Another reason is that a budget makes it clear that we can't have it all. You have to make trade-offs. So what matters to you, from the small moments that give you pleasure to the bigger objectives you hold dear? For instance, two of my priorities are taking the family to a bookstore on a regular basis and visiting our far-flung families. The Hills could cook the week's meals on Sunday and use their accumulated savings for a weekend trip with their kids or an evening alone at a fancy restaurant. "Do the Hills want to travel? Do they want to fix up the house?" asks Janet Bodnar, a columnist and senior editor at *Kiplinger's Personal Finance* magazine. "Write it down and look at the pros and cons. They may find that they like to travel so much that the house could wait or vice versa. But they are going to have to make some choices. They can't have it all."

The budget process I'm describing also keeps the envy factor at bay. Although "keeping up with the Joneses" has been a powerful motif throughout U.S. history, the sentiment seems to have grown during the heady economic expansion of the 1990s. Living standards have never been higher. Real median household income topped a record $40,000 in 1999; a record two-thirds of all households own their own home; and median household net worth is at an all-time high of $75,000. These figures are terrific. Yet one-fifth of the population amassed immense fortunes compared to the rest of the population. Dot-com millionaires, venture capitalists, Wall Street financiers, and stock option beneficiaries are tapping into their newfound wealth and spending it on starter castles, luxury cars, and high-tech toys. The spending spree has priced middle- and working-class Americans out of many desirable neighborhoods and communities, and, to keep up, far too many families without comparable incomes or stock holdings are borrowing beyond their means. "You have to be realistic and realize that you can't have it all unless you have got a Bill Gates–size income and budget," says Eric Tyson, author of *Personal Finance for Dummies*. "You are always going to know people who have more, who can spend more and do more. But you have got to decide what your priorities are."

At the same time, the way to cut back on the power of these money and consumption influences and wants isn't a wholesale retreat from society. Anticonsumer romantics have long admired Henry David Thoreau, who lived for two years, two months, and two days in a cabin he built in woods owned by his friend Ralph Waldo Emerson. In *Walden,* his account of that experience, he writes, "I went to the woods because I wished to live deliberately, to front only the essential facts of life and see if I could not learn what it had to teach." It's worth noting, however, that Thoreau's cabin was walking distance from town, his mother, and a hot meal.

A budget keeps you focused on your priorities, not an advertiser's message or a neighbor's luck of the stock option draw.

WHERE IS THE MONEY GOING?

So far, we've talked about priorities—deliberately. The actual budget is nothing more than an organizational tool for meeting priorities, much like a daytime calendar you use at work or the kids' school and activity calendar on the refrigerator. But now it's time to get down to nitty-gritty money management. Keep a record of your spending for several months to find out where your money is going. This is a boring task. But it doesn't go on forever. Indeed, once you've got a working budget, it's no longer necessary to minutely follow your expenses for the rest of your life. Now, after you have done all the up-front work, don't expect an overnight personality transplant. That's a recipe for failure. Keep the budget simple and your expectations realistic. You will stumble. So what? Don't put too much pressure on yourself to get the perfect budget in place right away, say within the space of three to six months. That's asking way too much of yourself and your family. Unless you are in the grip of a financial crisis that demands drastic steps, give yourself a year or two or even three. A budget is something you incorporate into your life gradually. And your budget will evolve as your circumstances change. Indeed, a budget review is important during any of life's major transition points, such as having a child, changing careers, or preparing for retirement.

But at this stage, you're trying to paint as complete a money snapshot as possible. Follow your spending in a way that is comfortable for you. There are several excellent computer programs for tracking your spending down to the penny. But data gathering on the computer is not for everyone. I'm far from a Luddite, but I've known far too many people who have started out keying in their data down to the penny with high hopes, only to fall short in maintaining their data entry week in and week out. So if you enjoy booting up your computer and get satisfaction from data entry, use the Internet or a software program. If not, monitoring your spending with an old-fashioned notebook and doing some quick addition and subtraction on a $10 calculator is more than adequate.

Of course, you'll want to include all your big expenses, such as mortgage payments, utilities, and insurance bills. But the trick is to be diligent enough to capture money spent on gas, coffee, and snacks. For instance, the $3 you spend every morning on a cup of coffee and a plain bagel comes to some $1,000 a year. The $5 you fork over for a weekday lunch at the food court costs you some $1,200 a year. Your spur-of-the-moment book and magazine purchases could easily hit $50 to $75 a month. ATM fees can reach $1 to $5 a week and late fees for video rentals $3 to $10 every couple of weeks. "The money can dribble out of your pockets without you even realizing it," says Grace Weinstein, a financial writer based in New Jersey. Adds Ruth Hayden: "What really breaks our budget, and studies have been done on this, is the weekly living expenses. It's the sieve."

The Hills have an idea where their money is going, but they don't how much. They spend a lot on Pampers and formula, usually bought in small quantities at the corner grocery. They don't buy in bulk or at a warehouse store. The Hills are so busy that they eat out a lot and have take-out dinners. When they do go to the grocery store, they just quickly get what they need and dash out again. It's an expensive way to live. The Hills are far from alone. Consumers spend about half their food budget these days on take-out and restaurant food.

Of course, it's not just what you spend. The other side of the equation is how much you make. What is your income? It's not the figure your employer says you earn. What is your monthly income after paying for employee benefits and after Uncle Sam and the state (and in some cases the city) have taken their share of your earnings? It's a humbling moment when you realize just how little you are actually taking home free and clear to draw on as you wish. Imagine if your employer told you that the $40,000 or $80,000 salary offer was actually $10,000 or $20,000 less in take-home pay. There's a reason why you are working so hard and earning a decent salary, yet always feeling that money is tight. By the way, I don't think earning more money is always the way out of a financial pinch. Yes, it's nice to make a higher salary. But the tendency when you earn more is to spend more. That's why doctors, lawyers, and other well-paid professionals often find themselves deep in debt. But if you have a budget that has become a habit and you end up making more money, your standard of living will go up and your financial goals will be much easier to achieve.

After a month or two, you should have a detailed blueprint of your take-home income, major expenses, and weekly and daily spending habits.

CREATING A BUDGET

Priorities established and data in hand, you're ready to create a budget. There are all kinds of worksheets on the web, in the bookstore, and at your library to help you make sense of the money coming in and the money going out—and how big a gap exists between the two. The electronic or paper worksheets will also offer you some basic guidelines, such as 30% of net income for housing, 20% for food, 18% for transportation, 10% for savings, 5% for clothing, and so on. These guidelines are useful, but don't take them too seriously. Rather than take too much time worrying whether you are above or below average, I'd prefer you go through your spending carefully. "Once you see where the money is going, you decide which of those things are meaningful to you, which of them are really important to continue, and where you might be able to cut back," says Grace Weinstein.

The Consumer Credit Counseling Service of San Francisco offers a representative budget worksheet. Here's the basic outline of their exercise. It starts with the essential expenditures, calculated on a monthly basis: housing, food, insurance, medical care, transportation, child care, miscellaneous (such as laundry, pet care, and union dues), income taxes, and savings. You add it all up. Then you start putting down the discretionary expenses on a monthly basis: personal (beauty salon, cosmetics, and the like), entertainment (cable TV, movies, and dining out), and miscellaneous (gifts, booze, and Internet service). Next comes all your unsecured debt, namely credit cards. That's followed by your total monthly income and your net income. You're now in a position to calculate the bottom line: your monthly net income minus your total monthly expenses. Maybe you're spending less than you make, but even so you probably want to shift what you are spending your money on. More likely, since most people put together a budget only when they are feeling financial pressure, you're spending more than you make. But once you know the size of the gap, you can start fiddling with the numbers to see where you can cut back. By the way, you don't need more than grade school arithmetic to calculate a budget.

Financial educator Ruth Hayden has designed a terrific budget scheme for intelligently balancing cash flow and personal priorities. Her first category is what she calls the "monthly have-tos." These are the bills you have to pay every month, such as your mortgage, student loans, credit card bills, and utilities. It's a standard category in all budgets. While we traditionally think of these monthly how-tos as fixed obligations or essential expenditures, there is some financial flexibility here. For example, many urban and suburban households pay $300 to $400 a month on their two phone lines, two cell phones, and an Internet connection. Perhaps you can go down to one phone line or cell phone. If that's not possible, maybe convert one of the cell phones to a cheaper plan tailor-made for infrequent and emergency usage. If interest rates come down, you might get the opportunity to refinance your mortgage at a cheaper rate. If you have two cable hookups, you could always go down to one. And so on.

Ruth's second category is the "nonmonthly have-tos." These are essentially the sums you spend to maintain your work and home life. The payments aren't routine, but if you don't make them during the year, your standard of living will suffer. Some common examples include license tabs for your car, cleaning the furnace, visiting the dentist, and taking your car in for a tune-up. While these expenses are irregular, you know you will spend money on all of them during the course of a year. Convert these yearly expenses into a monthly cost. Again, when you go over your spending you will see some room for maneuver. For example, the state government sets the license tab fees, but you could go to a barber rather than a hair salon. It makes no sense to skimp on the dentist, but your aging car may no longer need collision insurance (but keep the liability coverage).

Next are the basic "weekly living expenses." This is the budget-killer category. It's here that you write down the $100 weekly grocery bill, the $22 check at the dry cleaners, and the $15 to gas up your car. How many take-out meals a week? Yes, this is where the daily dose of caffe latte goes, and the afternoon Snickers bar. This is where much of the Hills' money is disappearing.

Convert these weekly figures into monthly sums. There is always room to shift spending patterns to squeeze out some savings. For example, the Hills could make one lengthy excursion to the grocery store every week, instead of several late-night dashes during the week. Before they go, one or both of them could take an inventory of what they need for the coming week, make a list, and walk the grocery store aisles with list in hand. Melody could brown-bag her lunch a couple of times a week. "If you are not going to be cooking every night or you are not going to be cooking once a week for a week's worth of meals, you may be having soup and sandwich a couple of nights a week," says Janet Bodnar. "That's okay. Cereal is okay, too, especially when you have little kids."

Ruth calls her final expense bracket "choice" or the "non-monthly choice" expenses. The common term in budget language is "wants," but that sounds too indulgent or as if this spending doesn't matter. But it does. You and I could live off a diet of bread, spinach, and a can of tuna every day. But I don't want to and I'm sure you don't, either. You can protect yourself from frigid Minnesota winters for $50 or so by shopping only at a used clothing store, but it's nice to get a fleece vest at Old Navy or a down coat at REI. Indeed, the choice category is where your values are often most apparent. This is the spending that makes it worthwhile to work hard. No matter what our income level, we like to exercise discretion with some of our spending. For instance, vacations are important to the Hills. They enjoy traveling to different places, and this is an integral part of their relationship. Rather than create a budget that says they won't travel, they could become more budget-conscious about their trips. They could decide to book their flight weeks in advance and stay over Saturday night to get a cheaper fare. Perhaps they might take more weekend vacations close by, rather than lengthy trips thousands of miles away, at least during this stage of their lives when they are raising a young family. "Trips might be with a coupon, overnight in a hotel, and sitting in a Jacuzzi," says Ruth. Turn this number into a monthly figure, too.

Ruth's final section is savings, from the emergency fund that protects you if something goes against you to the retirement account that is a buffer between today's life and tomorrow's. Savings include a life insurance policy to protect loved ones who are financially dependent on you if you die prematurely; a disability insurance policy that safeguards your income in case you get injured or ill; a retirement savings plan to preserve your standard of living in your twilight years; and easily accessible money in a savings account, money market mutual fund, certificates of deposit, and the like for those times you need an emergency infusion of cash.

We could label this the "savings" category "guilt." It's where people look first to make cuts, rather than exercise more imagination elsewhere in their spending. It's also where many of us have accumulated the most regrets. If only we had started putting money in a retirement savings plan three years ago. If we had just saved that $1,000 a year rather than spending it on trinkets, we'd be so much better off financially now. Sometimes, when money is truly tight, you have to cut back on savings. But to the extent possible, rather than touch savings, I would make as much of my savings automatic as possible. For instance, about half the people in the workforce have their retirement plan contribution taken out of their paycheck before it is deposited into their checking account. After a while, they don't even miss the money. Many homeowners have their mortgage payments automatically withdrawn from their checking account. Aaron Hill's student loans are deducted from his pay. Just about any financial institution, from mutual fund companies to credit unions, will take money out of your checking account monthly and put it into a designated savings account, from an equity mutual fund to a certificate of deposit.

Finally, it's time to calculate your monthly "spendable" income. That's the amount of money you have to spend after taxes, after savings, and after any tax-deductible benefits at work. Of course, for most people, their spendable income won't balance out with what goes into the five categories. Here's where values and priorities, supplemented with some common budgeting tricks, come into play to bring income and expenses into balance.

ADOPTING A BUDGET

By now, I hope you still have hair. And if you have been going through this exercise with a spouse or partner, I trust you two are still talking to each other. A tip: Don't try to do too much in any one sitting. Set up a regular once-a-week meeting where both of you come together for a defined period of time to work over the budget. Afterward, do something together you both enjoy. Reward yourself—and remind each other why you got together in the first place. No couple can design a budget without constant communication and willing compromise, leavened with a dose of humor.

You now know your spendable income, your savings, and your expenses. You also have a good idea where you want to go. The next-to-last step is preparing to join the cash economy. The checkbook should stay at home. You use the checkbook to pay the bills. The credit card is put away. For everything else, cash is king. You, or you and your partner, will draw down a cash salary every week. For whatever reason, maybe because you can feel the dollar bills leave your hand, it's harder to spend cash than it is to write a check or use a credit card. If you don't use all the cash, say because you saved some money at the grocery store, stockpile it. The less you spend on weekly expenses, the more you'll have to spend on the fun stuff.

You're ready to rumble. However, you've done only 20% of the work. The remaining 80% is actually jumping off the log. It's taking the step to follow the budget, modify it over time, and incorporate your goals and values into your everyday spending and saving habits. Managing finances differently doesn't come overnight.

Since Aaron and Melody like to travel, we flew them and Jaalam to Minnesota for a follow-up meeting. I joined up with them at the Mall of America, the world's largest shopping mall. They were optimistic about creating and following a budget. "We knew that we needed a budget, but we never really pushed to make it work," said Melody. "So this time we feel like we are really going to push forward and really going to follow those steps and see what happens, see if there is extra money at the end of the rainbow."

They were writing everything down and getting a sense of where the money was going. Both said they would continue to travel, but perhaps at cheaper rates or for shorter periods. In-

A chapter on budgeting is a good place to put ten common money mistakes.

1. **LOADING UP ON CREDIT CARD DEBT.** It's easy to run up a huge bill and tough to get rid of it. Don't carry a balance on your credit card.

2. **WAITING TILL TOMORROW TO SAVE FOR RETIREMENT.** Hey, the car is at the repair shop and you need new furniture, so you hold off saving for retirement. Big mistake. If you are not compounding interest, you're compounding the burden of saving for retirement.

3. **NOT INVESTING.** Sure, investing in the stock and bond markets is nerve-racking. But investing your savings in the markets allows your money to grow over time. Equities should be the foundation of any long-term savings plan.

4. **TAKING ON A BIG MORTGAGE.** Owning a home is the American Dream, right? But don't strap yourself for cash by taking on a huge mortgage. You don't want to work just to pay the mortgage.

5. **LEASING AN EXPENSIVE CAR.** Always wanted a fancy car but couldn't afford it? Now you can lease it. Leasing may look cheap, but it's actually quite costly. There are better uses for your hard-earned money.

6. **AVOIDING TAXES AT ALL COSTS.** Can't let Uncle Sam get any of your hard-earned money? Problem is, most schemes for avoiding taxes are bad investments. No one goes broke paying taxes.

7. **TAKING A COLD CALL.** Give cold calls the cold shoulder. The old adage is right: If an offer is too good to be true, it is. The deal is more likely to be a financial nightmare.

8. **SHUNNING A BUDGET.** A budget lets you take control of your finances. A budget makes your money work for you.

9. **TRUSTING FINANCIAL ADVISERS.** Financial advisers can be helpful, but don't take any money advice or buy a financial product you don't understand. Trust yourself.

10. **THINKING "IT'S ONLY MONEY."** No, money is many things, including your values and priorities. For you and your family's future, managing your money well is important. Take the time to make sound money decisions, and you'll have more time to enjoy life.

stead, getting their house the way they wanted it to look would take up more of their time and money. "Maybe for a couple of years we need to slow down with travel and get the house fixed up," said Melody. "I'm tired of the way it looks now."

How about on the food front? Both said they planned on getting more organized. But they did laugh at how much of a challenge grocery shopping and cooking were for them. They were going to try to write down what they needed before they went to the grocery store. They were even trying to cook some meals on the weekend for the week ahead. I could tell it was going to be tough. But the incentive was clearly there, especially with another baby just a short time away.

Resources

How to Turn Your Money Life Around: The Money Book for Women, by Ruth Hayden (Health Communications).

For Richer, Not Poorer: The Money Book for Couples, by Ruth Hayden (Health Communications). Both of Ruth's books are terrific, and both have a detailed analysis of her philosophical approach to money and practical details of her budgeting technique.

The Wall Street Journal Lifetime Guide to Money, edited by C. Frederic Wiegold (Hyperion). Chapter 1 has a good overview of getting your financial house in order, including figuring out where the money is going.

Making the Most of Your Money, by Jane Bryant Quinn (Simon & Schuster). Chapter 2, "The Ultimate Wish List," will help you make sense of your current financial picture and your goals.

Personal Finance for Dummies, 3rd edition, by Eric Tyson (IDG Books). A basic resource for anyone taking control of his or her finances.

Quicken or quicken.com. Many people are deeply devoted to their Quicken. It's how they keep track of their income, expenses, and investments.

Microsoft Money or moneycentral.msn.com. The competitor of Quicken. Check out the web site's "family finance" for tips on creating a household budget.

financecenter.com. Plenty of finance calculators, including several for figuring out various budgeting issues.

fincalc.com. Another site with good calculators.

cccssf.org. The Consumer Credit Counseling Service of San Francisco has a basic budget worksheet.

3

Buying a Car

She's got a competition clutch with the four on the floor
And she purrs like a kitten till the lake pipes roar.

—Beach Boys

Rachel Baer lives in a small apartment in a section of Minneapolis full of independent coffee shops, small restaurants, and plenty of young people. She wanted a new car. Now, this was not a frivolous, spur-of-the-moment purchase. Far from it. Her 1985 Toyota Camry had more than 125,000 miles on it, and the car was guzzling a lot more than gas. "I'm at the point where I'm putting so much money into it that I'm not sure if it's worth it," she said. "And I don't know if I'll have another big repair around the corner."

In the past, Rachel had always paid cash for cheap used cars. But now she had a good job with public television making some $25,000 a year. She was thoughtful during our conversations about cars, and I got a strong sense that Rachel was not easily intimidated. Yet like many people I know, she was nervous about buying a car and had a lot of questions. Should she buy a new car or a used one? How could she avoid a lemon if she decided on a used car? What sort of options should she pay for? With Minnesota's brutal winters and icy roads, should she pay extra for four-wheel drive or all-wheel drive? "I'm from Atlanta," she said. "I'm not really comfortable driving in snowy conditions."

She had thought about what model she might like. Rachel had always owned Japanese cars, and she was definitely intrigued by a Subaru. General Motors' Saturn also appealed to her, especially with its no-haggle pricing and reputation for good customer service. No matter what, she wanted something practical and not too big or luxurious. It had to be a comfortable car for her large, friendly golden retriever. She was certainly more utilitarian in her attitude toward cars than most people. No frivolity here. "I don't care about color. I don't care if it has automatic. I don't care about sunroofs and CD player," she said. "I want something that gets me to where I want to go."

Like most of us beginning the process of looking for a car, Rachel had looked at some car magazines and investigated cars on the Internet. I like visiting car lots when the dealership is closed to look around without a salesperson hovering around. But eventually, you have to visit the dealership when it's open for business. Rachel was apprehensive about going to a showroom. It's partly that she dreaded bargaining with the dealer. What price should she offer a dealer, and how much room would there be to negotiate? But her normal showroom jitters and concerns were compounded by her gender. Dealers have a bad reputation when it comes to working with women as customers. My wife and I shopped for a new car when we moved to New Jersey in the early 1990s. Yet even though it would be her car and she was largely paying for it, some salesmen insisted on talking to me and ignoring her. Obviously, we took our business elsewhere. "They have such a bad reputation," said Rachel. "There are a lot of stereotypes that might hold a grain of truth. Yeah, I'm nervous."

Of course, once you have picked out a car you have to pay for it. Cars are expensive. The average purchase price of a new car is some $23,000, and the typical used car runs about half that figure. For most people, a car is the most costly investment they'll make after a home and college. Rachel couldn't afford to pay all cash for a car. Should she lease? Borrow from a bank? Or go with the manufacturer's loan?

Rachel has her no-frills vision of a car, and her plain tastes may not be yours. Yet her bottom line is the same as for anyone in the market for a new or used car: She didn't want to be taken advantage of, and she didn't want to overpay. I certainly empathize with her. I don't get any pleasure from haggling over prices, and cars are a mystery. I can put the key in the ignition and drive away safely. I always buckle up and make sure the kids have their seat belts on. But a car engine is a closed book. I don't have a clue how fuel injection or an antilock braking system works.

Still, you don't need to be a gearhead to be a savvy car buyer in today's world. This is not your parents' car market of limited choice, arrogant manufacturers, and sleazy dealers. No, you have more choice than ever before, and the competition for your business is heated. A wealth of solid information is easily available on magazine racks, at the bookstore, and especially on the Internet. And you're in the driver's seat when you tap into the power of research and competition. Put somewhat differently, with knowledge and competition you can greatly reduce the financial risk of paying too much for a car and limit the risk of buying the wrong car.

AUTO NATION

Americans love their wheels. In recent years, sales of new cars have averaged around 15 to 16 million a year. Some 130 million cars are registered, and more than 50 million households own two or more cars. In most parts of the country, we use cars to get to work, shop for groceries, and get the kids to soccer games. Cars are practical, a way of getting from point A to point B. But for many people, a car is also a statement or anti-statement. The kind of car we drive tells the world that we are successful, fun-loving, hardworking, conservative, or frugal. A car has long been central to our economy and our culture.

The good news is that consumers haven't had it this good in years when it comes to buying a car. Thanks to fierce competition among domestic and overseas carmakers, prices have been remarkably stable over the past several years, especially after adjusting for improvements in standard equipment. A car offers a lot of value for the money, considering the huge improvements in auto technology. Automobiles are a whole lot better than even a decade ago, let alone three decades ago. Air bags and seat belts are now standard, and braking systems have improved markedly. Computer-controlled engine management systems are designed to let cars start and run smoothly under all weather conditions; cars are genuinely reliable for at least the first three years of driving, and when something does go wrong, sophisticated onboard diagnostic technology allows a repair shop to find the problem easily.

These technological and manufacturing improvements lie behind a dramatic transformation of the car market: For the first time, used cars are a viable alternative to new cars for many people. Yes, the term "lemon" and "unscrupulous" once were almost synonymous with "used car" and "used car dealer." Did you ever see the movie *Matilda,* with a nasty, foul-mouthed Danny DeVito as the crooked used car dealer who spun back the odometer, put sawdust in the engine, and used other tricks to con customers into spending good money on a clunker?

The used car market is dramatically changing for the better. In addition to the improved quality and durability of cars, the growing popularity of leasing means that used car buyers can find plenty of two- and three-year-old motor vehicles on the market. A car today should easily do 150,000 miles with just routine maintenance on the tires, battery, brakes, and the like, along with fixing the occasional alternator or air-conditioning problem. Since major design changes are relatively infrequent in the car industry these days, you can be in style and still pay less than full price. The car has been time-tested out on the road, and the bugs have been worked out. "In the old days, buying a used car meant buying someone else's problems," says Jack Gillis, director of public affairs at the Consumer Federation of America and author of a series of consumer buying guides to cars. "Today, there are so many different reasons why people get rid of perfectly good cars."

An even bigger transformation in the car and light truck market is the explosion in high-quality, easily accessible information, especially on the Internet. Dealers no longer hold all the cards. At the library, in the privacy of your home, or at your computer at work, you can gather all sorts of reliable information on pricing, options, warranties, and safety ratings. You can figure out on your own time whether it makes more financial sense for you to lease or to buy. On the Internet, you can find car loans, get price quotes from dealers, and even purchase your car. Rachel found the Internet invaluable for her auto research.

We're still at the early stage of the Internet's impact on the car market. The day is coming when you'll be able to boot up your computer and bypass the dealer by placing an order directly with the manufacturer for a car with the options you want. But at this early stage of the Internet revolution, the World Wide Web is still best for gathering information and running the numbers. Indeed, within a few years much of the knowledge about figuring out a realistic car price to begin negotiating with the dealer will be obsolete. The Internet is forcing the industry to abandon the traditional, highly inflated "manufacturers suggested retail price" and adopt posting the "invoice price" charged the dealer or other market-based prices. Buying a car on the Internet remains a bit tricky, especially with used cars.

Nevertheless, the Internet puts you in control.

FINANCING YOUR PURCHASE

A car is a big investment, so let's talk money. Cash is king. All cash is almost always the cheapest way to buy a car. But few of us have $20,000 or so in savings to plunk down for a new automobile. Even a used car at half that price stretches most budgets. So we end up wrestling with whether to lease or to borrow.

Leasing is an extremely popular option. About a third of all new car purchases are financed by taking on a lease. Open up any Sunday newspaper and look at the car ads, and you'll see why: With most leases you put very little money down and enjoy low monthly payments. When you lease a car, you are essentially renting a car for two to three years. You don't own it. You return the car at the end of the lease. Of course, you can choose to buy the car at the end of the lease, but many people simply lease another vehicle.

Leasing doesn't appeal to me. It can turn into a world of perpetual car payments. Leasing works mainly for people who drive no more than 12,000 to 15,000 miles a year, depending on the lease terms. It's all too easy to underestimate how much you will drive a car over the next two to three years. You also should be very neat. Otherwise, you'll suffer from a bout of sticker shock when the lease is up and you have to pay the dealer for any excessive "wear and tear." Early termination of a lease is costly. "When you lease a car, you have all the headaches and responsibilities of car ownership, but none of the benefits," says Jack Gillis. "At the end of that lease period you have nothing."

An important reason why I don't like lease financing is that the financial terms—the total cost of the lease to you—are often opaque. I prefer keeping my finances simpler and more comprehensible. Indeed, leases often aren't as cheap as they might appear at first glance or when you are looking at the car ads. What's more, if you borrow to buy a car and, yes, pay out a few more dollars a month, at the end of the loan you own the car, a tangible asset. You can continue driving it. You can sell it. You can give it to your kids. It's yours. With a lease, you either buy it when the lease is up or, more likely, take out another lease.

Still, leasing is an attractive option for some people, especially if they work in a profession where a new car is important to make a good impression on customers, such as real estate. So let's take a brief excursion through the world of lease financing. Your monthly payment is figured by calculating the difference between the vehicle's price (the so-called capitalized cost) and what the vehicle is estimated to be worth at the end of the lease (the residual value). The lease is financed at a rate of interest, typically called the "lease rate," the "lease charge," or "money factor." Your up-front costs usually include a first month's payment, a refundable security deposit, taxes, registration, and any other charges. There is also a capitalized cost reduction, a fancy term for what is essentially a down payment on the car.

Always compare different lease offers and negotiate terms. Insist that all the costs be laid out and the underlying financial calculations explained to you clearly. You should also take the information home with you, check in on leasing calculators on the Internet, and think about the contract you're about to enter at your leisure. If the dealer pressures you to make up your mind right away, go to another dealer. The Federal Reserve Board recommends considering the following factors when comparing lease offers:

- the agreed-upon value of the vehicle (a lower value can reduce your monthly payment)
- up-front payments, including capitalized cost reduction

- the length of the lease
- the monthly lease payment
- any end-of-the-lease fees and charges
- the mileage allowed and per mile charges for excess miles
- the option to purchase at the end of the lease or earlier
- whether the lease includes "gap" coverage that protects you in case the vehicle is stolen or totaled in an accident

Got that?

Borrowing is simple. There are plenty of lenders willing to do business with you. Shop around for the best loan terms available. Check out your credit union if you belong to one, and several local banks. The automakers' financing divisions often offer the best deals, though. The financing terms do make a difference. Take this example (you can play with the numbers all different kinds of ways). Let's say you buy a car for $20,000. You put $5,000 down and take out a $15,000, three-year loan at 9%. Your monthly bill is $477 and your total interest cost $2,172. At a 6% interest rate, your monthly tab is $456 and interest payments will run you $1,428. Putting down a bigger down payment saves you a lot of money. Let's keep our example the same, but this time you put down $10,000 and borrow $10,000. At 9%, your monthly payment is $318 and the interest tab $1,448. At 6%, the comparable figures are $304 and $952.

FINDING THE RIGHT CAR FOR YOU

Like any other investment, whether buying a house or a mutual fund, it pays to do your research before spending any money. Research takes a lot of time, from several weeks to several months depending on how busy your schedule is and how quickly you need a car. My own experience is that research on the Internet can eat up enormous amounts of time, so plan accordingly. While much of your information will come from the Internet and published materials, don't forget to talk to friends and acquaintances about their cars. Their auto adventures and dealer insights will add to your stock of knowledge.

A thoughtful exploration of the car market goes beyond unearthing solid information about models, prices, and finances. You should also investigate your hopes, dreams, and anxieties. The value of research is that it helps us keep our desires and budget in balance at that moment when the dealer is manipulating our longings and we start rationalizing spending more than we planned. Research limits your risks.

Take your time narrowing down your choice. What kind of transportation do you need or want? Sedan? Sport utility vehicle? Minivan? Compact? When we lived in Brooklyn and parked on the street, we owned a compact car that was easy to parallel park. We also didn't get upset (well, not too worked up) when neighborhood kids played basketball on the hood. But several years later we got a minivan when we found ourselves in the suburbs and transporting our kids and their friends to soccer games and other events. An acquaintance of mine loves cars and enjoys taking long drives through the countryside, and he's willing to spend big bucks on a Mercedes.

Once you've decided on the type of car you need, you should home in on several comparable models, such as a Saturn, a Toyota Corolla, and a Honda Civic, or a Ford Explorer, a Jeep Cherokee, and a Chevy Blazer. This way, you have some bargaining leverage when it comes time to negotiate with a dealer or dealers. "Never narrow your choice down to one car," says Jack Gillis. "That's when you lose the psychological advantage of being able to walk away from a bad deal."

You'll also need to decide what options are important to you. Some features help a car maintain its value, as well as being sensible in their own right. Check out safety ratings and fuel economy. Safety features such as dual air bags (side air bags if they are available), antilock brakes, and three-point seat belts in the backseat are standard in most cars. I don't even think of these as options, but as necessities. Keyless remote entry is a nice safety feature, since you can easily make sure your car is locked and you can unlock it quickly. Automatic transmission helps on resale, since many drivers prefer automatic to manual transmission.

Rachel had wondered about four-wheel drive and all-wheel drive (computer controls automatically shift to four-wheel drive if conditions warrant). The improved traction from either can be a worthwhile feature if you live in one of the northerly or more rugged parts of the country. Both cost more, but you'll usually get about half of your investment in four-wheel or all-wheel drive back at resale. Air-conditioning is standard on many cars today. Once I owned a car without air-conditioning (my wife and I were trying to save money), but I wouldn't do that again. Have you ever been stuck in a three-hour crawl across Staten Island trying to get back home to Brooklyn in August without air-conditioning? It's not conducive to good marital relations. Other options involve personal preferences and budgets. Do you want leather or fabric seats? Four doors or two doors? Standard or fancy trim?

Your work at this stage of the process isn't done yet. All the car experts agree: The test drive is critical. The test should be a lot longer than a quick trip around the block or the dealer's lot. Take it for a long test drive, and if you have a family, make sure they are with you. Drive out on the highway, tour around several neighborhoods, and pull into your driveway. Put a couple of suitcases or boxes in the trunk and take them out. Have your kids get in and out of the car. Before we bought our minivan I toyed with the idea of a sport utility vehicle. I liked one in particular. But the kids were clearly uncomfortable in the backseat when I took them with me for a test drive. No way I was going to buy that car. "The things that most of us dislike about our cars are things that you could have avoided if you had taken a good long test drive," says Jack Gillis.

SHOULD YOU BUY NEW OR USED?

A new car looks good. The upholstery smells clean. There's not a scratch on the paint or a nick on the windows. Besides the clean looks, between quality improvements and today's comprehensive warranties, you should get about three years of trouble-free driving with a new car. For many people, the warranty alone is reason enough to buy new. But emotions, status, and the desire to own the latest high-tech machine also come into play. After all, if a car were just to get us from home to work in the morning and back home again in the evening, we could just drive all-black, slightly updated Model Ts. But we like new car designs, different colors, and high performance. "Some people want a new car because it's their right to have a new car," says Paul Brand, a former race car driver and auto expert. "They have worked hard."

Problem is, you will spend a lot of money on a new car. A Volkswagen Beetle GL lists for $16,000 before taxes, a Honda Accord 3.0 LX Sedan $22,000, and a Lincoln Navigator 4WD some $46,000. Used cars are much cheaper. The best place to purchase a used car is from a friend or someone you are familiar with. You know their driving habits, and you'll get an honest answer about how the car has been treated. Both you and the seller come out ahead financially because you cut out any payments to a middleman.

Of course, our pool of friends ready and willing to sell us the car we want when we need it is limited. Luckily, the used car buying experience is improving. New car dealers have moved into the used car business in a big way, especially with formerly leased cars. Many established dealers will offer extended warranties on their used cars. The used car superstores are a competitive force, too, since they offer consumers a lot of choice, no-haggle pricing, and often a warranty. Rental car companies hold frequent sales. The traditional used car dealers are still in business, but it's more of a "buyer beware" market. Jack Gillis recommends doing business with a used car dealer that has been active in the community for a long time. You can also search for used cars on the Internet. An Internet-based used car search is a quick way to check out what's available in a certain make and model in a metropolitan area. The web also lets you comparison shop used cars hundreds, if not thousands, of miles away.

THE USED CAR CHECKUP

Still, a used car is likely to be somewhat beat up. It is damaged goods. Perhaps its previous owner had a lead foot or neglected to change the oil regularly. It may have been left outside during bad weather or driven constantly on bumpy roads. Problems could lurk in the fuel line, the brakes, the transmission, or elsewhere, all hidden from view.

This is critical: When you decide on a used car, take it to a mechanic you trust and have the mechanic check it out very carefully. The inspection with an independent mechanic will help you avoid a lemon. If a dealer won't let you take it out of the lot to a mechanic after filling out the appropriate paperwork, go elsewhere. The $50 or $100 the mechanic will charge you is well worth it. The mechanic will run a computer diagnostic on the car, and you'll get a detailed printout of the car's condition. Go over the report with the mechanic, and get the mechanic's personal input. Let's say the written report points out some modest problems. You can get an itemized repair estimate and use it in your negotiations with the dealer.

I learned from Paul Brand how to do a ten-minute "walk-around," a self-inspection of a car that anyone can do—including nonmechanics like me. The inspection is a quick way to narrow your choices in a used car lot. It will save you a lot of money ($50 to $100 for inspecting every used car that intrigues you can add up to big bucks quickly).

- Has the car been in a wreck? Look carefully at the paint job. Is it uniform in color? Are the panels straight? Are the gaps between the doors and the body uniform? Don't worry about a ding or two. It is a used car.
- Search for any corrosion. Check carefully for any rust. For example, look and feel along the inside edge of the door seam, along the fender lip, under the carpet, and inside the trunk.
- Kicking the tires is a pretty useless practice. But do see if the tires are worn down uniformly. Do you see an unusual wear-and-tear pattern that could indicate a potential problem?
- Open the hood. You don't have to be a mechanic. This is just another visual and touch test. Brand believes the engine is a good place to discover the personality of the previous owner. How clean is it? Check the air filter and oil filter. Pull out the dipstick and see if the oil is clean. Look for any leaks under the car. How are the belts? Are there any splits or cracks? All you are looking for is signs of abuse or neglect.
- Start up the motor and let it idle for a while. Did the car start cleanly? Is it idling smoothly? Try out the gears. Does it go directly into gear? Can you easily shift into reverse? Check out the lights, radio, power windows, and other features. Is the seat comfortable? Any evidence of rain leaks?

Move on if the car falls short at any point during this examination. There are plenty of alternatives available. But if it does pass this simple test, take it for a test drive. And if you are still pleased, you should then drive it to a mechanic to run a series of diagnostic tests.

THE PRICE IS RIGHT

You've done your homework, narrowed down your choices, and taken several test drives. Now, what price should you pay for your new set of wheels? It's a critical part of the car-buying process, unless you decide on a fixed-price Saturn or choose a no-haggle dealer. Luckily, good pricing information is readily available through the Internet, in the bookstore, and in your local library.

First, forget the sticker price or the "manufacturer's suggested retail price" that's stuck to the window of a car in a dealer's lot. I don't know why they even bother with the MSRP. I guess it's the "there's a sucker born every minute" philosophy of retailing. Imagine going to Wal-Mart or Target and taking off the shelf some household product with a price tag of $30. But you know how the system really works, so you ask the cashier if $30 is the real price, and the cashier says no, now that you ask, it's actually $20. No wonder car dealers have such a dubious reputation. They still insist on posting the MSRP, but what you want is the dealer's "invoice" cost or the factory invoice. It's essentially the price that the dealer pays the manufacturer for cars and trucks. You can get that price from a variety of sources on the Internet, including price data on all the options and package deals. Just as important, you want to know about any fees dealers might try to tack on to a car's price, plus any rebates or manufacturer incentives you may qualify for. I would print out the information if you get it off the Internet or through a consumer car-buying service and carry it with you to the dealership.

Of course, as in any market, supply and demand affect prices. If dealer lots are full of a certain model, you can often get it for 3% or so over invoice. But if it's a hot car and you are determined to own one right after the new model is introduced, you may have to fork over the full sticker price—or more. Car buyers can stack the odds in their favor for a better price toward the end of a model year. Dealers often try to clear out their lots to make room for the automakers' new cars. You can also check out one of the car-buying sites on the Internet, for either a new or used car. You submit your request, and within a few hours you will get by e-mail or phone a firm bid from a nearby dealer. You visit the dealer if you like its bid, check out the car, and close the deal.

Unfortunately, women like Rachel are still at a disadvantage when they go to a dealership. The Consumer Federation of America estimates that over 90% of car salespeople are men, and their research confirms that far too often they will not treat a woman's question with the same respect they do a man's. At the same time, the Consumer Federation of America has found that women are generally smarter car buyers than men. "Women end up doing far more research and, unlike men, make a far less emotional decision," says Jack Gillis. "Men will be the ones that buy on color, style, and emotion, not women."

The same phenomenon is at work in the world of investment clubs. Women's investment clubs outperform their male counterparts. The reason: Women tend to research their investments carefully, while far too many men are willing to make snap judgments. Still, the point is not to stereotype or reverse-stereotype too far. It is that research is one of the best ways of cutting down on the risk of making a bad purchase, whether it's a stock or a car.

Now, even the most active car buyer is in the market only every two or three years; many of us shop for a new car once a decade. Dealers are buying and selling every day. The dealer almost always has an advantage over the most diligent researcher. There is a gap between reading about something and living it. Dealers are always coming up with new and inventive ways to earn a profit as more and more people become savvy to the importance of invoice prices, rebates, and other incentives.

The bottom line: There is no substitute for tapping into the power of competition or, to put it somewhat differently, the willingness to walk away. When you have narrowed down your choice to several models, armed yourself with all kinds of pricing information, and test-driven your selections, it's time to seriously shop around. Reject any high-powered sales pitches, and take your time. Dealers are in business to sell cars, and in most markets there are many dealers eager to close a sale. Some dealers may be willing to earn a smaller profit margin than others. "The used car and the new car dealer is trained to let you feel that you are not in control," says Paige Amidon, head of the *Consumer Reports* car-buying service. "The most important thing is to tell the dealer, 'Quote me your best price for this car. I'm going to shop here and at other locations. If you give me your best price, I'll be back and buy the car here.' " Competition is to your benefit.

SIGNING ON THE DOTTED LINE

You've got a deal, but you're still not done. Indeed, you're about to walk into the crucible of the negotiated deal, the car dealer's office (thank goodness for no-smoking laws). Suddenly you have to sign all these forms. The temptation is just to sign them and get it done with. But read the papers carefully, ask questions, and don't forget that you have already researched what you want and don't want. Don't be swayed by any last-second pitch. And watch out for last-minute fees. "It's definitely one of the higher-pressure situations you will find yourself in," warns Paige Amidon.

What about the service contract the dealer will offer you at this time? A service contract is essentially an insurance policy that covers everything the warranty doesn't. I would steer clear of service contracts. If it's a reliable car, the manufacturer's warranty is all you need. If you are worried about repair costs beyond what's covered by the warranty, put the money you would pay for a service contract into a money market mutual fund or savings account. When the repair bills start, you will have accumulated a nest egg to pay for them. Credit insurance, rustproofing, fabric protection, and similar extras offered by dealers usually aren't worth purchasing. "Most of those just aren't worth the money," says Paige Amidon.

Your focus up till now has been on getting the best price you can. Only when you are done with your purchase (or before you start the process of getting a new car) do you discuss your trade-in. Again, you need to do your research. First, look up the value of the car. Three good sources are the *National Automobile Dealers Association Official Used Car Guide—Consumer Edition,* the *Kelley Blue Book,* and *Edmund's Used Car Prices and Reviews.* You can find them at your library or online. Compare the wholesale price to the retail price of your car. If there is a big difference, say $1,000 or $2,000, between those two figures, you may want to try selling your car on your own. But a lot of people don't want the hassle of auctioning off their car themselves. In that case, knowing what it is worth will help you negotiate the trade-in value with a dealer.

CAR INSURANCE

You need car insurance. It's smart finance, and it's mandatory anyway. Unfortunately, prices on car insurance vary widely, even for policies that offer essentially the same coverage. You will have to ask around to get a good policy. Solicit quotes from several agents or insurance companies. You can get quotes off the

Internet at many of the comprehensive auto-information web sites. Many state insurance departments publish a guide to auto insurance, including the rates offered by companies in the state. You can save yourself several hundred dollars a year by being a smart insurance buyer. Always ask if the insurer is offering a discount—or charging a premium—for the kind of car you will own or the type of driver you are. For example, many companies offer good-driver discounts. In sharp contrast, sports car owners should expect to pay a premium. It's a good idea to take as high a deductible as you can afford. The relationship is simple: The more you self-insure, the lower your premium. It can make a big difference to your premium payments if you decide on a $100 deductible or a $500 deductible.

Insurance terminology is abstruse, and a policy includes several different kinds of coverage. Simply put, the auto insurance policy limits your losses if something goes wrong. Different states have varying requirements, but here are some of the basics. To start with, everybody needs liability insurance. Bodily-injury coverage protects you in case you are sued for hurting someone in an accident. It also covers medical expenses and lost wages if the passengers in your car are injured. *Consumer Reports* recommends that the typical middle-class family have at least $100,000 per person and $300,000 per accident. But you may want to go much higher, perhaps by buying supplemental coverage through an umbrella policy. A supplemental policy pays for losses that are greater than are covered under your auto or homeowner's policy. A $1 million policy costs about $200 a year.

Property-damage liability covers damage against property, such as another car, a fence, or a mailbox. You can purchase up to $100,000 in coverage and then supplement it with an umbrella policy. Motorist coverage against uninsured and under-insured drivers is a good idea, too, and many states require it.

Comprehensive and collision insurance protect your car. Comprehensive physical damage insurance is your safety net against fire, flood, and other disasters—including damages when your car is stolen. Collision insurance pays for car repairs or the replacement of your car. If you are driving a new car, you'll want plenty of collision insurance. But collision insurance becomes less necessary as the car ages. A common industry measure is that you can drop your collision and comprehensive coverage if the cost of your premium is more than 10% of the vehicle's value.

The Insurance Information Institute, an industry trade group, offers these nine tips for saving money on your auto insurance policy.

1. Comparison shop. Prices for the same coverage can vary by hundreds of dollars from company to company. But check out the insurance companies' financial ratings, too.

2. Ask for higher deductibles. For instance, hiking your deductible from $200 to $500 could reduce your collision and comprehensive cost by 15% to 30%.

3. Drop collision and/or comprehensive coverage on older cars.

4. Buy a "low-profile" car. Cars that are expensive to repair, or that are a preferred target of thieves, have higher insurance costs.

5. Take advantage of low-mileage discounts. Some companies offer discounts to motorists who drive fewer than a predetermined number of miles a year.

6. Consider insurance cost when making a move. Insurance costs tend to be lowest in rural communities and highest in cities, where there is more traffic congestion.

7. Find out about automatic seat belt or air bag discounts.

8. Ask about antilock brakes. Some states require insurers to give discounts for cars equipped with the brakes. Some insurance companies offer discounts nationwide.

9. Inquire about other discounts. Insurers may offer discounts for no accidents in three years, to drivers over 50 years of age, for taking driver-training courses, and to young people for good grades.

Many states have "no-fault" insurance, a tactic for keeping premium costs down by eliminating many lawsuits. It doesn't matter who is at fault in an accident; if you are hurt in an auto accident, your losses or bills are covered by your insurance policy. In a "fault" state, if the accident was the fault of the other driver, you would collect from his or her insurance company. The rules for no-fault insurance vary by state.

RACHEL'S CAR

Rachel did get a car. She ended up buying a 1995 Subaru Impreza, a stick-shift, all-wheel-drive station wagon, for $8,500.

Remember I mentioned that Rachel did a lot of her research on the Internet? Well, she found her car on the Internet. She was talking to her sister about her frustrating search for the used Subaru she wanted. She couldn't find a manual shift, only automatic. And she hadn't unearthed a station wagon. Her sister asked Rachel to e-mail her her specifications. Her sister then did an Internet search and found the used Subaru Rachel wanted in Atlanta, where her parents live.

Rachel had test-driven several cars in Minneapolis, including a Suburu Impreza. She knew how it drove. Rachel had her dad pick up the car and test-drive it for her. He also had his mechanic check it out. Imagine, it was cheaper for Rachel to fly to Atlanta and drive it back home in two days than it was for her to buy a comparable car in Minneapolis. How did Rachel finance her car? She put $5,000 of her savings toward the car and borrowed $3,500 from her parents. And they put her on a strict repayment plan.

The last time I saw Rachel, she and her dog were enjoying their improved creature comforts. I asked her how the dog liked the Subaru. "She is happy," said Rachel. "She is not going to have as much free rein in it as I let her have in my Toyota. No rawhides, no wood, and no shedding. She can shed—just kidding."

IN SUMMARY

Rachel had a lot of questions at first, but in the end she got the car she wanted for a reasonable price. Her experience proves that you don't have to be a gearhead or a savvy negotiator to be a smart car buyer.

Take control of the process. And that means get good information. Rachel used the Internet, a terrific source for information that greatly expands the geographic size of your marketplace. But you can also use the library, read the newspaper, and consult publications like *Consumer Reports* and the books by Jack Gillis.

Find out what the dealer paid for the car and start your pricing negotiations there. Pass on the dealer's warranty. The carmaker's warranty is enough. Take a long test drive. Rachel didn't test-drive the actual car she bought—her dad did—but she drove one like it.

When it comes to paying for your car, don't let the low monthly payments on a lease be the driving force behind your financing decision. Consider borrowing, since leasing gives you all the headaches of car ownership with none of the benefits. If you buy a used car, have a mechanic check it out first.

Above all, tap into the power of competition.

Resources

There are a lot of good new car and used car buying books.

Consumer Reports New Car Buying Guide (annual), by the editors of *Consumer Reports* (Consumer Reports Books). For many people, this is the bible of car buying. This organization truly believes in an educated, informed consumer.

Consumer Reports Used Car Buying Guide (annual), by the editors of *Consumer Reports* (Consumer Reports Books).

The Car Book: The Definitive Buyer's Guide to Car Safety, Fuel Economy, Maintenance, and Much More (serial), by Jack Gillis with Ashley B. Cheng, Karen Fierst, and Amy B. Curran (HarperPerennial). Jack Gillis is clear and insightful. He has a genuine knack of boiling down information to its essence. After all, we are in the market to buy a car, not to get a Ph.D. in car buying.

The Used Car Book (serial), by Jack Gillis with Scott Beatty and Karen Fierst (HarperPerennial).

Smarter Insurance Solutions, by Janet Bamford (Bloomberg Press). Janet's book is the best on all aspects of insurance. Check out her chapter on buying auto insurance.

The Internet is a tremendous resource for consumers in the market for a new or used car. This is one area of the new economy where reality meets the hype. Certainly, there is a wealth of information, and the Internet is terrific for trolling for car data, price facts, and well-thought-out advice. You can even shop for a car on the web. But there is no guarantee that you will get a better price on the Internet than you will at a car dealership.

consumerreports.org. Want the latest invoice price on a car you're interested in? What about manufacturer rebates or incentives? Ten ways to check a used car so you don't end up with a lemon? You can easily spend a couple of hours at this site.

edmunds.com. This is another well-known source for all kinds of data on new and used cars. Again, this is the kind of site you can profitably spend hours on, going through car data. No need to visit a dealer until you are ready. Edmunds.com has a very good discussion of the trade-offs between leasing and borrowing.

carpoint.msn.com. I spend a fair amount of time on the Internet. It is becoming more user-friendly. Carpoint is a good example of the trend. It offers a virtual auto show, new car reviews, a payments calculator, and so forth.

autobytel.com. You can research the car you want and then send your specifications to Autobytel.com. An accredited Autobytel.com dealer near you will find what you want and give you a price. You check out the car, and, if you like it, you purchase it at the agreed-upon price.

kbb.com. What is your trade-in worth? The *Kelley Blue Book* online gives you that information. Plus much more.

intellichoice.com. Decent side-by-side price comparisons, plus car reviews.

autoconnect.com. This site has a lot of used cars, invoice pricing, and side-by-side price comparisons.

autoadvantage.com. New cars and more.

leasesource.com. Want to plug in some numbers on a lease? Do some comparison shopping? Read some articles on leasing? Stop by here.

kiplinger.com/calc. *Kiplinger's* is a well-known personal finance magazine. Its web site has quite a few online calculators, including several for car buyers.

hwysafety.org. Far too many people die on our roads every year. The Insurance Institute for Highway Safety and the Highway Loss Data Institute have posted a lot of good safety information.

nhtsa.gov. A sobering site. The National Highway Traffic Safety Administration has gathered together its crash test data and safety information. It also contains depressing statistics on the economic and social cost of automobile accidents.

bog.frb.fed.us/pubs/leasing. The Federal Reserve Board's consumer guide to leasing. A good explanation of the difference between leasing a car and buying a car.

nada.org. The National Automobile Dealers Association offers car news, industry statistics, and buying guides at its web site.

insure.com. A good starting place for auto insurance news and information.

insweb.com. You can calculate your auto insurance needs and shop for a policy online.

4

Buying a Home

Ah! There is nothing like staying at home
for real comfort.

—Jane Austen, *Emma*

A place to call your own: It's the American Dream. But a home is also the most expensive and complicated investment most Americans ever make. Homeownership offers rich rewards and plenty of risk.

Katie Schneider and Mark Larson were starting a life together in Minneapolis. They were engaged to be married. They both had new jobs, she as a multimedia producer at an international public relations firm and he as a sports magazine publisher. And they were looking to buy their first home.

Mark and Katie lived in a clean, modern one-bedroom apartment. Although their apartment was relatively nondescript, it was in one of the city's more attractive neighborhoods close by a major lake, with bike paths, walking trails, and canoe rentals. They had a vague wish list of the kind of home they would like to live in: an older home with charm and character, a three-car garage, a bathroom on the first floor, a fireplace, at least three bedrooms, and on a quiet street. Mark and Katie imagined living in the house for only two to three years. They planned on making some modest do-it-yourself renovations and then selling the improved home at a hefty profit. "I see it as an opportunity to buy a house that is in some need of repair, make those repairs, make some updates, and then get out with some equity," Mark said.

The conversations they'd had about a home, their vision of a comfortable place to spend quality time in, and their strong expectation that it would be a profitable investment are typical of first-time home buyers around the country. After all, many of our parents rode the post–World War II middle-class real estate boom. I've met numerous people who have done exceptionally well in real estate in New York and California. However, for everyone who has scored a real estate killing, there are many more who have done only middling well—and buried many of their homeowning money mistakes.

Mark was intrigued by the idea of buying a duplex. A friend of theirs who had made money in commercial real estate recommended they purchase a duplex, rent out the top half, pay for their mortgage (or much of it) out of the rental income, and take advantage of the business expense write-offs available to landlords. But their friend did point out that as a landlord seeking renters it's preferable to own a duplex on a busy street with a lot of traffic. "Is that the kind of neighborhood we want to live in?" asked Katie. "I'd rather have something that's not on a busy street."

Mark and Katie puzzled over all the classic concerns. Both wondered about finding a real estate agent they could trust. Katie wondered how she could tell if a house was in good condition or a lemon. "I can tell if the floors are in bad shape," she said. "But if the electricity is outdated or if the heating system is going to need to be replaced, I don't know those things." Mark worried about finding a good mortgage. He said that they couldn't come up with the traditional 20% down payment. He figured they could manage 10% to 15%. "I don't want to be in over our heads," he said. "I want to do it the right way."

Mark and Katie were asking the three most important questions facing any home buyer, whether your first time or the tenth: How do you choose the right house? How do you calculate how much you can afford? And how do you finance your purchase? But their expectations were unrealistic. There's no way they could find, in the city, an affordable three-bedroom home with a three-car garage, character, quiet, and a fireplace that will make their financial dream come true in two to three years. Homeownership doesn't work that way.

HOME ECONOMICS

The stock market grabs almost all of the money attention these days. Yet when it comes to investing, many people care a lot more about their home. For one thing, few people develop the kind of emotional and psychological attachment to stocks that they do to their homes. We identify with our homes and shape them to our tastes and personalities. We can invite our friends into our home and keep other people out. A home and domestic well-being are almost the same thing.

For another, a home is the second-largest item on the household balance sheet after equities. A record two-thirds of American households own their own home. All age and income groups have shown housing gains in recent years. For example, minorities made up a third of first-time home buyers in 1998 versus a fifth in 1985, according to the Joint Center on Housing Studies at Harvard University. Even assuming the inevitable national recession and an accompanying downturn in the housing market, it's likely that the nation's homeownership rate in the early decades of this century will climb higher, perhaps matching Maine's 77% homeownership rate—currently the highest among the states.

Yet a decade ago, the sentiment was that home prices were in for a long stagnation at best and a downward spiral at worst.

A big reason for the pessimism was demographics. Home prices would fall as aging baby-boom home sellers confronted too few young home buyers. For instance, David Weil and Gregory Mankiw, economists at Harvard University, forecast in a famous academic article that housing prices would drop by some 3% a year between 1987 and 2007, after adjusting for inflation. Instead housing prices were largely unchanged between the mid-1980s and the mid-1990s, and they rebounded strongly after that.

The dismal forecast didn't pan out for a numbers of reasons. Interest rates came down sharply. Buying a home became far more affordable as fixed-rate 30-year mortgages fell from an average of almost 10% in the late 1980s to the 7% to 8% range in recent years. Household incomes rose sharply, thanks to the long economic expansion and low unemployment rates. The strong stock market also helped support the demand for homes. Immigrants, who are flocking to America in record numbers, are eager home buyers, too.

What kind of investment return can homeowners expect over the long haul? I'd keep my expectations modest and not count on anything spectacular. Of course, there are those moments when a real estate market will skyrocket, as in Boston and Los Angeles in the late 1980s and in San Francisco and Portland in the latter part of the 1990s. But in general, I wouldn't count on doubling your money on real estate. Here's one potential measure of residential real estate's long-term return: From 1850 to 1992, the after-inflation return on homeownership was 2.5% a year, according to a study by economist Karl Case of Wesleyan College. The data come from 16,000 unencumbered land sales in Middlesex County, Massachusetts.

Another, slightly lower figure comes from one of the better economists I know, Mark M. Zandi, chief economist and a founder of the Regional Financial Associates, an economic consulting firm. Like any market, whether it's oil or housing, home prices come from the interaction between supply and demand. He argues that on the supply side, if the demographics do turn out to be somewhat negative, home builders will cut back on new construction as demand slackens. On the demand side, the single most important factor driving the housing market is the growth in household income. Americans will demand as much housing as they can afford. After making some reasonable projections (personal income growth of 4% a year and consumer price inflation of 2.5%), Zandi forecasts that house price gains will average about 1.5% a year, after subtracting inflation. "Real house price gains during the next 20 years are thus expected to be more than twice as strong as during the past 20 years," he says.

THE LONG-RUN HOUSE PRICE OUTLOOK

Annual rate, after adjusting for inflation:

1970s	2.3%
1980s	–0.4%
1990s	0.9%
2000s	1.5%
2010s	1.2%

DATA: Regional Financial Associates.

THE RENT-VERSUS-BUY DECISION

A home is a good investment if you live in it long enough to ride out any market downturns. A home comes with good tax benefits, too, especially the deductibility of mortgage interest payments and no capital taxes due on home sale gains under $500,000. You automatically increase your savings as you pay down your mortgage. Still, no matter what the big economic picture, everyone decides to buy a home based more on his or her own hopes and dreams. A home is a neighborhood, schools, a commute, and a nesting place you get to decorate your way. Your lifestyle choices and the state of your personal economy determine what you buy just as much as interest rates and tax benefits. "If you're a person who has the ability to invest and earn 25%, 30% a year on your money, and if all that's important to you is making money, live in a cardboard box," says Roger Harrington, a mortgage consultant. "But if you do want to enjoy your home, your castle, and have a reasonable financial investment program on the side, and be able to buy food and take care of your family, having a nice home is just wonderful."

Homeownership is not for everyone. You should calculate whether it makes financial sense for you to rent or buy. The calculators are easily available on the Internet, or you can just use paper, pencil, and a handheld calculator. In essence, you want to compare the cost of renting to the after-tax cost of owning. With rent, your calculation should include your security deposit, the monthly rent payment, and any anticipated rent increases. With homeownership, there is the price of the home, the mortgage, the down payment, closing costs, maintenance and taxes, your tax rate, how long you expect to live in the home, the anticipated appreciation of your investment, and several other factors. You then compare the cash flows between the two and see whether it's better for you to rent or buy. I advise taking the time to play with the numbers. Ideally, you should run a range of scenarios, plugging in different rates of appreciation, home improvement costs, interest rates, and other factors to develop a sense of the financial possibilities. Also, review your other goals and competing investments to make sure this is the right trade-off for you.

Time is among the most critical factors, though. The longer you intend to stay in a home, the better the financial advantages of ownership look. The risk of taking a loss are simply too great if you don't have time on your side. "I advise people that if you plan on buying a house and you anticipate being in it somewhere around three years, give or take a couple of months, don't buy the house," says Allen Cymrot, head of Cymrot Realty Advisors and a longtime real estate investor who lives in the San Francisco Bay area but still carries more than a trace of a Brooklyn accent. "Find a nice place to rent."

Of course, buying a home is an emotional decision. Deep down, most people want to own a house. It's a place we can change any way we want without asking for a landlord's permission. A home is a refuge from the pressures and tumult of the outside world. A place of our own is also a very visible, tangible sign that we are moving up in the world.

The choice to own a home may be emotional. But keep your emotions in check while shopping. There are many risks and pitfalls when making the biggest purchase in your life.

HOW MUCH HOUSE

All home buyers, whether it's their first purchase or their fourth, enjoy thinking about the kind of environment and amenities they'd like. But let's look at some numbers. A traditional criterion in the real estate universe is being able to put down 20% of the purchase price. It's a good cushion, and lenders won't require you to buy private mortgage insurance to protect them against the risk that you'll default. It wasn't all that long ago that if you couldn't afford a 20% down payment ($20,000 on a $100,000 loan) it was tough to get a mortgage. Today, lenders will do business with you even if you put down only 3% or less (although I strongly advise against such low down payments for most people).

Here's another measure of how much house you can afford to buy. The standard ratio on how much debt you can take on is that no more than 28% of your income should go toward the mortgage, and that includes principal, interest, taxes, and insurance. Mortgage lenders also use this rule of thumb: No more than 36% of your income should go to your mortgage (principal, interest, taxes, and insurance) and all your other long-term debt, including car loans, motorcycle loans, credit card debts, student loans, and any other kind of debt you might owe. Of course, if you have an extremely secure job you could carry the upper limit of these lending industry guidelines. On the other hand, if your income varies widely or job insecurity is endemic to your profession, these financing standards are far too generous.

The Internet is full of affordability calculators (at the end of this chapter are some of the web sites I like). You can ask a broker or a lender to run the numbers for you to find out whether you qualify for a loan—and for how much. You simply tell a banker your income and your expenses and how much of a down payment you plan to make, and then the banker will say you are prequalified for a mortgage of so many thousands of dollars. It's a first cut estimate, and relatively meaningless. The bank isn't on the hook. But prequalification allows you to realistically target your home price range.

As you narrow down your choices, you should consider getting your mortgage financing in place with preapproval. A lender makes a conditional mortgage agreement with you, and it's a good idea. The lender will examine your income, your expenses, and your credit record—everything except the home that you're going to buy. The lender approves you for a mortgage up to a certain amount. In essence, both you and the seller know that you will get the mortgage you need to buy a home, assuming a satisfactory home inspection and some other critical tests are met.

My guess is that you will be stunned at how much home you can afford—really, how big a mortgage you can qualify for—when you run the numbers. I disagree with the folk wisdom that you should buy as much house as possible, even if that means not making a 15% to 20% down payment. I realize many first-time home buyers can't pull together 20%. Even so, get as close as you can or downsize your expectations.

The risks of stretching financially are substantial. A home is expensive to own. For one thing, as soon as you move in, you'll see that the furniture you've accumulated over the years looks wrong in your home. You'll probably need a lot more furniture if you are moving from an apartment into a house. After all, you could be going from a one-bedroom apartment with a living room and an efficiency kitchen to a small house with three bedrooms, kitchen, living room, dining room, and basement. For another, you may love tending your garden and taking care of the lawn. But that pleasure costs money. The same goes for maintaining the home. Before long, you're fixing the deck, paving the walk, remodeling the kitchen, painting the walls, and tiling the bathroom floor. At the same time, you want to start saving for your kids' college education and your retirement, and you're beginning to realize that your parents are going to need your help. "Lenders will give you enough rope to hang yourself," says Roger Harrington. "You really do have to apply the discipline to yourself. It's wise to set up a budget and say this is where I need my money, this is for food, this is for education, this is for utilities, this is for investments, and this is for savings. You've got to set the limits on yourself, because generally the lenders won't do it for you."

It's no fun being house-poor. The risks are too great. Lean toward the financially conservative side and make sure that homeownership doesn't prevent you from meeting other important financial goals.

FINDING A HOME

A home is nothing but a series of trade-offs for all but gazillionaires. The rest of us have to make many compromises.

Mark wanted a three-car garage and Katie was attracted to a charming Victorian-style home. Yet three-car garages go with new construction, and Victorian homes with one-car garages, usually detached from the house and in some disrepair. Older homes have smaller windows, fewer bathrooms, and modest closets. But they also have wood floors, cozy alcoves, and appealing artistic flourishes of a bygone era. In many parts of the country, living in an older home means you can walk to a newspaper store, a coffee shop, a small grocer, and a nearby park. Newer construction often comes with bigger yards, no sidewalks, bike paths, more privacy, and a car trip for shopping— even for a cup of coffee. One of the biggest decisions you'll make when shopping for a home is whether to buy a newer home or a vintage abode.

Money obviously plays a role, too. Depending on where you live, a house with three bathrooms, including one on the first floor, might cost $200,000 and up. If your budget is $150,000, one of the bathrooms probably has to go. An eat-in kitchen that comfortably sits four at a table may mean buying a home with a price tag of at least $100,000. Wood floors, wood trim, and decorative touches like stained-glass windows might add $20,000 to the cost of a home in some areas. Real estate markets are very local, but within your area you will get a good idea of what various amenities add to the price of a home during your shopping expeditions.

I've found taking advantage of open houses to be useful, especially early in the looking process. You can get a feel for what is available at what price range after spending a couple of afternoons on your own checking out the open houses. It's also smart to take a local community home-buying class, perhaps offered by a nonprofit organization or a community development board. They are cheap and informative.

To minimize the risk of becoming overwhelmed, make a checklist of what you want. How much do features like a fireplace, three-car garage, or first-floor bathroom matter to you? As you look at homes in your price range, decide where you are willing to compromise and where you aren't. When you are looking at houses, it pays to write down your impressions. File your notes with the seller's sheet detailing the home's basic layout and any other information the real estate agent can give you. Believe me, if you don't keep a written record, everything starts blurring together. You and your spouse will end up having conversations like this: "I really liked the laundry-room-and-mud-room combination at the home on Sycamore Street." "No, that wasn't Sycamore. That was Harvard Place. Sycamore had the fireplace you liked." "It did not. You're thinking of . . ." Buying a home is stressful enough. Don't compound it with disorganization.

And if you are buying a home as a couple, talk to each other. Two people can bring very different expectations to the home-buying process. For instance, Mark seemed to look at a home more as an investment and Katie more as a lifestyle choice. You'll be making personal trade-offs with your partner just as much as you'll make trade-offs about house features. The home-buying mantra for couples should be "communicate and compromise."

I would strongly encourage you to research the public school system even if you don't have kids and don't plan on having any. Many families put a high value on good public schools. Similarly, is the neighborhood convenient to work for people who are employed in the local area or commute to their job? Again, there are trade-offs. Homes in communities with good schools and easy commutes are easier to sell because the demand is always there, but they are also more expensive to buy.

When you get serious about a community and several homes in it, talk to the neighbors and ask them what they like and don't like about the area. Most people are candid if you solicit their opinions. Ask them about crime, and also look up the local crime statistics at the library or on the Internet. I would also visit the homes and neighborhoods that have captured your imagination on a stormy night or rainy day, as well as when the sun is shining. You could be living in that home in all kinds of weather and seasons. As much as possible, you'd like a sense that the house will feel warm and cozy in wintertime and cool and open during the summer. "You're never going to get everything you want in the house," says Allen Cymrot. "But there's a certain acceptable grade that allows the house to take care of your personal needs."

Of course, you can't anticipate every contingency. You can't get rid of every uncertainty. You're just trying to eliminate the risks that truly trouble you or are unacceptable to you. I remember when my wife and I bought our first home. We were living in a 350-square-foot apartment in Manhattan. Good location, but lots of cockroaches. Newly married, we moved across the river to Brooklyn to get more space. We picked out a recently renovated two-bedroom apartment in Carroll Gardens, an old, mostly Italian neighborhood. The apartment was a second-story walk-up in a five-story brownstone. What we did not anticipate is how steep those stairs would seem after we had our first child.

A FIXER-UPPER

What about buying a home that needs a lot of work, doing all the repairs on your own, and selling the upgraded home at a substantial profit? All of us would love to profit from sweat equity. I know someone who has followed such a blueprint several times, and he has done very well financially. Yet fixing up homes is a passion for him. It's not a chore. But how much sawdust are you willing to live with? How good a craftsman are you? People will pay up only for professional-quality improvements. They will flee from amateur repairs. What's more, you need a pretty hefty

profit to justify the investment. If you buy a small house, reno-
vate it, sell it in three years, buy a slightly bigger house, remodel
it, and sell it in a few years, and so on, you will incur a lot of closing costs, legal fees, mortgage fees, and all the other expenses
associated with real estate transactions. Those costs will add up
over time. There are different methods of making money in real
estate, but there are no easy ways to pocket a profit.

Mark did visit some friends of his parents who had re-
habbed a home sometime after we had met for the first time.
He was stunned at all the work that had gone into improving
the property. "There is no way," said Mark. "I mean, he's a professional carpenter and it took him seven years to finish the
place." Mark also doubted that these homeowners would get
everything out of the home that they had put into it.

Don't get me wrong. Remodeling, repairing, and renovat-
ing a home are fine. In today's world, many people are choosing to overhaul their homes rather than move. Why not?
They're happy with the community. They like the schools. They
don't feel like moving, but they would like a bathroom on the
first floor or a bigger family room and kitchen. Americans
spend about $150 billion a year on home improvements (about
2% of gross domestic product), according to Harvard's Joint
Center for Housing Studies at Harvard University. You can get
your money back on certain home improvements, too. For example, Remodeling Online's 1998–1999 Cost vs. Value report
indicates that a minor kitchen remodel will return 94% of your
investment within one year of the home improvement. In sharp
contrast, a home office will only return about 64%. Swimming
pools are at the bottom of most lists.

THE REAL ESTATE AGENT

First-time home buyers are always stunned at how many people
get involved in the transaction. Signing on with a real estate

agent marks the beginning of letting go of your fantasies and entering a world of lenders, lawyers, title insurers, inspectors, and other professionals. But you will work most closely with a real estate agent, so do your homework and choose wisely.

Like everything else in today's society, the real estate business has become more complicated, including how brokers are compensated. But the bottom line remains the same—you want a competent broker. Before signing an agreement with anyone, interview several brokers and get recommendations. In most cases, the seller pays the commission cost.

The traditional real estate agent, similar to the one your parents used and still the most common type, is an agent of the seller. The agent shows you around to different homes, and you develop a certain rapport with him or her. But the agent has a fiduciary responsibility to represent the seller whose home you visited. The agent has a legal obligation to get the best possible price for the seller. After all, it's the seller who pays the real estate agent's commission. Of course, agents want to get a deal done, and part of the agent's job is to find common ground between buyers and sellers. "They can take you to lunch, they can drive you around, they can kiss your kids, but they are not the agent of the buyer unless you specify that," says Julie Garton-Good, once a real estate agent herself and now a real estate author and lecturer.

A "buyer's" agent is increasingly popular. A buyer's agent is just that—an advocate for the buyer. For instance, a buyer's agent can talk frankly about what he or she sees as the pros and the cons of the homes you visit, something conventional agents are restricted from doing. One potential drawback: Typically, a buyer's agent wants you to sign an exclusivity agreement—you'll work solely with that agent for a stated length of time. The exclusivity agreement puts a premium on making sure you want to work with this broker—so keep the exclusivity time frame relatively short. And recognize that the agent has an incentive to pressure you to close a deal as the expiration of the exclusivity agreement looms. A buyer's agent is often the best choice. Although the buyer can owe the buyer's agent a fee, it usually ends up being paid by the seller. The seller's agent typically agrees to split the commission with the buyer's broker.

Some brokers and agents represent solely the seller or the buyer. Many "single agents" swing on both sides of the real estate street. They may be a buyer's agent for some customers and a seller's agent for others. In sharp contrast, "dual" agents are matchmakers for both the buyer and the seller in the same transaction. However, most experts agree that the dual agent relationship sets up an almost impossible conflict-of-interest situation, so I would steer clear of that association. Discount brokers are a growing force in the industry. In essence, discount brokers get you access to the list of properties in your area, but then you are on your own. In all cases, you want it fully disclosed to you who the agent represents.

The market for real estate services has become more diverse and flexible. You have more choices than before. When you work with a real estate agent you can contract with them to do everything or a few things. You get to decide. The Internet holds the promise of giving the real estate buyer even greater choice and control. But for now real estate online is best used for research, education, calculations, and information. Yes, more and more people are trying to sell their homes on the Internet. The numbers who are managing to do it are small but growing rapidly. The real estate industry is putting up a valiant fight to keep the Internet from eroding commissions. But it won't be long before the Multiple Listing Service—the valuable information that carries all the homes for sale and their price tag—is widely available on the Internet. Still, whether Internet home buying grows in popularity or not, you must visit in person the homes that you are interested in.

Whom should you use? I've used a traditional real estate agent and a buyer's agent. Although I think real estate agents are overpaid relative to what they bring to the transaction (especially in a strong housing market), my personal experience with the professionals I dealt with was positive. Still, I was more comfortable with the idea of working with a buyer's agent—after I'd done a lot of research on the Internet. Using a broker or agent who represents you—the buyer—limits your risks of not getting the knowledge a real estate professional can bring to the process. The risk-reward trade-off certainly leads me in that direction.

THE INSPECTION

Katie voiced a concern all of us share when we are looking for a home. How do you know the plumbing works, the flooring is sound, the boiler will fire up in the winter, and the roof doesn't leak? You will see a lot that is right and wrong with a home when you walk through it. When you get serious about a couple of homes, if you know someone who is in construction, good at home remodeling, or an experienced home buyer, ask him or her to come along with you and look at the house. They may see things that you have missed.

It's time to make your bid. The seller has the home on the market for, let's say, $136,000, the average price of a single-family home in a metropolitan area. You tap into your broker's or agent's professional expertise to get an idea how much you should bid. You should have a good idea what the home is worth after looking at comparable home sales data in the area. You and the seller start negotiating after you've made your bid, hoping to find common ground. As in any negotiation, keep your emotions in check and be prepared to walk away. This is the moment to remember the price guidelines you spent so much time establishing. Don't let your competitive juices run amuck, your annoyance at the seller overtake your judgment, or pressure from the real estate agent sway you into paying too much for your income and lifestyle. You will regret it later on. Believe me.

When you put in your offer for the home, it's contingent on the home passing inspection. Now, when real estate markets are hot and homes are going for above the seller's asking price, some agents will take you aside and recommend putting in a bid without an inspection clause. They'll tell you it will increase the odds that the seller will favor your offer. That may be true. But I say forget it. This is a huge purchase. You could be living in it for many years. You're only asking for trouble by waiving an inspection. It's unlikely that you'll lose the house by insisting on an inspection clause—but even if you do, eventually the market will cool off and you'll find a house you like even better.

Not all inspectors are created equal. Many inspectors are moonlighting, and the quality of their work can vary widely. Julie Garton-Good recommends choosing one who has been certified by the American Society of Home Inspectors. Other trade groups that require training are the National Association of Home Inspectors and the National Institute of Building Inspectors. The inspector can't rip the house apart. But an experienced inspector will look for trouble spots, signs of damage that hint at a bigger problem. He or she will look at the roof and the gutters, check the wiring, inspect the boiler, and so on. He or she will give you a detailed report on what they found. The deal is off without any financial penalty or liability to you if the inspector unearths unacceptable problems. Alternatively, you can decide the trouble spots uncovered by the inspector are tolerable so long as the seller reduces the purchase by an amount to cover future repairs. For example, if the inspector says the roof will need to be replaced in a year or two, you can ask to have the purchase price cut by the price of a new roof. If the seller says yes, you've got a deal. If the seller says no, you can either walk away and move on to another potential home or decide to go through with the purchase anyway.

Your offer should include at least two other contingencies. First, the deal should be subject to your getting approved for a mortgage (if you are turned down by a lender, you aren't on the hook for any money to the home seller). Second, the seller must prove that they have clear title to the property.

FINANCING THE PURCHASE

A mortgage is a real deep-breath moment. You are about to deal with some of the biggest checks of your life. It's like winning the lottery in reverse, the same vertigo, only you're not going to Disneyland. Unless you have very generous parents or a rich uncle or have hit a mother lode of stock options at work, it's amazing how much money you'll borrow to own a home.

Mortgages are complicated. They come with different interest rates, loan terms, and maturities. You should get an amortization table from a mortgage lender or pick one up at a bookstore. The amortization table lays out the principal and interest payments on a loan and makes it easier for you to compare different loans. The World Wide Web is invaluable for researching different loans and calculating the many trade-offs you face.

At root, picking a mortgage involves thinking about what risks you are comfortable taking with your finances, and how those risks fit with your other financial goals. For instance, an adjustable-rate mortgage is often cheaper (at least initially) than a fixed-rate mortgage, but your monthly outlay can change from year to year. Check whether the mortgage has a prepayment penalty. A prepayment penalty is a charge a lender will impose if you pay off a loan early. You want a mortgage with no prepayment penalty or a very short penalty period. The mortgage market is so competitive it's a financial penalty you don't have to incur.

There are several hundred mortgage options available, but underneath all the razzle-dazzle are several basic mortgages. Everything else is built around these basic mortgage types. Here's a brief overview of the four basic options.

30-year fixed-rate mortgage: The most popular with consumers is the traditional 30-year fixed-rate mortgage. It's the industry mainstay. The big advantage of a fixed-rate mortgage is that you know what your monthly payments will be for the life of the loan. It doesn't matter what happens elsewhere in the world of finance—your monthly payment is locked in. If interest rates go up, that's your lender's problem. If interest rates go down and stay down, you can always refinance and take out another fixed-rate mortgage at a lower rate. "The best advice I can give is, if you can fix a rate that you can afford and know that's going to be your rate, take a fixed-rate mortgage," says Allen Cymrot.

15-year fixed-rate mortgage: The 15-year fixed-rate mortgage is gaining adherents. The reason is simple: You save a lot of money in the long term. If you buy a $200,000 home with $50,000 down and a $150,000, 30-year mortgage at an 8% rate of interest, your monthly payment will be about $1,100 and your total interest bill will be $246,232. If instead you have a $150,000, 15-year mortgage, your monthly payment will be $1,433, but the interest tab will come to only $108,026.

Here is an alternative strategy to the 15-year mortgage. Take out a 30-year fixed-rate mortgage, thus locking in the lower monthly outlay. Then write a second check for one-twelfth your average mortgage tab each payment period. Tell the lender to apply the second check to paying down principal. Borrowers who make 13 payments a year rather than 12 will pay off a 30-year mortgage in about 22 years, saving a considerable sum in interest payments. For instance, the interest savings on our $150,000 mortgage amounts to nearly $69,000. The big advantage of this approach is flexibility. Let's say your financial circumstances change. Perhaps you lose your job, you need a new car, your children need extra tutoring, or an investment opportunity presents itself. You can always go back to the 30-year payment schedule with no penalty. By the way, if you plan on accelerating your mortgage payments, don't fall for a lender's offer to set up a biweekly payment schedule for $300 to $600. Why pay anything? Just send the lender another check on your own, with a note that the money is to go toward principal.

Adjustable-rate mortgage: The interest rate on an adjustable-rate mortgage, or ARM, floats according to fluctuations in some well-known fixed-income security. Common interest rate benchmarks include six-month, one-year, and three-year Treasury securities. The lender charges an interest rate typically somewhere between 1% and 4% above the benchmark index. Your interest rate can't go up or down by more than 1 to 3 percentage points at the interest rate adjustment date, and the adjustable-rate mortgages come with a lifetime cap. With an ARM, the initial interest rate is usually less than the rate on a 30-year fixed-rate mortgage. The low rate saves you money up front. Still, anyone taking out an ARM is betting that the interest rate environment will be favorable for the duration of the loan. Even if you save money with an ARM, it is a riskier loan than the conventional mortgage. Your monthly outlay can change yearly, sometimes for the better and sometimes for the worse. Some adjustable-rate mortgages allow you the option of converting the ARM into a fixed-rate mortgage. Problem is, that rate is always higher than the current fixed rate available on the market. So it's usually not a feature worth paying for.

You also need to be aware of negative amortization. It occurs when your monthly payment isn't enough to cover the principal and interest and the lender tacks the difference onto the loan. Some ARMs have negative amortization, some place caps on it, and others are structured so it doesn't happen. Make sure you understand this feature of any ARM you are considering. Competition in the market is eliminating negative amortization. You don't want negative amortization, and there are plenty of ARMs out there without it.

A mortgage two-step: These adjustable-rate mortgages offer some of the stability of a conventional mortgage. The two most popular are the 5/25 and the 7/23. In the first instance, the interest rate is fixed for the first five years at a rate below the rate on 30-year mortgages. It then floats yearly for the remainder of the loan. This can be a good mortgage for people who are moving into a new area. It's helpful to know what your monthly outlay will be while you get settled into your new hometown, and then, assuming your finances are in good shape, you can absorb the risk of a floating rate after several years. Similarly, if you relocate every couple of years because of work, a two-step mortgage gives you mortgage payment stability at a cheap rate. A 7/23 two-step mortgage is fixed for seven years, and then it floats for the next 23 years.

BUYING THE HOME

First-time home buyers, unless they are masters of high finance, are probably going to balk at trying to scare up $100,000 to $200,000 in mortgage money. But shopping is shopping, and mortgage money is widely available. Banks, thrifts, credit unions, mortgage brokers, and other lenders are falling all over themselves to offer consumers mortgages. What's more, mortgage lending on the Internet is growing fast, although from a small base. High-tech forecaster Forrester Research expects online mortgage loans to increase from $18 billion in 1999 to more than $91 billion in 2003. Online mortgages should bring down the cost of acquiring a loan.

So shop around. It's not enough to look at interest rates and the length of the loan. For instance, lenders charge different fees for processing your loan application. The terms of adjustable-rate loans can vary significantly. You will also have to decide how many points you want to pay. A point equals 1 percent of the loan amount. In other words, one point on a $100,000 loan is $1,000. Points typically range from 1 percent to 3 percent, and the more points you pay, the lower your interest rate. Lenders offer all kinds of point and interest rate combinations. For example, if you expect to move out of the house in the not-too-distant future, it may make sense to get a no-point or one-point mortgage. No-point loans are also popular when interest rates are high because the borrower expects to refinance the mortgage loan at a later date when rates have come down. But if this is the house of your dreams and you plan to stay forever, you may want to pay 3 points to lock in a lower interest rate.

The Internet is a terrific source for finding and comparing mortgages in your area. Several national mortgage search services offer for a modest fee a detailed listing of the mortgages available in your region, including the terms of the loans, the processing fees, and the closing costs. Check out the ads in the newspaper. And be ready to make a lot of calls as you narrow down your list of potential lenders.

Two terms you will hear a lot are "mortgage banker" and "mortgage broker." A mortgage banker is what most of us think of when we set about getting a home loan. It's a bank, thrift, or some other financial institution where a loan officer takes our loan application, approves it, closes the deal, and services the loan. A mortgage broker also processes your loan application, but the broker isn't a lender. Instead, the broker shops your loan application around to various institutional lenders and investors. The mortgage loan business is intensely competitive, so you should be able to get the kind of mortgage you want and good customer service.

If you can't make the traditional 20% down payment, the lender will usually insist on private mortgage insurance. It protects the lender against the borrower defaulting on the loan. Private mortgage insurance is costly. It's not deductible. Premium prices vary, depending on the type of loan and its terms, but the typical premium on a 30-year fixed-rate mortgage ranges between .25% and 1% of the annual loan amount. There really is nothing good to say about PMI except that it is a necessary evil if you can't or won't put down 20% of the purchase price. A new federal law requires private mortgage insurers to automatically cancel your PMI once the equity in your home is at 22%. Once the equity in your home is at 20%, contact your private mortgage insurer and find out what you need to do to get your PMI canceled.

In recent years, an alternative to PMI has sprung up. It goes by the name 80-10-10. You take out a mortgage worth 80% of the purchase price. You put down 10% in cash. You borrow another 10%—a so-called second mortgage—and that money goes to the down payment. You now have a 20% down payment and no private mortgage insurance. And the money you borrowed to make the down payment is tax-deductible. Which is better, PMI or 80-10-10? You should have someone run the numbers for you or do it yourself on a web calculator. PMI often, though not always, comes out ahead, especially now that it is easy to drop once your equity reaches the 20% threshold.

You've done all this work. Finally, it's time to sign legal documents—more legal documents than you've ever seen—and hand over a check for a sum of money you can't believe. This is a high-pressure situation, but you can't get intimidated. Everyone else in the room has done this countless times, and they are looking to get paid. But remember, they need your signature to get their money. This is your last chance to raise questions. So know what you are signing and, if you are dissatisfied, sit back, put the pen down, and seize control of the situation. Although it is not necessary in all states, it's often smart to hire a real estate lawyer to check out the deal struck between you and the seller. The lawyer also comes to the closing and represents your interests.

Pay close attention to all the closing costs. Your lender, by law, should have given you a good-faith estimate of all the fees, but the number of charges is astonishing. Fees can include title search fees, lender's processing fees, appraisal fees, attorney's fees, and so on. For instance, average closing costs for a home mortgage in late 1998 were $765 for an appraisal, credit report, application fee, document preparation, and flood certification, according to HSH Associates, a publisher of mortgage and consumer loan information. Here's the rueful advice from one homeowner. "Watch the fine lines when you do your closing, because they seem to want to add in all kinds of little things," he said. "I don't know, legal fees, abstract fees, all these things they never really tell you about when you are originally going in."

MARK AND KATIE

When I first spoke with Mark and Katie, they had a very ambitious vision of homeownership. They had a lot of plans for their first house—especially Mark. But they seemed rather chastened by our experts' views. Mark abandoned the idea of imitating *This Old House.* A major renovation was for another day. "It's inevitable whenever you buy an older home or an existing home you are going to have to redecorate," he said. "But I think we will be looking for a house that is pretty much in move-in condition."

He had wondered about buying a duplex rather than a single-family home, a town house, or a condo. But the difference between owning a home and being a landlord is comparable to that between driving a Volkswagen Beetle and a Peterbilt. As with any small business, there are many financial risks that come from renting out property. You might not find a tenant for a long time, you could get saddled with a destructive tenant or one who is late with the rent money, and you have many repair responsibilities that eat up cash.

A landlord is a good occupation, and many entrepreneurs have done well at owning rental property. But it also takes a special kind of person, one who doesn't mind late-night calls from irate tenants because the toilet's overflowing. You also need the ability to do at least some repairs on your own to keep your costs down, and deep enough pockets to maintain the property's value. "If you want to be a landlord, you really had better think about it, talk to people who have done it, because it can really ruin your life," says Roger Harrington.

Mark had dropped the idea for now. He was still interested in investing in rental property down the road. But first, he acknowledged, Katie and he needed to learn how to handle owning a home. Plus, they were getting married. "We don't need to throw into that a duplex and all that responsibility," he said. "I don't think it's what we are after right now."

Mark and Katie were compromising on what they wanted out of a home. For instance, the idea of a three-car garage was gone if they ended up staying in the city. They were also widening their house search, checking out several suburban neighborhoods. "We have to weigh everything and see how it balances out and what's important to us," said Katie.

Perhaps most important, Mark and Katie realized that a home was a longer-term commitment than three years. The choice between an older home and a new one depends on personal taste. But the financial numbers just don't work out if your ownership time frame is too short.

In my experience, every first-time home buyer makes a number of costly mistakes. The biggest ones are purchasing a too-expensive home, picking a house that's the wrong size for the family, and buying a home that is hard to sell. But these mistakes are easily avoided if you do homework and stay calm. Before you spend a big chunk of your savings on a house, invest in your choice. Think about where you want to live and what you can afford. And then, as the process picks up, monitor your real estate agent, keep close tabs on your lender, insist on an inspection, and, no matter what, closely watch all your costs. Perhaps most important, constantly review the trade-offs you are making, and stay comfortable with your decisions. And then enjoy the fruits of all your hard work.

Resources

Home Buying for Dummies, by Eric Tyson and Ray Brown (IDG Books Worldwide). A knowledgeable and insightful tour through the home-buying world.

All About Mortgages: Insider Tips to Finance or Refinance Your Home, by Julie Garton-Good (Dearborn). This author is tops when it comes to real estate. I like this and her other guide to home buying and selling. Both are written in a question-and-answer format.

The Frugal Homeowner's Guide to Buying, Selling, & Improving Your Home, by Julie Garton-Good (Dearborn).

10 Steps to Home Ownership: A Workbook for First-Time Buyers, by Ilyce Glink (Times Books).

100 Questions Every First-Time Home Buyer Should Ask: With Answers from Top Brokers from Around the Country, by Ilyce Glink (Times Books). She covers all the basic home-buying questions in her books.

hsh.com. The site of HSH Associates, a mortgage adviser based in Butler, New Jersey, has a national survey of closing costs so you'll know if a lender quotes you too high a figure. Its home-buying articles are excellent. HSH is a resource I use all the time on mortgage and real estate questions.

smartcalc.com. This site's interactive calculator allows you to plug in numbers so you can figure out whether it makes sense for you to refinance.

homeadvisor.msn.com. One of the most complete real estate sites on the web. A good rent-versus-buy calculator.

homefair.com. Thinking about moving to another part of the country, perhaps for lifestyle reasons or for a job? You can do a lot of research right here. The web site includes a cost-of-moving calculator.

ashi.com. The web site of the American Society of Home Inspectors.

todayshomeowner.com. Once you own the home, you'll need to maintain it and make modest improvements. The web site created by *Today's Homeowner* magazine is full of good information and well laid out.

mbaa. The Mortgage Bankers Association of America offers home-buying tips and planning tools for the first-time home buyer. I especially like the articles by the "Mortgage Professor," otherwise known as Jack M. Guttentag, professor emeritus at the Wharton School.

realtor.com. The Internet site of the National Association of Realtors.

loanguide.com. A good place to go for calculators and data.

fanniemae.com. Click on Fannie Mae's consumer section, and you'll find a wealth of home-buying and refinancing information.

5

A College Education

The educated person now matters.

—Peter Drucker

$624,000. Ouch. That's what the bill for tuition, fees, room, and board could be for Joel and Missy Levintman to send their five kids to four-year private colleges, assuming a 4% annual cost increase. The public university bill would still be $236,000. Norman, their oldest, is a 17-year-old high school senior about to head off to college. Behind him are 13-year-old Donielle, nine-year-old Jessie, and the six-year-old twins, Briana and Shira.

The Levintmans have a decent family income, but not that kind of money lying around in their estate. Joel is a single-practitioner lawyer and a twice-monthly conciliation court judge. Missy is the education director at her synagogue. She also teaches Hebrew at an afternoon community school and at Carlton College. The Levintmans place a very high value on education. It's a clear priority. For instance, Norman tutors Hebrew at the Jewish community center, and Donielle and Jessie are in after-school study programs. The kids attend summer camp in Israel. "We believe that in order for them to achieve what they want to achieve they need to be highly educated," says Joel. "But as I sit and think about it, starting next year I'll be paying for college until I'm probably about 63 or 64 years old."

Joel and Missy are looking at 16 years of college payments. With so many children at different ages, they are somewhat shell-shocked, but determined. When we were talking, it was readily apparent that their children are going to get college diplomas. Their goal was to make it happen and limit the financial burden. The Levintmans hadn't put much money aside for Norman, or for any of the other children. Like many middle-aged, middle-income folks with kids, they found that the rigors of everyday life made it tough to save. Yet as middle-income parents, Joel and Missy doubt that their children will qualify for financial aid.

They had a lot of questions: What kind of planning can they do for their younger children? Where should they invest their savings for future college expenses? Should the money be in their name or the kids' names? How readily available are scholarships? Is a private college completely out of their price range? "And is there some hat somewhere with a rabbit in it that we can pull out?" laughed Joel.

Joel and Missy were eager to do more because they wanted to give their other children greater options than they could give Norman. For instance, he had expressed an interest in attending Brandeis, the private liberal arts college in the Boston metropolitan region. But tuition, room, board, and other expenses for attending Brandeis seemed to put it out of financial reach. Instead, Norman applied to the University of Wisconsin in Madison, also a good school and far cheaper. The University of Wisconsin was Norman's first choice, too. "It would feel really bad to have to say no to them simply because of the price," said Missy. Joel added: "Ultimately what I want each of my kids to have is the benefit of every possible opportunity that they can have."

I can see every parent reading this chapter nodding his or her head in agreement. I know I am.

In almost every episode of *Right on the Money,* either on-camera or off, parents grill me about saving and paying for college. On *Sound Money,* the public radio show I co-host, I once got a call from a listener so anxious about the soaring cost of a college education that she wanted advice on the best way to set money aside now—even though she didn't have any children yet!

Sending kids to college, like owning a home, is a big part of the American Dream. The Levintmans even contemplated raiding their retirement plans so that their kids could go to the college of their choice. Paying for college is financially hard on families. But don't despair or let long-range projections of total college costs overwhelm you. Yes, save what you can. But when it comes to paying for college, the options available to parents and students are surprisingly abundant. A college diploma is a more attainable certificate of achievement than many people realize—or fear.

THE SHEEPSKIN PAYOFF

The price tag for a college sheepskin has gone up sharply over the past two decades. For much of the 1980s and 1990s, college costs rose at double and triple the rate of overall consumer inflation. But many parents started rebelling against steep price hikes, and cost containment, total quality management, reengineering, and restructuring are all the rage these days in academia. The annual rate of college cost inflation has slowed to double the rate of consumer inflation—still a rapid rate of increase. The share of median family income required to pay for a four-year public college in the 1980–81 school year was 40% for low-income families, 12% for middle-income families, and 5% for the well-heeled. By the 1999–2000 school year, according to the College Board, those figures are now 61%, 17%, and 5%, respectively. The comparable numbers for a four-year private college in 1980–81 were 93% for low-income, 28% for middle-income, and 12% for high-income families, and in the 1999–2000 school year are 162%, 44%, and 14% respectively. No matter how you slice it, college is expensive.

The cost of a college education may be steep, but so is the return. Don't sell a college education short, because the economic payoff from a degree is substantial. For the past two decades, those with a college education or technological skills have been well paid while everyone else stagnated. Today's male and female college graduates earn a substantial wage premium of 44% and 51% over those with only a high school diploma. College graduates enjoy greater job security and lower unemployment rates than workers with a high school diploma or less. Economists estimate that the lifetime real rate of return from all that money invested in a four-year college education ranges from 11% to 15% annually—a hefty return. "For many people, it's the most valuable investment they are going to make," says Michael McPherson, dean of Macalester College, a private liberal arts college in Minnesota. "And that's before adding in other benefits offered by an education, such as scientific breakthroughs, the cultivation of the arts, and a more vibrant society. I think students come out of college as better citizens, as more thoughtful members of their communities, maybe with different cultural tastes and cultural tendencies than they would have otherwise."

AN EDUCATION PAYS

Median earnings, 1998
Full-time year-round workers 25 years and over

	Female	Male
Less than 9th grade	$14,132	$18,553
9–12 (no diploma)	$15,857	$23,438

High school graduate (includes GED)	$21,963	$30,868
Some college, no degree	$26,024	$35,949
Associate degree	$28,377	$38,483
Bachelor's degree	$35,408	$49,982
Master's degree	$42,002	$60,168
Professional degree	$55,460	$90,653
Doctoral degree	$52,167	$69,188

DATA: Census Bureau.

Students and their parents are heeding the market's message that an education pays. College enrollment is at record levels. The proportion of high school graduates enrolling in college after graduation jumped from 49% in 1979 to a record 67% in 1997. Between 1985–86 and 1995–96, the number of associate degrees increased by 24%, bachelor's degrees by 8%, master's degrees by 41%, and doctor's degrees by 33%. In a high-tech economy, the demand for educated workers will remain strong.

People tap into a variety of financial resources to pay for college. If students had to finance college strictly out of their parents' budgets or out of their own pockets, they would be pretty constrained, especially in lower-income households. In addition to savings, parents and students pay for college with scholarships (aid offered on the basis of merit that isn't paid back), grants (aid based on need that isn't paid back), loans (financial aid that must be paid back), and student employment (usually low-wage work). For instance, Norman currently earns the minimum wage plus tips as a bellhop, and he plans on working part-time while in college. Financial aid awarded for the 1998–99 school year was $64.1 billion, up 85% in a decade, according to the College Board. Students are relying more on borrowed money than before to pay for college, with more than half of financial aid made up of loans. Taking on some debt makes sense, since a college education should improve students' earnings prospects; but borrowing too much can lead to financial turmoil and trouble later on.

THE FINANCIAL AID PIE

Student aid, 1998–99 academic year
Current dollars
Total $64.1 billion

	Billions	Percent
Federal loans	$33.7	52.5
Institutional and other grants	12.2	19.0
Federal Pell Grants	7.2	11.3
State grant programs	3.5	5.5
Federal campus-based programs	2.7	4.2
Other federal programs	2.4	3.7
Nonfederal loans	2.4	3.8

DATA: College Board.

The basic financial aid formula is simple: Start with the yearly cost of college. Then subtract the parents' and student's contribution. The remainder is defined as need. Meeting the need means getting a combination of scholarship, grant, loan, and work. You can go on the web and play with various numbers to get an idea what your financial aid package might look like.

Unfortunately, the details are abstruse and complicated, much like the U.S. tax code. Indeed, the financial aid system that developed in the post–World War II era was initially modeled after the U.S. progressive income tax, and, like the tax code, it has evolved into a messy stew of rules, regulations, exemptions, incentives, and penalties. "In some ways it's astonishing, if you think about it, that colleges have succeeded in getting people to fill out all of these forms," says McPherson. "Imagine going to your car dealer and they said, well, before I'll let you know how much this car is going to cost you have to tell me how much your house is worth, where you work, how much you earn, and then I'll tell you how much it's going to cost you!"

Sadly, the system's complexity fuels a strong suspicion that the procedure is deeply unfair, a formula easily gamed by any family with deep pockets and few scruples. The cost of a college education is high enough that a cottage industry of consultants has grown up to help people navigate the system. Still, I'm skeptical about the stories of wealthy doctors, lawyers, and other well-heeled families hiding assets so that their kids can qualify for a generous financial aid package. Yes, there are abuses. But most of the proposed schemes I've looked at involve bad, and even foolish, financial maneuvers.

The risk-reward ratio clearly favors going to college, despite the costs and the frustrations. The rest of this chapter will detail different ways you can limit your risk of disappointment or financial trouble.

APPLYING FOR COLLEGE

Let's say you haven't done much to save for college, and your high school junior is about to take the SAT's. Are you sunk? Hardly. What follows are some tips for getting your teenager off to college. Later, I'll deal with how to better prepare for the college bill by saving for college.

Norman had applied to only one college, the University of Wisconsin in Madison. It's where he really wanted to go. His uncles had graduated from the University of Wisconsin in Madison, and many of his friends were enrolled there. He did have a safety valve, though. Since Norman would find out early whether Wisconsin accepted him or not, he had time to send in an application to the University of Minnesota if the news was negative. He had looked at Indiana University, but it didn't seem worth the higher cost compared to the cheaper tuition option of the universities of Wisconsin or Minnesota. (Wisconsin and Minnesota have a reciprocal higher education tuition agreement.) Despite the steep price tag, his mother had encouraged him to apply for the joint Columbia University/Jewish Theological Seminary program. But Norman had no interest in pursuing it.

However, it's a sound strategy to apply to several colleges. It's well worth the extra time and extra fees to put out five or six applications, including one to a school your family can swing without financial aid. You should also consider a school or two where your student might stand out, which might increase his or her chance for merit aid. And don't rule out applying to a more expensive school just because it seems financially out of reach—assuming your student would like to go there. A number of high-priced schools are willing to design generous financial aid packages. Your actual out-of-pocket cost (as opposed to the published sticker price) may be comparable to the lower-cost options. For example, Deena Katz, a well-known financial planner based in Coral Gables, Florida, is on the board of Adrian College, a small liberal arts college with about 1,100 students in Adrian, Michigan. She notes that the cost of attending Adrian is more than $18,000, but about 85% of its students get some kind of financial aid. "You can't judge the institution by the sticker price," says Katz. "You really need to look and see what kinds of programs they have available for college-based aid, including scholarships and other kinds of merit funding." Adds Macalester's McPherson: "The first thing I would advise is, don't foreclose your options early on when you are thinking about what schools to apply to. Because good colleges will try to come up with a financial aid package that will allow you to afford the college."

Another advantage of applying to several schools is that it gives you room to negotiate when it comes to the financial aid package. Colleges call it "dialing for dollars," and it is increasingly commonplace. No one is going to think you are wrong in trying to cut a better deal for your son or daughter. The tuition, room, and board charges are substantial enough that it's worth the effort, too. "If you have an aid offer from two competing schools, you can often go back and say school Y is offering me an extra $5,000 in aid," says Kristin Davis, a senior associate editor at *Kiplinger's* and author of *Financing College.* "Can you do something about that?"

Here's another increasingly popular option: the "two-plus-two" step. Your student attends a lower-cost two-year private college or public community college. The student then transfers to a brand-name four-year college for the final two years of his or her college education. His or her college sheepskin comes from the better-known school, but the diploma comes at half price.

FIGURING OUT YOUR FAMILY CONTRIBUTION

The Levintmans were skeptical that Norman would qualify for financial aid. Many middle-class parents share that sentiment. But every college guidance counselor, admissions officer, and college expert I've talked to agrees: Everyone should apply for financial aid. The Federal Student Aid form put out by the U.S. Department of Education is free, and it's available online and at colleges, in high school guidance counselors' offices, and in most libraries. Admissions officers highly recommend filling out the application early (after January 1 for the school year starting in September).

The financial aid calculation starts with the cost of attendance (including tuition, room, board, books, transportation, medical expenses, and the like). The computation subtracts the expected family contribution from both parents and student, a figure derived from formulas that take into account your income and assets. The formula also subtracts your living ex-

penses and taxes in coming up with your expected family contribution. Still, many middle-income folks are stunned at the
amount of money colleges and universities expect them to pay.
Many families feel they are living on the financial edge, but according to the federal government's formula they're living fat
and easy. You should prepare yourself by running some numbers on your own on a web-based financial aid calculator. Most
university web sites offer a financial aid estimator, too.

FILLING IN THE GAP

Now let's look at how to close the gap between the family's
contribution and the cost of attendance, starting with grants.
Grants are based on the student's financial need, and the
money doesn't have to be paid back. Unfortunately, the long-
term trend has been away from grants and toward loans. The
federal government's main grant program is the Pell Grant,
aimed at low-income students. The maximum grant in the
1999–2000 school year was $3,125 (the sum varies depending
on how much Congress appropriates for the program). The average Pell Grant is approximately $1,900, but how much you
get depends on your financial need, as well as the cost of attending school and whether you're a full-time or part-time student. The value of the Pell Grant has declined substantially over
the past two decades, after adjusting for inflation. According to
figures compiled by the College Board, in the 1970s the Pell
Grant covered about three-quarters of the average cost of a
public four-year university and one-third the average cost of a
private university; today, the maximum Pell Grant covers only
one-third the average cost of a public college and one-seventh
the average cost of a private one. The other well-known federal
grant program is the Federal Supplemental Education Opportunity Grant. Colleges and universities dole out the money to

their poorest undergraduates. The grants range from $100 to $4,000 a year.

Scholarships are highly desirable, too. It's worth trying to find a scholarship, although all the evidence suggests there isn't tons of money waiting to be plucked. Scholarship money, while welcome, usually comes in relatively small denominations. Many companies, especially larger corporations, offer scholarships to employees' children who earn good grades. Trade unions, industry groups, community foundations, charitable organizations, religious establishments, and the like also offer scholarships. Merit scholarships are increasingly available at all but the top-tier schools for applicants with outstanding grades or talent. I remember when I researched scholarships more than two decades ago. It was a painstaking, laborious process of going through tome after tome with small print and user-unfriendly indexes. Today, the Internet has made searching for a scholarship much easier, but that also means that many more people are trolling for scholarship money.

Financial aid often includes student work. The Federal Work-Study Program provides jobs for needy students. Most schools have a job placement office for any student looking to earn some money on the side. Of course, the big question is how much a student can work before the job cuts into academic performance. I've known too many people trying to hold down a 40-hour-a-week job and go to school. They're exhausted, and they don't get anywhere near the kind of education that they should considering how much money they are paying. Research suggests that ten hours a week or less won't hurt the grades of freshmen. For other undergraduates the figure is 15 hours a week. The research made a definite impression on Norman. "I actually work more than that now in high school," he said. "But I don't think I would exceed that at college, because classes are more important."

LOANS

Loans play an increasingly large role in financial aid. The federal government dominates the higher education loan business, but all states also have their own loan programs. I'll focus on the main federal programs, but you should check out your state's loan options. Borrowing does carry risk, so be cautious and responsible when it comes to taking on student loans. "If things don't work out well for you, then you have accepted a burden, and you are going to have to shoulder that burden later in life or you are going to pay a price if you default. It's going to hurt your credit," says McPherson. So keep careful track of your loan burden.

Let's review the main loan options. The federal Perkins Loan is geared toward low-income students, and these loans are a critical part of a financial aid package. For instance, students with Pell Grants get priority with these loans. Perkins Loans come with an attractive interest rate, currently 5%. Interest and principal repayments can be deferred for nine months after graduation. Undergraduates can borrow a maximum of $15,000.

The Stafford Loan is the mainstay federal student loan. A dependent undergraduate can borrow a maximum of $23,000 for college education. Need-based subsidized Stafford Loans are available. The federal government pays interest on the subsidized loans while the student is enrolled in college. Interest and principal payments can be deferred for six months after graduation. Unsubsidized Stafford Loans are widely available for those who apply for financial aid. Interest payments and principal can be deferred until six months after graduation (but interest does accrue immediately with these loans). The interest rate charged on Stafford Loans can vary from year to year, but the current cap is 8.25%.

Parent Loans for Undergraduate Students, or PLUS Loans, are federal loans geared for parents with dependent under-

graduate students. Parents with good credit histories can borrow yearly the difference between college costs and financial
aid. In other words, if the college bill is $10,000 and financial
aid equals $6,000, the parents can take out a $4,000 PLUS
Loan. The interest rate varies, but it can't exceed 9%.

Several organizations that specialize in education loans,
such as Sallie Mae and Nellie Mae, also offer supplemental student loans to creditworthy borrowers. Two common loan alternatives to student loans are a home equity loan and borrowing
from a retirement plan. Interest payments are deductible on a
home equity loan. It is an option mostly pursued by well-off parents with a hefty chunk of equity in the home. The other option
is borrowing against a 401(k) plan. You then pay yourself back,
since you are the lender. It's risky, though. Many people never
pay themselves back, so they end up incurring a financial
penalty. They also lose out on their retirement money compounding on a tax-deferred basis over time. Plus, if you lose your
job you often have only a few months to restore the money
you've borrowed or you will get hit with an early-withdrawal
penalty and an income tax bill. If you don't save for your retirement while you're earning an income, there is no going back.

There is nothing wrong with students taking out loans. Sometimes you have to spend money to make money. Borrowing is
scary for a lot of students, but a college loan is an investment that
should pay off in increased earning power. Parents can always
supplement a child's income later on to help pay off the loans,
too. "It's okay to have your children take a job or assume some of
the debt to get themselves through school," says Deena Katz. "I
think they will appreciate it."

SAVING FOR COLLEGE

If you have younger children, time is on your side. Save for your
children's college education, even if it's only a few dollars a

week. The earlier you start saving, the more money you will accumulate. For example, any money the Levintmans set aside for the six-year-old twins will have a long time to compound. But even if your children are already teenagers, it still pays to save. Invest in a mix of stocks, bonds, and money market or other interest-earning accounts. Go for growth in these investments, especially the longer your time horizon. The closer college entrance is for your child, the more conservative your portfolio should be, since you'll be writing checks soon. As an example, here's the asset allocation in the Missouri Higher Education Savings Program, run by TIAA-CREF, the leading manager of state-sponsored college savings plans. (TIAA-CREF underwrites *Sound Money,* the public radio personal finance program I co-host.) TIAA-CREF's money management philosophy is deeply informed by academic research. The asset allocation devised for a newborn is 75% stocks and 25% bonds. The asset allocation changes in a more conservative direction until someone with two years or less before college is invested 50% in a money market mutual fund, 10% in an equity fund, and 40% in a bond fund.

A POSSIBLE ASSET ALLOCATION FOR COLLEGE

Investment Horizon	Year of Birth	Money Market Fund	Equity Fund	Bond Fund
1–2 yrs or less	pre-1984	50%	10%	40%
2–3 yrs	1984–85	15	15	70
4–5 yrs	1986–87	5	25	70
6–7 yrs	1988–89	0	35	65
8–9 yrs	1990–91	0	40	60
10–11 yrs	1992–93	0	45	55
12–13 yrs	1994–95	0	55	45
14–15 yrs	1996–97	0	65	35

16–17 yrs	1998–99	0	70	30
18–19 yrs	2000–01	0	75	25

DATA: TIAA-CREF. Based on the Missouri Higher Education Savings Program. Assumptions: inflation, 3%; real return on equities, 7%; real return on bonds, 3.5%; real return on money market funds, 2%.

Of course, you can—and should—slice and dice this illustration any number of ways, depending on your risk tolerance and financial resources. The portfolio may be too aggressive or conservative for your taste. It could be too risky a portfolio for low-income parents. Conversely, if your financial circumstances are more secure, you might want to take a greater degree of investment risk than illustrated here. Remember, you may have more investment time than you think, since you don't have to lock in all your gains at freshman year. Your child will go to school for four years. I would stick with high-grade plain-vanilla investments. Don't be lured by sales pitches for costly products you don't need in the name of college savings, such as buying life insurance. A bad idea. And you can afford to be somewhat aggressive in your saving and investing strategy because there are other financial options available to you if the markets take a downturn at the wrong time.

I advocate regularly investing some college money in a broad-based stock index fund, such as the Wilshire 5000. You'll match the performance of the stock market and do better than the majority of money managers year in and year out. You will also pay rock-bottom fees—and high fees subtract from long-run performance. In addition to equities, you should diversify your college savings portfolio with high-quality bonds and a blue chip money market fund. If you are managing the money yourself, and you have several children, Deena Katz recommends keeping all the college investment money in one large portfolio, rather than segmenting it into a different portfolio for each child. It's easier to create a well-diversified portfolio that matches your assets with the coming college tuition bill if everything is under one umbrella. It's also easier to see your investment trade-offs.

Most people purchase bond mutual funds or U.S. Treasury securities for the fixed-income portion of their college savings portfolio. Both are good ideas, but you might want to consider Series EE savings bonds. Now, many financial advisers don't like savings bonds—they're dull, plodding investments. You'll never razzle-dazzle anyone with savings bonds. Yet they offer an intriguing package of benefits. You can buy savings bonds in small denominations (the minimum is $25), with no commission and no risk of default. Your money grows tax-deferred until you cash in the bonds and is exempt from state and local taxes. And, depending on your income and other conditions, your Series EE earnings may be completely or partially excluded from taxes if the money goes toward tuition and fees. For instance, in 2000 a full exclusion is available to single taxpayers with an adjusted gross income (which must include the interest earned on redeemed savings bonds) below $54,100. The benefit is eliminated for anyone with an adjusted gross income of $69,100 or more. For a married taxpayer filing jointly, the tax exclusion is reduced for anyone with a modified gross income above $81,100. It ends for joint filers with an adjusted gross income of $111,100 and more. The new I bonds offer the same education advantage as the Series EE. But an I bond is inflation-indexed. It offers a fixed interest rate above inflation as measured by the consumer price index. The bond's principal is adjusted as the consumer price index changes. Thus the value of your money in an I-bond cannot be eroded by higher consumer prices.

STATE-SPONSORED COLLEGE SAVINGS PLANS

State legislatures heard their constituents complain about the high cost of college, and a majority of states have created tax-deferred college savings plans. The early plans were mostly a bad deal for consumers. But the latest generation of so-called Section 529 plans (named after the part of the tax code that deals with them) is definitely worth a close look. You will need to look over the details of your particular state's plan closely, since plans vary considerably.

Parents open an account for a beneficiary. Typically, it's a youngster, but these plans are also used by adults saving to go back to school. The money compounds tax-deferred until the money is withdrawn to pay for qualified educational expenses. The withdrawn funds are taxed at the student's presumably lower tax rate. Depending on the plan, you could get a break on state taxes. The money is usually invested in a mix of stocks, bonds, and short-term interest-bearing securities. A huge advantage of these plans is that anybody can contribute to the child's account, including parents, grandparents, relatives, and friends, and in some states the maximum in an account can exceed $100,000. There is an unusual gift benefit with Section 529 plans that intrigues a growing number of grandparents. Federal tax law limits gifts to $10,000 and under without triggering a gift tax liability. However, with these plans you can gift $50,000 in one year, and then the contribution will be taken as a $10,000 gift over each of the next five years. The federal gift tax isn't triggered and the investment money gets to work faster. Contrary to widespread belief, you are not locked into attending school in your state with a state-sponsored savings plan. The accumulated savings are available for any college—public or private—and in any state.

These plans do have some drawbacks. The biggest is that you don't have any say in how the money is invested. If you feel you can do better on your own or don't like the plan's investment approach, I would steer clear of a Section 529 plan. Like an Individual Retirement Account, or any other tax-deferred plan designed to encourage a social goal, the government imposes steep penalties if the money isn't used for education expenses. Typically, a state will impose a 10% penalty on any withdrawals used for other purposes, plus any income tax liability. The money in the plan is counted as part of the parents' (or donor's) assets in calculating financial aid. However, when the money is withdrawn it is considered part of the student's taxable income, and under the current financial aid rules, student income is treated less generously than the parents' income. The financial aid formula takes into account 35% of the student's money per year versus nearly 6% for the parents. Finally, some states charge high fees to plan participants. So make sure the fees are competitive with what you could do on your own.

There is another type of state-sponsored college plan: prepaid college tuition. Yet locking in today's tuition turns out to be a less appealing option than the savings plans. Yes, you don't have to worry about future college inflation, which, as we have seen, has been considerable. Yet you might still do better investing in the market. These plans often put limits on where your child can go to college. (If your child does go to a different school, you'll get your money back plus interest, which may not be such a good deal.) The main attraction of prepaid tuition plans is that it is a very low risk way to save for college.

The federal government offers a tax-deferred college savings plan called the Education IRA. You can put aside up to $500 a year in a tax-deferred account to pay for educational expenses. The benefit phases out for joint filers with incomes between $150,000 and $160,000 and for single filers between $95,000 and $100,000. You cannot contribute to an Education IRA the same year that you make a contribution to a state college savings plan or vice versa. The money is withdrawn tax-free when it is used to pay for qualified education expenses. The money in an Education IRA is considered the child's asset.

Individual Retirement Accounts also allow you to withdraw money before age 59½ from a traditional IRA (funded with pretax dollars) without penalty to meet college costs. You will owe income taxes on the money you take out, though. It's far better to take advantage of the other available options and let your retirement money continue to compound. With the Roth IRA (funded with after-tax dollars), you can take out your annual contributions with no tax or penalty consequences. For instance, if you had made a $2,000 contribution a year for 10 years, you could take out $20,000 from your Roth IRA free of any complications. The question is whether you want to draw down your retirement money to pay for your kid's college education. It's a bad trade-off to use your retirement account to pay for college. "To me, raiding the retirement plan is a last-ditch effort," says Deena Katz. I agree.

SAVE IN WHOSE NAME?

Outside these tax-deferred accounts, the big debate is whether to save in the child's name or in the parents' name. For example, the Levintmans had some money set aside in their children's names and other money earmarked for college but in their name. They wondered which was more prudent financially. Saving in the child's name is tax-savvy. The first $700 of investment earning is free of taxes when the student is under age 14. The next $700 is taxed at the child's rate and anything above $1,400 at the parents' rate. However, once your child reaches age 14, everything above $700 is taxed at his or her rate. It's easy to save in a child's name. All you do is open a custodial account at an investment firm, discount brokerage, online broker, bank, or other financial institution. Just fill out a simple form and deposit the minimum starting balance, usually not more than a few hundred dollars. Since youngsters can't buy and sell securities, you control the account through the Uniform Gifts to Minors Act (UGMA) or the Uniform Transfer to Minors Act (UTMA). But the money is the child's

when he or she reaches adulthood, 18 to 21 years of age depending on your state.

But the drawbacks to saving in your child's name are substantial. The money is your child's. You have no control over
what your child does with it once he or she is an adult. If Johnny
or Jane decides to spend the money on a car or starting a restaurant rather than on college, that is his or her prerogative. The
current financial aid formula also assumes that more of the
money in a child's name will go for college versus the sums of
money you have put aside in your name. Of course, the financial
aid rules may change. I still think it makes more sense to have
discretionary savings in the parents' name. If your children end
up qualifying for scholarships or decide that college is not for
them, at least the money is available for your retirement. You
have more flexibility when you save in your own name.

This is a good place to deal with a critical question I get all
the time, on radio and on television. Does it make financial
sense to save for a college education at all? No question, the financial aid system penalizes savers. It's a bitter realization.
Some parents don't set aside money for their children's college
education in the belief that they will get a better financial aid
deal. I disagree with that trade-off. First of all, there's no guarantee you'll come out ahead financially. Second, students and
parents are far more comfortable applying to the more expensive schools when there is a savings cushion. The third, related
reason is that by saving you are buying an incredibly valuable
option for your children—the financial ability to go to any college they want, assuming they get in. The risks associated with
not saving are too great. So save, please.

TAX CODE BENEFITS

A few wrinkles in the federal tax code are geared toward easing
the college tuition bill. (Many states have their own variations.)

The Hope Scholarship Tax Credit is a two-year benefit worth a maximum of $1,500 per year for anyone in a postsecondary education program for a degree or certificate. The credit phases out for joint filers with an adjusted gross income between $80,000 and $100,000, and for single filers between $40,000 and $50,000.

The Lifetime Learning Tax Credit is for college juniors and seniors, graduate and professional school students, and adults returning to college. The tax credit equals 20% of up to $5,000 in tuition and fees, with a maximum benefit of $1,000. The credit will increase to 20% of $10,000 after 2002. The same Hope income limitations apply to the Lifetime Learning Credit.

Student loan interest payments are now deductible for the first 60 months of required repayment. The maximum student loan interest deduction is $2,000 for 2000 and $2,500 for 2001 and afterward. The deduction is phased out for joint filers with incomes between $60,000 and $75,000 and single filers between $40,000 and $55,000.

THE DEBT BURDEN

The cost of a college education is so high that even if you do everything right there is always the risk that your child will have a huge debt burden long past graduation day. So even while your student is in college and struggling to read Chaucer in Middle English or master calculus, you should both lay out a realistic strategy for paying off the student loans. Once again, there are options. But all students need to be frank about how much they'll earn after graduation. After all, a repayment plan that works for someone with a degree in economics may not be affordable for someone with a diploma in drama. The benchmark is that you should be paying no more than 8% of your income toward student loans. But 10% to 15% of monthly income is becoming more common with the increase in loan size. For example, let's say you borrowed $24,750 for your undergraduate education, at an 8% rate of interest for ten years. According to calculations by the Minnesota Higher Education Services Office, assuming student loans represent no more than 8% of your income, you should have no problem meeting the $300 monthly payment on a salary of $45,000. But on a $24,000 salary you'd be struggling.

The good news is that there are a number of loan repayment options that offer flexibility—for a price. The standard student loan is a fixed monthly payment for ten years. All the other options involve trading off lower monthly payments for a higher overall cost of a college education. Let's say you owe your undergraduate alma mater a total of $25,000 at an interest rate of 8%. That's about $300 a month for ten years for a total bill of nearly $36,400. Now let's say you stretch out the loan repayment to 15 years, and you adopt a graduated payment plan. In the early years, your monthly bill drops to some $167 a month. That sounds great, doesn't it? But the total cost of your education has risen to $47,460. Still, a graduated repayment plan builds upon the fact that income grows with experience and promotions.

Another option is income-contingent loans. Your loan obligation fluctuates with your income, guaranteeing low monthly payments when you don't earn much and high payments when you do. The amount you owe monthly is calculated every year and depends on your income, family size, and the size of your loan. If it's a federal loan and it's still outstanding after 25 years, the government forgives the rest of the debt.

An extended repayment plan lets you increase the length of your loan from 12 to 30 years. You must pay a monthly minimum of $50. Again, increasing the length of your loan increases the cost of your education.

You can consolidate your loans. You take all your old loans and repackage them into one loan. One bill. One check. Consolidation makes sense if you get a lower interest rate or you need to slash your monthly outlay by lengthening the terms of your loan—again, at a price of paying thousands of dollars more in interest. However, you can always accelerate your payments without penalty if your income takes a turn for the better.

If you think you are teetering near default, don't hesitate. Contact your lender. You can always restructure your debt, and you may qualify for a deferment or forbearance if you are unemployed or suffering from some other economic hardship. Your lender doesn't want to see you default any more than you do.

Default is costly. If you default, your school and whatever entity holds your loan may sue to recover the money. They will also notify the national credit bureaus, and the default will trash your credit rating. The agency that holds your loan could force your employer to deduct payments from your paycheck. In addition to the money you owe, you could be liable for any expenses incurred to collect the loan. The U.S. Department of Education can ask the IRS to take your tax refund if you get one and apply it to the loan. And if you ever decide to return to school, don't bother applying for any federal student aid. Still, even if you've defaulted, it pays to contact your lender. There are ways to rehabilitate your loan. By the way, student loans are not discharged in bankruptcy, so don't try that route.

THE LEVINTMANS

The Levintmans face an enormous college bill, and it isn't going to be easy to pay the freight. Yet when I met with them again, there was an energy and optimism that contrasted sharply with the worry and confusion they had displayed at our first meeting.

Several ideas had struck them. For instance, they liked the idea of combining savings for all the children under one umbrella. Joel was going to research state college savings plans, especially for the twins. Norman had decided to apply to several more schools. Both he and his parents liked trying to carve out some negotiating room. Joel was convinced the family should fill out the financial aid form. He was open to Norman's taking out some student loans. "It certainly makes sense, because at that point he is an owner of his education as opposed to simply a beneficiary. And there is a certain value to that," he said.

Norman agreed, although a bit reluctantly. "The thought of student loans intimidates me a little bit just because I don't want to start my life in the hole," he said. "I didn't like it, but I understand it."

They were also on the web. "My sense is, there is a light at the end of the tunnel," said Missy.

Joel laughed. "I agree. As Missy said, there is a light at the end of the tunnel. The tunnel is 16 years long, but there is light at the end of the tunnel."

As we've seen, college is expensive. But you have a choice of when to pay for your children's education. As a parent, you don't have to pay for the whole thing yourself. Now, if you're lucky, your child may get a scholarship, but there are plenty of other options, least of which is that your child can contribute. Your child may work, take out a loan, or both. There are also loan options available to you and lots of savvy ways to use cash, your home, and other assets to pay for college.

Start saving now. If you invest money for college, consider your time horizon. Go for growth with these investments. When your children are young, you may want to put a hefty chunk into the stock market. As they get older and college bills loom large on the horizon, put the money in more conservative investments. And in general, put the money in your name, not in your child's. Many parents believe they won't qualify for financial aid. But who knows? So apply—no matter what your income. The same goes for private scholarships and merit-based aid.

Think in terms of options, not limitations.

Resources

Financing College, by Kristin Davis (Kiplinger Books). A senior associate editor at *Kiplinger's,* the personal finance magazine, Davis covers the waterfront with her book. Well researched and well thought out.

The Complete Family Guide to College Financial Aid, by Richard Black (Perigee). Black is director of financial aid at the University of California, Berkeley. A three-decade-plus veteran of the college aid business and a parent of four children, he brings a wealth of insight to financial aid. This is a short, clearly written book. It reduces financial aid hieroglyphics into plain English.

College Planning for Dummies, by Pat Ordovensky (IDG Books). How should your youngster go about finding the right college? How many colleges should he or she apply to? Odovensky offers a practical guide to the college planning process.

Take Control of Your Student Loans, by Robin Leonard and Shae Irving (Nolo Press). A very clear, concise guide to the confusing world of student loans.

The Guerrilla Guide to Mastering Student Loan Debt, by Anne Stockwell (HarperCollins). Anne had a lot of student loan debt, and out of her struggles to repay it came this book. It's smart and feisty.

The Student Aid Game: Meeting Need and Rewarding Talent in American Higher Education, by Michael S. McPherson and Morton Owen Shapiro (Princeton University Press). Why is it so expensive to go to college? What is driving costs ever higher? How has the financial aid business evolved, and where should it go? This book is not a primer on student loans like my other picks but a thoughtful, thorough book on the hot-button issue of paying for college. The authors are two of the country's foremost education economists.

collegesavings.org. A source of information on state savings plans for college.

collegeboard.org. A gold mine for parents and students confronting the transition from high school to college. Among its offerings: financial aid calculators, a college search engine, and a scholarship search guide.

ed.gov. The Department of Education's web site has mountains of data on long-term trends in education. It also has the Student Guide to Financial Aid, information on applying for grants and scholarships, and a list of Internet resources for parents, as well as information about student loans and the various payment options (including consolidating your loans). Spend some time here. It will be worth your while.

finaid.org. It's free. It's clear. And the information is comprehensive when it comes to student financial aid.

fastweb.com. A database of more than 400,000 scholarships.

adventuresineducation.org. This site, created by the Texas Guaranteed Student Loan Corporation, is a genuine public service for harried parents and students. You don't need to be from Texas to take advantage of its knowledge.

salliemae.com. Sallie Mae is a giant, publicly traded financial services company in the education-loan business. It offers financial calculators, from an accrued interest calculator to a repayment estimator. The web site also has decent discussions about what to do if you are having trouble keeping up with your payments and other student loan problems.

6

Saving for Retirement

Grow old along with me!
The best is yet to be,
The last of life, for which the first was made.

—Robert Browning

Weekend mornings, Pat McKeown likes to go mountain biking with his wife and three kids. During the long days of summer, he'll even ride the ten-mile commute to work. Not surprisingly, Pat would like to do even more biking when he retires. He and his wife, Terri, would also like to take long road trips during their retirement years in the small used RV parked in their backyard.

But right now, they're working hard. Terri is a freelance graphic designer whose career is beginning to take off. Pat is director of information systems for a medium-sized medical publishing company. For the first time in their marriage, Pat and Terri have some extra money each month. Terri's income has gone up, and they're finally out from under the usual debt burdens, such as car loans. Like many 40-something parents, Pat and Terri want some of the cash to go toward saving for retirement. "My dad retired from the railroad, and he has a monthly income coming from a pension. Now, that's probably not going to happen with me," reflects Pat. "Social Security may be there, but not with the kind of monthly income my parents are getting. We have to depend essentially on the money we put away ourselves."

He's right—and it's a scary change. Investing today to secure a decent standard of living tomorrow is a huge responsibility, and for every person diligently managing his or her retirement portfolio there are hundreds more winging it. It's increasingly up to you, not your employer or the government, to provide for your later years. And, of course, there is a basic question: What are your dreams for when you're older? The answers have implications for the kinds of risks you are willing to take with your money.

For their retirement savings, the McKeowns are relying on Pat's 401(k) retirement savings plan at work. He's automatically setting aside a slice of every paycheck into the plan, and his company matches a portion of his contribution. But in this world of self-directed retirement savings plans, he has to decide how to invest the money, something he isn't comfortable doing. Pat is educated and literate. So is Terri. But the stock and bond markets are largely alien to them. For instance, in the first half of 1998, Pat had half his retirement savings invested in stocks and half in bonds—a reasonable portfolio allocation. Yet the U.S. stock market took a stomach-churning dive that year with the collapse of the Asian stock, bond, and currency markets. Pat couldn't take the volatility in the stock market. He abruptly switched all his money into fixed-income securities. He knew it wasn't sensible to act precipitately with his investments, and that completely abandoning equities wasn't a good move with retirement savings. But he got nervous. "Everybody said stay in [stocks] and I said, nah, I'll switch over," said Pat. "But I know long-term bonds are not a good place to keep the money."

Terri supported the skittish switch. Investing makes Terri uncomfortable. It's simply too risky. Like many people, Terri sees the stock market as a casino where fortunes are won and lost with bewildering speed and for incomprehensible reasons. Her idea of gambling is occasionally buying a lottery ticket whenever the prize money hits mega-millions level. The stock market is for rich people and speculators, not for middle-class people working hard for their money. "I'm not a gambler," she says. "It seems like a big gamble to me to be in the stock market," she says.

Terri is self-employed. Yet even though there are tax-sheltered retirement savings plans for freelancers and other independent contractors, she hasn't set one up. Indeed, only recently did she become aware that she had the option of establishing her own pension plan. Many social commentators blame America's lack of adequate savings on our infatuation with shopping and desire for instant gratification. Perhaps there is some truth to that, although I'm skeptical. But a far bigger reason for hesitating to put money at risk in the stock and bond markets is unfamiliarity with the world of investing. Wall Street appears too complicated for much of Main Street. "I have to admit, I don't have a great understanding of the financial world," Terri said. "It's baffling to me."

The retirement savings problem goes far beyond knowing how much to save and how to invest it. Pat and Terry have other financial responsibilities that compete for their money. For example, besides paying for their daily living expenses and family vacations, the McKeowns are contributing to their 19-year-old's college education. They expect their other two children, a sophomore in high school and a sixth-grader, to earn a sheepskin, too. Pat and Terri would like to pay for their children's college education, or at least limit their student loan debt burden. It's a 12-year financial obligation with little break. The price tag of putting three children through a public university is almost $100,000 at current prices, and their total college bill will be considerably higher, since college tuition costs are inching higher year after year. Like many parents, they wonder whether their savings should go toward college or retirement.

The difficult balancing act between buying a secure future and paying for today isn't limited to needs and responsibilities. We also consume for pleasure, from owning a high-tech bike to attending the theater to buying a fancy pen. For example, now that their finances are improving, Pat and Terri are interested in owning a bigger house. They currently live in a modest home on a tree-lined street. Both are content with their current living arrangements. But they have looked at some "gorgeous" homes to see what's available. Pat and Terri also wonder if a bigger, more expensive home might make a better long-term investment.

To make sense of it all, the McKeowns once visited a financial planner. Their hope was that the planner could help them sort through their financial questions and offer up some sound money guidance. The financial planner's advice boiled down to this: Put away a few hundred dollars more a month. Don't you marvel at snap-your-finger recommendations? Overweight? Diet. Not getting enough exercise? Run. The less-than-helpful experience soured both of them on financial planners, and the retirement issue returned to the back burner.

The McKeowns hadn't really focused on how they wanted to spend their golden years, either. And planning well for retirement isn't possible without a strong sense of what you want to do at that stage of your life. During our conversations, we talked about biking and traveling more during retirement. They had some vague notions of spending quality time together, enjoying a more leisurely pace, perhaps continuing some sort of part-time employment or picking up a hobby. Clearly, both Pat and Terri lacked a long-term vision or goal. "I really haven't thought about retirement that much," Pat said. "You get so tied up in family, the kids, and the job."

Pat and Terri are typical of many couples. Time is a luxury, and even when you carve out financial planning moments, confusion reigns. How much should you save? Where should you invest the money? How can you bring about a better balance between today's financial demands and the need to create a retirement nest egg tomorrow? Still, the odds are that as long as you are putting money into a retirement savings plan, you're muddling through. But you can do better than that by seizing on a proactive planning approach toward your old age and by taking a broad perspective on retirement.

In this chapter, I'm going to extend the preparing-for-our-old-age discussion beyond saving and investing for retirement. Planning for retirement is the touchstone, the risk-and-reward centerpiece, of long-term financial security. Yet your long-term safety net should add up to more than judging your saving habits and tallying up your assets. Long-term financial security includes insurance and estate planning. You can't anticipate every contingency. Plans go awry. Insurance and estate planning are vital for limiting your downside risk if something bad, such as death or injury, happens.

THE EVOLUTION OF RETIREMENT

If you feel the national obsession over retirement, and the intense personal pressure to save, is different from what your parents and grandparents dealt with, you're right. But their experience contrasted sharply with their own parents'. There's nothing new about getting old, but the way society copes with aging has changed dramatically, and over the past century, it's been mostly a positive story of improving financial security. But the risks surrounding old age are changing.

The first pension plan in the United States was started in 1759, for the benefit of widows and children of Presbyterian ministers. A century later few people had a pension. American Express offered its employees the first corporate pension in 1875, and by 1932 about 15% of the workforce was covered by a pension. Only the very wealthy associated old age with leisure. For everyone else, the word "retirement" suggested ill health, involuntary unemployment, and a humiliating dependence upon family, charity, or community organizations for shelter and food.

Retirement changed dramatically in the decades following World War II. The Social Security Act of 1935 extended a financial safety net to everyone. The elderly gained universal health care coverage with Medicare in 1965. Corporate America embraced the tactic of offering workers tax-sheltered pension benefits during the strong economy of the 1950s and 1960s. The pensions were mostly "defined benefit" plans. The employer took all the investment risk and committed to a fixed payout of money, a pension stream typically based on a salary-and-years-of-service formula: The longer you worked at a company, the better your pension income. The retirement rate of American men older than 64 rose from 25% at the end of the nineteenth century to over 80% today. The elderly poverty rate in 1959 was 35%; it has since declined by more than two-thirds. Retirees developed a distinct lifestyle—mass migration to sunbelt communities, travel in RVs and bus tours, long mornings spent on the golf course and in other recreational pursuits. Hollywood, comedians, and social critics of both the left and the right often target the tastes and choices of the aged. Yet the development of retirement is one of the great social achievements of the twentieth century, writes Dora L. Costa in *The Evolution of Retirement:* "For most individuals retirement is no longer a time of withdrawal from all activities and of dependence on family and friends; rather, it is a time of discovery, personal fulfillment, and relative independence. In the past, such an experience of retirement was limited to the wealthy few who could afford it. Now it is an option available to the majority of workers."

At the turn of the millennium, retirement is changing once again, thanks to a shift in pension design and an evolution in lifestyle expectations. The risk of declining living standards in retirement is greater for baby boomers and subsequent generations than it was for the World War II and Korean War generations. The reason: Companies are retreating from offering their workers expensive defined benefit pension plans in favor of lower-cost "defined contribution" plans, such as 401(k)s. Employers expect workers to take responsibility for funding their retirement plan, and the employee absorbs all the investment risk.

To be sure, thanks largely to the soaring stock market of the past decade, workers have done exceptionally well in their retirement savings plans. With about half of all households owning stock and two-thirds their own home, median household net worth is at a record $75,000, calculate economists at Regional Financial Associates. The average 401(k) account balance was $47,004 at year-end 1998, up 26% from 1996, according to the Employee Benefits Research Institute. But markets fluctuate, and the risk of disappointing returns is real. For example, following the great bull market of 1949 to 1968, the average stock fell by 75% from 1968 to 1974. In a similar vein, the Dow Jones Industrial Average at year-end 1964 was 874 and at year-end 1981 was 875.

Your long-term financial security is more dependent on the markets than before, and whether you eat caviar or cabbage during retirement will largely rest on the investment choices you make during your work years. Worse, if you don't save out of inertia or ignorance, your financial resources will be meager and your vulnerability to any setback disturbingly high. Retirement is a more perilous concept than in the past half century.

One of the best ways to limit your risk is to learn the basics about investing. But other powerful societal trends also offer options for intelligently managing your risks. The most striking is the change in the retirement concept from a kick-back-at-60 to a more active period of life. Many baby boomers are preparing to stay engaged in the workplace, perhaps by working part-time, changing careers, starting their own business, or going back to school. "Retirement isn't giving everything up and moving to the warm climate and lying out in the sun," says Ross Levin, president of Accredited Investors Inc., an Edina, Minnesota, financial consulting firm. "It is becoming a transition state, not an end to itself."

The results from a survey of baby boomers by the American Association of Retired Persons (AARP) are striking. The AARP found that fully eight in ten baby boomers plan on working at least part-time during their retirement; a mere 16% don't expect to work at all. A little over a third expect they will work part-time for enjoyment and engagement; nearly a quarter will work part-time mainly for income. Others see themselves starting their own business (17%) or working full-time at a new job (5%). Half say they expect to devote more time to community service or volunteer activities during retirement, and more than seven in ten boomers anticipate engaging in a time-consuming hobby or special interest. "People are thinking much more about what they want to get out of life and how they want to maintain their health than they are thinking about the traditional stop at 62 or 65," says Tom Kingston, president of the Wilder Foundation, a nonprofit organization providing research and innovative living resources for seniors.

The transformation of retirement is being helped along by generational changes. We're living healthier and longer lives. Americans are smoking less and exercising more, and are better educated than their parents. The Census Bureau's intermediate forecast predicts that women who reach 65 in 2010 will live another 20 years on average. The comparable remaining life span for men who hit 65 is another 16.8 years. "People need to start planning for what they are going to do when they have this incredible amount of time in front of them, so they enjoy it and aren't miserable," says Harold Evensky, a bow-tied financial planner based in Coral Gables, Florida.

The work world is changing in ways that make it easier for the elderly to labor longer if they want. It is a lot less taxing physically to work with computers or on the Internet than it is to labor on an assembly line or in a mine. Indeed, working longer is one of the best ways to reduce the risk that comes from managing an investment portfolio on your own. Starting a second career, shifting to part-time work, or joining the staff of a nonprofit organization lets your retirement money compound for a longer period of time. Your income, even if it is sharply lower than what you made when younger, reduces the sums you need to withdraw from your portfolio. "If people choose to continue to work even after 'retirement' this will bolster the resources available to support living standards in retirement," writes William G. Gale, economist at the Brookings Institution, in an essay titled "Are Americans Saving Enough for Retirement?"

DO YOU NEED A FINANCIAL PLANNER?

At this point, you're probably wondering, should I just hire a financial planner to get my long-term retirement plan in order? The planner can be my guide rather than this book and the other resources listed at the end of the chapter. Yet most of you probably don't need a financial planner. You can take care of your financial responsibilities on your own with a little education, discipline, and common sense.

It may not be the biggest mistake in the financial universe, but simply turning your money over to a professional and assuming he or she will do all the work ranks high. Blind faith is a recipe for money trouble. The only way a relationship with a financial planner will work is if you are reasonably well educated about finances yourself. That way, you and the planner can have a rewarding dialogue, and the money will be managed with your personal goals in mind and not by some formula generated for the average consumer. But the level of education required to ensure a successful relationship with a planner is usually enough to let you sensibly manage your money on your own.

Still, if your finances are complicated and a lot of money is at stake, hiring a highly educated financial planner is smart. Another reason for turning to a planner is time. Our lives are hectic, the law is constantly changing, and we may need to delegate some financial tasks.

But finding a professional you can trust is tough. Just about anyone can call himself or herself a financial planner, from the con artist to the dual Ph.D. in math and finance. The best way to search for a financial planner is to network. Talk with colleagues and neighbors you trust and see who they work with. You can also contact one of the main financial planning organizations, such as the Financial Planning Association. Three good credentials are Certified Financial Planner (CFP), Chartered Financial Consultant (ChFC), and Personal Financial Specialist (PFS). Any of the three tells you that the financial planner has had rigorous training, passed a minimum competency exam, and participates in a continuing education program.

Now, once you do find several professionals, check them out and interview them. Get references and follow up on those references. Have they had legal trouble? Do they handle clients with your income and assets? What is their financial background and education? And, of course, how do they get paid? Financial planners can get compensated in several ways. Commission-only financial planners get paid when you buy the investments they recommend, such as stocks, bonds, mutual funds, and insurance products. At the other end of the payment spectrum are the fee-only planners. They make their money by charging you a hefty fee, but they don't make anything off the investments you purchase. A hybrid payment schedule is the fee-plus-commission.

These planners charge a fee for telling you what to do, and they also earn commissions when you buy the investments they recommend. The planner could also use a fee-offset schedule. In that case, the planner reduces his or her fee by the commissions they earn.

In one sense, it doesn't matter how a financial planner is paid, so long as everything is well disclosed and the charges are transparent. Far more important is finding someone who is skilled and honest and who does business with clients just like you. Still, I lean toward fee-only planners. They are better able to make objective investment recommendations than their commission-oriented peers. Once you have found a financial planner with the skills and experience you need, it's important that you have a rapport with this person. You need someone who will listen more than talk.

Most of you reading this book can do your own financial planning, though.

A RETIREMENT BLUEPRINT

The other day, my wife and I sat in our family room looking at house blueprints in one of the many home-building magazines. We had a comfortable time together studying the different layouts, pointing out the ones we liked and discussing why others left us cold.

Couples should have somewhat similar discussions when thinking about retirement. What do you want to do in retirement? What do you want your lifestyle to be? A guiding principle for old-age planning is the life you live now. Think about the activities you like. Then figure out how you can continue doing versions of those activities in your later years. Let's say you live in Maine, and the rhythm of your days and years is marked by spontaneous visits and holiday traditions with nearby family and friends. You don't want to give up those relations. Perhaps you should plan on staying where you are rather than migrating to the sunbelt. But it snows in Maine, and its winters are frigid. You might want to prepare to move to a town home complex where somebody else does the shoveling, or maybe even an assisted living community where someone will drive you to shopping when the roads are icy. Maybe you want to launch a less stressful second career in your late 50s or early 60s as a professional photographer, a fund-raiser for a non-profit organization, or a seasoned consultant to young entrepreneurs. Now is a good time to start accumulating the skills you'll need. "Once you have looked at this total picture and once you've seen where you want to be 20 years from now, you can work backward and from there create a plan that's going to be effective for you, that's going to bring congruity between your actions and your values," says Ross Levin.

Of course, the trade-offs you'll face as part of your retirement planning will evolve over time. Many young people get into debt over their heads. They end up focusing their energies on erasing their daunting interest bills and set aside less for retirement. The daily $2.50 splurge on a cappuccino isn't eliminated so that they can live better in their later years; it's cut back as part of a budget discipline to get rid of debt. A family with elementary school kids will struggle to put something aside for their children's college education. This is a good place to confront a common question asked by the McKeowns: Should they save for their children's college education or their retirement? Each is a critical financial goal, yet there isn't enough money to accomplish both. However, in almost all cases it is a mental mistake to turn personal finance questions into either/or propositions. Instead, many of the most important choices lie on a spectrum, and the decision is where to give priority and emphasis at our current stage in life.

Rather than think in either/or terms, concentrate on the range of risk-and-reward trade-offs. For example, the McKeowns will end up saving for both college and retirement. But the financial priority is retirement. Students heading off to college have many financial options when it comes to paying for their tuition, room, and board. Many qualify for a financial aid package composed of student loans, grants, and work. Presumably, they'll start earning an income once they graduate with a college sheepskin in hand. But you have only so much time to salt money away for your twilight years. What's more, if it turns out that you end up making a far higher income and enjoying fatter investment returns than you ever expected, you can always chip in and pay off some or all of the student loans.

Everyone wants to know: How much money will I need in retirement? Another way of saying the same thing is: How much should I save to achieve my goals and financial security? What is the right formula? A familiar guideline is that you'll need to replace about 70% to 90% of your preretirement income when you stop working to maintain your current standard of living. In other words, if you earn $60,000 a year, you should plan on a retirement income of $42,000 to $54,000.

The 70% to 90% guideline is a reasonable starting point. But whether you will need more or less depends on what you want to do. Some people may need only 60% of their preretirement income ($36,000 in our example) if they own their own home outright, their idea of a good time is to take long hikes or bike rides, their tax bite declines, and many work-related expenses disappear. Other people may need 120% (or $72,000) of what they earned before retirement if their tax rate goes up because they have done so well with their investments and their goal is to travel to all the exotic spots in the world they dreamed of visiting but couldn't find the time for when they were younger. It's a useful exercise to run some numbers against your goals and come up with a broad probability range of estimates and scenarios. Your choices and estimates will become more realistic the closer your retirement date.

RETIREMENT SAVINGS PLANS

Good financial advice is tailored toward the deeply personal and individual. Everyone has different goals, tolerance for risk, job security, income, and wealth. Yet here is a piece of financial counsel that applies to all of us: Participate in a retirement savings plan.

A "defined contribution" retirement plan is a convenient, disciplined, and tax-savvy way to save. Perhaps your employer offers one. If not, you'll have to set up a retirement savings plan yourself. In an employer-sponsored plan, you determine how much money you want automatically deducted from your paycheck, subject to legal limits. The money that is siphoned off into your account is pretax dollars, and, therefore, it lowers your taxable income. Your investments in a retirement savings plan are protected from federal, state, and local government taxes until you withdraw the money during retirement. Your company will offer a menu of mutual fund investments, ranging from a handful of stock, bond, and short-term fixed income fund options to several hundred choices. Here's the best part: Many companies offer their employees a "match"—your employer contributes to your retirement plan, perhaps as much as 100% of what you put in, perhaps 50% or 25%. Even 25% is the best return anyone can make on a consistent basis in any investment. Not even the Wizard of Omaha, billionaire Warren Buffett, the greatest stock picker of the past half century, can match that kind of return month after month.

Now, for a variety of reasons, our retirement savings system is complicated. There are 401(k)s for the private sector; 403(b)s for nonprofits; 457s for state and local government employees; Keoghs, SEP-IRAs, and SIMPLE IRAs for small businesses and the self-employed; traditional Individual Retirement Accounts and Roth IRAs for those who qualify. These retirement plans all have different rules, regulations, and quirks. For example, married couples with an employer-sponsored pension plan and an adjusted gross income of up to $150,000 can contribute $4,000 into a Roth IRA. The income limit for the same couple for setting up a traditional IRA is $50,000.

The odds are you'll accumulate money in several retirement plans as your job opportunities multiply and your career takes off. In today's economy, it's not unusual for someone to work for a private company for a while, make a stab at starting his or her own business, do a stint in government, spend a few years at a nonprofit, and return to the private sector. The key is always to participate in whatever retirement plan is available to you at the time.

A RETIREMENT SAVINGS PLAN SKETCH

Here is a sketch of the major retirement savings programs. It's a lot to digest, but I want to give you an idea of what is available. These plans are all defined contribution plans. It's up to you to participate in a plan, and you have to decide where to invest the money. (Your employer may also offer a traditional defined benefit plan, a payout based on years of service. Great if you can get one, but I'll leave that to one side, since you don't manage the money.) You should get a much fuller accounting of your retirement savings plan from your employer and follow up with human resources (or management in a small company) if you have any questions. If you're self-employed and establishing a plan on your own, the mutual fund company or financial institution you're doing business with should supply you with a full, clearly written description of the plan. If not, take your business elsewhere. The bottom line remains the same—fund whatever plan you can to the maximum amount allowed by law. In almost all cases you can take money out of the tax-deferred retirement plan after age 59½ without penalty, and you are required to start spending down your savings at age 70½. If you take money out of the plan before age 59½, you will pay a 10% penalty, plus any taxes you owe on the tax-deferred savings you withdraw.

401(k): Established in 1978, the 401(k) is now the mainstay retirement savings plan offered by private companies. More than 37 million workers are enrolled in 401(k) plans. Pretax dollars are set aside every paycheck, and taxes on savings are deferred. The average 401(k) plan offers participants seven investment options, although the trend is toward ever greater choice. The maximum you can have taken out of your salary is currently $10,500 (that figure moves up over time, reflecting cost-of-living increases). The maximum amount that can go into a 401(k), including your contribution, any after-tax contributions you make, and your employer's contributions, is 25% of your compensation or $30,000, whichever is less. About 90% of all 401(k) plans at large companies, but less than half at small companies, let you borrow from your accumulated savings. 401(k) plans are portable—i.e., you can transfer your money into another 401(k) plan without penalty when you leave an employer. Or you can roll the money over into an Individual Retirement Account.

403(b): Unless you work for a nonprofit, the 403(b) isn't for you. These plans, also called tax-sheltered annuities, are geared to teachers, health care workers, public television and public radio employees, and workers at other nonprofit institutions. 403(b)s increasingly look like 401(k)s, with ample investment choices, payroll deductions, employer matches, borrowing provisions, and portability (including the option to roll over into an IRA). Participants in 403(b) plans have, on average, twice the number of investment options available to them as participants in 401(k)s, according to the Spectrum Group, a research and consulting firm. A 403(b) lets you save the same $10,500 as in a 401(k), but the plan offers its participants greater flexibility than a 401(k). If you fall within certain guidelines (such as being employed at the same place for at least 15 years), you can take advantage of a catch-up provision if you didn't take full advantage of the plan over the years. If you don't like the investment choices in your 403(b), you can transfer your contributions into an individual 403(b) custodial account—and the employer has no say in the matter.

457: If you are a state or local government employee, you might have a 457. Workers can defer up to 25% of their taxable income or $8,000 a year. The biggest benefit of a 457 is a generous catch-up provision prior to retirement. You can move your 457 savings into another public sector employer's 457 plan, but you can't roll over the money into an IRA when you leave your employer, as you can with a 401(k) or 403(b). 457 plans are offering participants more investment options these days.

Individual Retirement Account: The IRA is a quarter century old, and it opened up a retirement savings plan to many people who didn't have access to one at work. Still, an IRA isn't as generous as employer-sponsored pension plans. The maximum contribution is $2,000 ($4,000 for a married couple filing jointly). You need earned income to contribute to an IRA, but a nonworking spouse can put $2,000 into his or her own IRA. These plans are flexible. You can open an account with practically any financial institution. Your contributions are pretax, and the money compounds tax-deferred. You can't take the money out without penalty before age 59½, and you must start making withdrawals at age 70½. However, you can withdraw money without penalty for certain purposes (you will still pay income taxes). For example, there is no penalty if the savings are withdrawn for a first-time purchase of a home (with a lifetime limit of $10,000). Individuals covered by an employer-sponsored pension plan, such as a 401(k), can fully deduct their IRA contributions from taxes if they have a modified adjusted gross income of up to $31,000 (for singles) and $51,000 (for married couples). You can't borrow from an IRA. Anyone can establish a nondeductible IRA. The $2,000 contribution is not tax deductible, but the other rules are the same.

Simplified Employee Pension–IRA: Read this if you are a freelancer, an independent consultant, a sole practitioner, or if you moonlight for some extra income. The SEP-IRA is the retirement plan of choice for the self-employed—with good reason—and for business owners with a handful of employees. You can open a SEP with just about any financial institution, including banks, brokerage houses, insurers, and mutual fund companies. A self-employed individual can sock away 13.04% of net self-employed income up to $25,000. SEPs are extremely easy to set up, with minimal paperwork and low fees. You cannot loan yourself money from the account.

Saving Incentive Match Plans for Employees. The SIMPLE is a pension plan for companies with fewer than 100 employees. The federal government created the SIMPLE to encourage small businesses to offer their employees a retirement plan. The employee can put in a maximum of $6,000. The company must offer a match, with a high of 3% and a low of 1% (depending on certain employer choices).

Keogh plan: The Keogh is for the self-employed and small-business owners. The self-employed increasingly prefer the SEP, however, since the Keogh is more complicated and requires more paperwork than the SEP. Yet the Keogh allows for bigger contributions than the SEP, and its complexity also means it offers business owners and the self-employed greater options.

JUST DO IT

Many people find it tough to sign up for a retirement savings plan. Young workers, single parents, low-income employees, and new freelancers are often living paycheck to paycheck. The thought of setting money aside to draw down in three decades seems preposterous. Still, not participating in a retirement sav-

ings plan is a huge mistake. If money is tight, go ahead and en-
roll in the plan even if you put in only a few dollars out of every
paycheck. You can always increase the amount of money you put
in later on if your circumstances improve. But what you can't get
back is time—and it is with time that even small contributions
compound into large sums of money. Here's one calculation offered by the U.S. Department of Labor that emphasizes my
point. Let's say you put $1,000 a year into an IRA from age 20 to
age 30, and then you stop (bad idea, but for this example we'll
make that assumption). Your money earns a 7% annual rate of
return. When you retire at age 65, you'll have $168,514 in the ac-
count. A colleague starts saving at age 30 but puts $1,000 a year
into an IRA for the next 35 years, until age 65. He's contributed
more than three times what you did. How much does he have in
his account, assuming a 7% rate of return? His IRA is worth only
$147,913, or $20,601 less than yours.

When you participate in an employer's sponsored pension
plan, always check the "vesting" period. That's the waiting period before all the money in the plan is yours, including the employer's match. Depending on the plan, your vesting period
could be immediate or you may have to wait several years. If you
are thinking about leaving your job, see where you are in the
vesting timetable. Let's hope all the money is yours to take with
you. If not, consider waiting until you are fully vested.

The main defined contribution plans are portable. In other
words, you can take the money with you when you leave your
job. Typically, you'll roll over the money into your new employer's plan or into an Individual Retirement Account you
open up at a financial institution. (There is a $2,000 maximum
annual contribution limit to an Individual Retirement Account,
but there is no limit when it comes to a "rollover" IRA.) A common mistake is tapping into accumulated retirement savings
when you leave work and before age 59½. The government ex-
acts a significant penalty for the move. A mere 20% who re-

ceived a lump sum distribution from their retirement account rolled the entire sum into another tax-qualified vehicle, according to a study sponsored by the Pension and Welfare Benefits Administration. When you leave your job and take your pension with you, the whole sum should be transferred from your current employer directly to your new employer or into a rollover IRA. It's easy to do—all you have to do is fill out some forms. Another option: Many employers will let you keep the money in their plan even though you are no longer on their payroll.

It's up to the employer, but many 401(k) and 403(b) plans allow workers to borrow from their retirement account. Typically, companies will let you borrow only for a hardship reason, such as illness, or for your kid's education, or for a first-time home. You can't borrow to pay the bill for a dream vacation or a high-tech mountain bike. Loans can't exceed 50% of the value of your account or $50,000. You usually have five years to pay off your loan, although you can get 15 years if the money was borrowed for a home purchase. The interest rate you pay is usually the prime rate plus 1 or 2 additional percentage points. If the prime rate is 8%, the interest on your loan will be 9% or 10%. Your loan is repaid with after-tax dollars through automatic payroll deduction.

Some planners favor borrowing from your plan because, as the saying goes, you are borrowing from yourself and you repay yourself. But I would treat borrowing from a retirement savings plan as a last resort. Borrowing from a savings plan has several significant drawbacks. For one thing, if you leave work to go to another job or simply lose your job, most plans will require you to pay off the loan within 30 to 60 days. Otherwise, the government will consider the loan an early withdrawal and you'll pay a 10% penalty, plus income taxes on the amount you withdrew. The biggest penalty, however, is that the money you've borrowed isn't compounding on a tax-deferred basis.

WHAT HATH ROTH WROUGHT?

A new retirement option is worth delving into. It's the Roth IRA, named after its sponsor, Senator William Roth (R., Delaware). A Roth is unlike other retirement plans for working people because it is funded with after-tax dollars but all future appreciation is free from Uncle Sam's clutches. The Roth is a Hydra of rules and regulations that can trip up the unwary. But if you qualify, a Roth is a terrific retirement savings plan.

Who can open a Roth? You need earned income to contribute to a Roth. Single filers can contribute a maximum of $2,000 if their adjusted gross income is $95,000 or less. Single filers with incomes between $95,001 and $110,000 can make a reduced contribution. Roth IRA contributions are completely phased out after these sums. Joint filers with incomes of $150,000 and less can contribute $2,000 to a Roth ($4,000 for a married couple). Lower contribution limits are in place for joint filers with adjusted gross incomes of $150,001 to $160,000. As in other retirement plans, you can invest your Roth money in stocks, bonds, mutual funds, and similar investments.

In an unusual twist, you can "convert" your existing IRAs into a Roth without paying an early withdrawal penalty. You will owe taxes on your accumulated earnings. You can convert an existing IRA into a Roth only if your adjusted gross income does not exceed $100,000. The bottom line when it comes to conversion is whether you want to pay the taxes now and then let your money grow tax-free from here on out. One important guideline: You shouldn't convert unless you have other savings to pay the taxes you'll owe. You don't have to convert all of your existing IRA—you can convert as much as you like (although it must be an equal percentage from all your IRA accounts). But for many people, it makes sense to leave their traditional IRA alone and just start contributing to a Roth.

You can withdraw your earnings from a Roth IRA free of

taxes as long as the account has been in place for five years and you're over the age of 59½. You can also withdraw your annual after-tax contributions tax- and penalty-free at any time (but not the earnings). After five years, first-time home buyers can withdraw up to $10,000 of earnings from their Roth without penalty and tax-free toward their new purchase. As with any IRA, you can make an early withdrawal of earnings from your Roth to pay for qualified higher education expenses without penalty although you will owe income taxes on the earnings you take out. Unlike a traditional IRA, the Roth IRA does not require you to start withdrawing money at age 70½.

Let's deal with another retirement vehicle funded with after-tax dollars: a variable annuity. The baby boomers' search for tax-sheltered ways to benefit from the incredible stock run-up of the past few years has led to increased popularity for variable annuities. These savings vehicles are essentially mutual funds wrapped in tax-deferred insurance company accounts. Individuals buy variable annuities with after-tax dollars, but their contributions compound tax-deferred until retirement, when the gains are taxed as ordinary income.

Part of the appeal of variable annuities is a unique death benefit: When the owner of a variable annuity dies, the estate or beneficiary gets back the original investment, plus some guaranteed minimum return. So, if a variable-annuity owner invests $10,000 and dies when the investment shows a paper loss of $5,000, the estate or beneficiary still gets $10,000 (and, depending on the contract, any guaranteed minimum return). Of course, if the owner dies during a bull market and the $10,000 investment is worth $20,000, the heirs get the $20,000.

While the death benefit is clearly comforting to many people, it isn't worth anywhere near the price most insurance companies charge their customers for it, according to a study by Moshe Arye Milevsky of Canada's York University and Steven Posner of Goldman Sachs. They found that consumers are being charged as much as five to ten times the economic value of the guarantee for a basic return-of-premium variable annuity. Indeed, once the steep variable-annuity fees are taken into account, most long-term investors would do much better putting their money into a low-fee equity mutual fund or a mutual fund managed with an eye toward limiting the annual tax bite.

Let's take a closer look at the death-benefit guarantee. A variable-annuity holder pays an annual fee for the death benefit, typically labeled the mortality and risk-expense charge, or M&E fee. The average M&E fee in 1999 was 1.14%, according to the Variable Annuity Research & Data Service. The Morningstar Variable Annuity & Life Performance Report put the median M&E at 1.25% per annum. But how much should people pay for the death benefit? Not much, it turns out.

For one thing, the benefit probably doesn't make much sense for long-term investors. Market history suggests the odds are slim that the dollar value of your investment account will shrink over 10 to 30 years. For a more methodical and rigorous analysis, however, Milevsky and Posner used a sophisticated economic model to come up with the economic value of the death benefit in their study "The Titanic Option: Valuation of the Guaranteed Minimum Death Benefit in a Variable Annuity." Their bottom line: Most insurance companies are charging their customers too high a price. Their research shows that a typical 50-year-old male or female who buys a variable annuity with a simple return-of-premium guarantee should be charged a maximum of 3.5 basis points or 2 basis points, respectively, per year. (A basis point is one hundredth of a percentage point.) A variable-annuity contract with a 4% interest rate guarantee, which is obviously worth more, should charge a 50-year-old male 20 basis points and a 50-year-old female 12 basis points. Yet the industry average for the M&E fee is over 100 basis points! That's five times more than the benchmark fee that

Milevsky and Posner came up with for men, and nearly nine times the benchmark fee for women. In addition, other fees are associated with variable annuities, such as administration fees, records maintenance, and mutual fund expenses. The total average fee on a variable annuity is 2.23%, according to VARDS. Most variable annuities also carry "surrender" charges if you decide to bail out during the first couple of years. Taken altogether, the high fees associated with variable annuities is why most people saving for their retirement can find more attractive alternatives, from a 401(k) plan to a Roth IRA to a low-fee equity mutual fund.

Annuities have a long history. In ancient Rome contracts called *annua* promised an individual a stream of income in return for an up-front payment. Governments in England, France, and several other countries sold annuities in place of government bonds in the eighteenth century. In 1759, Pennsylvania chartered the Corporation for the Relief of Poor and Distressed Presbyterian Ministers and Distressed Widows and Children of Ministers to provide survivorship annuities for the families of ministers. It's safe to say that annuities are not about to disappear. And that's good, because some low-fee variable annuities are offered in the marketplace. Anyone stuck in a high-fee product should consider a tax-free transfer of his or her money into a lower-cost alternative—assuming he or she is past any surrender charges imposed by his or her insurance company. As with other investment products, competition is heating up in the variable-annuity retail market, so perhaps this product will evolve into an attractive retirement savings vehicle. But it's not there yet.

SOCIAL SECURITY

Let's not forget Social Security before we leave this review of retirement plans. Social Security is a financial behemoth that paid out $386 billion in 1999 to 44.6 million beneficiaries. Nearly all Americans age 65 or older receive Social Security benefits. Every pay period, Social Security affects 96% of the American workforce and their employers. More than twice as many workers are covered by Social Security as own mutual funds. Your Social Security benefit is a percentage of your earnings averaged over most of your working lifetime, and the benefit covers retirement, disability, family, survivors, and Medicare.

In a sharp break with the past, the Social Security Administration is sending out a benefits statement to all workers age 25 and older who are not currently receiving Social Security. The statement includes a year-by-year printout of your earnings as they have been reported to Social Security, plus an estimate of the benefits you and your family are eligible for now and in the future. Look over the statement carefully, and if there are any mistakes, contact the Social Security Administration to get them fixed.

The normal retirement age for 150 million workers went up starting in 2000. While you can still retire as early as 62 and collect reduced benefits, the age for collecting the full Social Security benefit will rise from 65 to 67 over the next 22 years.

INVEST, INVEST, AND INVEST

You've done your homework and explored your options. Now what? You've heard the old real estate saying that the only three things that matter with real estate are location, location, and location? Well, when it comes to retirement planning, the comparable mantra is invest, invest, and invest. I go into greater detail on investing in the next two chapters. Here, I want to focus on some of the most important principles when it comes to investing for retirement.

Many people are understandably intimidated about making investment choices. Terri McKeown certainly was nervous about the markets. Pat was unsure about the choices he had made. But investing for retirement isn't all that hard, so long as you keep your approach simple. To begin with, no matter what kind of retirement savings plan you are in, whether it's a 401(k), a 403(b), or an IRA, don't try to time the market or pretend you are a well-seasoned money manager. Focus on the investment decision that truly matters: how you divide your savings between stocks, bonds, cash (meaning money market funds, CDs, and the like), international equities, and real estate. Equities are the foundation of any retirement savings portfolio, but you still need to diversify. The basic idea behind diversification is to spread your risk. Take the place where you live as an example, such as Chicago, New York, or San Francisco. Imagine that your town had only one business, banking. Your city would thrive when banking was doing well, but the local economy would tank when banking was doing poorly. But cities have many good businesses, from manufacturing to media to transportation. So if banking is doing poorly, the economic fortunes of the city are not tied to just that one industry. The same goes with your investment portfolio. You don't want to tie your future standard of living to just one asset, like stocks. You want to put some money into a variety of assets, some of which will zig while others zag.

Invest for the long haul. It's hard to stay the course when the stock and bond markets head lower. Look at what Pat McKeown did. He got completely out of his stock portfolio when the U.S. stock market swooned during the Asian market meltdown. Yet the stock market climbed to record territory over the following year. Even if the market had continued to tank, Pat would have made a mistake. You can't let the market tell you what to do. Instead, concentrate on your needs and goals. The time to make investment changes is when your life circumstances change, not when the market takes an abrupt shift up or down. Are your children nearing college age? Did you retire? Lose your job? These

are the kind of life events that might dictate a shift in strategy—
not the latest swing in the market. Mark Fettig, formerly head of
the retirement savings plan business at Prudential Securities,
uses his brother as an example. A highly respected doctor, Fettig's brother flies into a panic with every downward shift in the
value of his stock market holdings. What should he do? Get out
of equities? "I say, John, you are smart. Long-term, have your
needs changed?" says Mark Fettig. "No? Well then, you
shouldn't panic into any change right here."

Pat's reaction to a down market does emphasize the importance of understanding risk. The essence of asset allocation is
mixing and matching your assets until you have a portfolio that
mirrors your risk tolerance. Risk isn't just your psychological
and emotional ability to weather swings in the market. It also includes whether you currently enjoy job security, are about to go
through your third corporate downsizing, or plan to continue
working well into your 70s. Luckily, a new generation of sophisticated software and Internet-based programs makes the
asset allocation side of investing easier than ever. You can use
web-based programs to play "what if" scenarios as you come up
with a reasonable asset mix. Now, many of these programs give
you very precise numbers. If you save so much for so many years
and earn a rate of return of such and such, you will have
$898,979.225 at age 60. A little skepticism is in order. These
programs are very sensitive to small changes in your assumptions, such as future inflation rates or the rate of return you will
earn on your money.

Since the essence of investing is uncertainty, you will want
to play with a range of scenarios. Calculators based on "Monte
Carlo" simulations are designed to do just that. Monte Carlo is
a mathematical technique that tests hundreds or thousands of
investment outcomes (depending on the program), all with an
eye toward assessing the probability of your portfolio's reaching
a desired outcome. Financial Engines, a web-based company

cofounded by William Sharpe, a Nobel laureate in economics, uses Monte Carlo simulations. Here's an example I used for a story on retirement for *Business Week*. Let's say you are a 50-year-old male, earn $100,000 a year, and have $600,000 in your 401(k). You want to retire at 65 with a retirement income of $80,000 annually, adjusted for inflation, but excluding any Social Security money. If you invest conservatively, what is the chance you'll reach your goal? And how much of a difference would it make if you invested more aggressively? You are saving 10% of your salary in a 401(k), with 63% of the money going into bonds and 37% into an equity mutual fund. According to Financial Engines, at age 65 you would have a 34% chance of reaching your goal. Now let's keep everything the same, except this time you invest 37% in a bond fund and 63% in stocks. You now have a 51% chance of achieving your goal at age 65. But your portfolio is more volatile, so there will be a lot more heart-stopping moments along the way. "Risk in many ways is the probability of not reaching the things that you want to reach, not meeting your goals," says Ross Levin.

A common investment mistake is not looking at your household portfolio as a whole. The problem lies with the way we get ourselves to save. Most, if not all of us, segregate our money into different "mental accounts." Here is my pot of money for retirement, another pot for my children's college education, another for emergencies, and so on. Similarly, many financial services firms will offer novice investors a model portfolio as a pyramid of assets. The layers of risk in the pyramid go with certain goals, such as retirement, college, and the down payment on a home. Mental accounting makes it easier for us to save. But the different parts of the pyramid will interact with each other—something you miss with the mental accounting strategy.

Every once in a while, you should get rid of the mental categories and throw all the money into one pot. The reason is that you may be too conservative or aggressive in your investment choices without even knowing it. For example, let's say you've saved $150,000 for your children's college education. Your students are heading off to college in three to five years, so you have divvied up the portfolio into 20% equity and 80% fixed income. It's a very reasonable asset allocation considering the time frame. You also have $150,000 in a retirement account, split into 75% equities and 25% bonds. Again, it's a sound asset allocation for a long-term goal like retirement. Each asset allocation sounds about right. But your household asset mix is 52.5% fixed income and 47.5% equity. Is that the right overall mix for your household? That may be far too conservative for you. You might be better off with an overall portfolio of 60% stocks and 40% bonds.

The balance between risk and reward in your household should reflect your total investment portfolio.

THE NEW FLEXIBILITY

Almost all of us understandably focus on saving and investing when it comes to retirement planning. One reason is that finding the money to save isn't easy. Another reason is that investing is a new, uncertain world for many of us. Nevertheless, one of the best retirement planning tools available is staying active longer than the typical retirement age of 60 or 62. The financial effect of allowing your retirement portfolio to compound for a greater period of time is significant. Take a median U.S. couple in their 50s. After accounting for their debts, the median couple have accumulated a net wealth of $325,000, including pensions, Social Security, and housing. Economists James Moore and Olivia S. Mitchell of the Wharton School estimate this median couple on the verge of retirement will have $380,000 by the time they hit 62. To maintain their preretirement consumption levels if they retire at 62, the couple will need to start saving an additional 16% of their annual earnings right now. However, if they delay retirement three years to age 65, their nest egg will swell to $420,000 and the required additional savings will drop to 7% of their annual income. Time is money.

Investing for retirement doesn't just mean money. Long before you say good-bye to full-time work at the office or on the assembly line, you should also invest in the skills, knowledge, and contacts you'll need to make a smooth transition to another phase of your life. Want to start your own business? Investigate your options and learn about how to put together a business plan before you take the leap into entrepreneurship. Always wanted to work for a nonprofit? Explore your options, generate some contacts now, and see where you're most needed. Invest some time in what you plan on doing down the road—you'll lead a better life and assure yourself a less risky one, too.

PLANNING FOR FINANCIAL SECURITY

Let's take a step back for a moment. We've immersed ourselves in the issue of saving for retirement. The reason you struggle today to set aside some money is to ensure yourself a financially secure future. The concept of long-term financial security extends beyond saving for retirement, though. Two other key topics are insurance and estate planning. Like retirement savings, both are all too easily deferred. But the triumvirate of retirement savings, insurance, and estate planning is critical for managing and limiting risk while improving the odds that you will achieve your goals.

Let's start with life insurance. Several years ago, I got a somewhat belligerent call on *Sound Money,* the public radio show I cohost, from a young professional with a good income, a stay-at-home wife, and two very young children. His challenge: Why buy life insurance? He had begun investing in the stock market and was doing well. Wouldn't it be better to invest in the stock market than waste money on life insurance premiums? My answer: I think you are crazy, and you are exposing your young family to an enormous financial risk if you should unexpectedly die.

There is only one reason to buy life insurance: to financially protect your loved ones from catastrophe. Some insurance agents will try to sell you a policy as a way to save for retirement or for your children's college education. Forget it. The financial world offers far better and cheaper ways to salt away long-term savings, such as retirement savings plans and mutual funds. No, life insurance is financial protection for your children and other family members who depend on you. Indeed, once your kids are off on their own, you may no longer need a life insurance policy.

How much life insurance should you own? The web offers a number of calculators for playing with numbers. The Consumer Federation of America recommends that a family with two children consider purchasing life insurance worth six to eight times family income. I lean toward the higher figure, considering the emotional and financial trauma from the death of a spouse.

What kind of life insurance should you buy? Life insurance comes in two basic flavors. One is called term insurance. It is a pure death benefit. Term insurance is cheap, but the premiums increase as you age. Term insurance meets my requirement of simplicity. The product is easy to understand and allows for comparison shopping to get the best mix of price and coverage for you. You'll want a low-cost, plain-vanilla policy from a blue-chip, financially strong life insurance company. Term insurance is ideal for most families. You can also stop funding a term life policy when you have built up sufficient assets and your children are off in the work world, setting up their own households. If you're concerned that you may want a longer-term policy, consider a convertible term insurance policy. It allows you to transform your term policy into a "cash value" policy.

Cash value is the other major kind of insurance. Cash value insurance always comes with a tax-sheltered savings component as well as a life insurance policy. Cash value life insurance is more complicated than term. There are all kinds of policies—whole life, universal life, variable life, variable universal life, and so forth. Depending on the type of cash value policy, the insurance company may invest the savings on your behalf, or you may choose from a menu of mutual funds offered by the insurer. The premium may be stable for the life of the policy, or you may vary your payments. Competition is bringing about improvements in the cash value insurance market, but in general these policies are expensive. Commission costs are steep, the policies' inner workings are often obscure, and premiums are much higher than term. Cash value life insurance is usually sold rather than bought. Unfortunately, about a quarter of all cash value buyers let their policies lapse after two years and about half drop the policy by the seventh year. The main reason is that the premiums are too costly to carry year after year.

Cash value insurance makes sense for some people. For instance, parents with a handicapped child often need insurance coverage well into their old age, when term insurance is prohibitively expensive. A life insurance policy can play a vital role in sophisticated estate planning, although you should work closely with a professional before doing anything. If you think a cash value policy is the way to go, take your time, shop around, and get competitive bids. Don't depend too much on any long-term projections about how much money you'll earn in the savings component of a cash value policy—remember, trees don't grow to the sky. Again, stick with financially healthy companies.

Here's a popular alternative to buying cash value insurance: Buy term insurance and invest the difference. For example, suppose the annual premium on the cash value policy you're contemplating is $1,000 and you could get a term insurance policy for several hundred dollars less. Buy the term insurance, and invest the difference on your own, perhaps in a mutual fund.

Do you have disability insurance? I hope the reply is yes, although for far too many people the answer is no. Disability insurance replaces a portion of your income if you are taken ill or injured and can't work. Insurance industry statistics show that only 40% of people have disability insurance compared to 70% with life insurance, even though the odds of being disabled during our working years are much higher than the odds of dying. According to the Health Insurance Association of America, about a third of people between the ages of 35 and 65 will be disabled for at least 90 days. Many employees are offered disability insurance through work. Social Security also administers a disability benefit. But if you are self-employed, or your employer doesn't offer a group disability benefit, you should investigate buying an individual disability policy. Disability policies typically replace about 60% to 70% of your income. There are a couple of features to look for when researching these policies. Make sure the policy covers your occupation. If you should become disabled, the benefit should protect you against inflation, and it should be guaranteed renewable or noncancelable so that you can be sure the coverage will continue.

HOW'S YOUR HEALTH?

Check up on your medical insurance. You're in luck if you work for a company that offers you health care coverage. You may be stuck with its policy, but nothing compares with employer-provided health insurance (until you are eligible for Medicare).

If your employer's benefit package doesn't include health insurance or you number among the swelling ranks of self-employed entrepreneurs, you still need health insurance, but you will pay a small fortune for it. Sometimes you can buy into a group health plan through a trade organization, community group, professional association, or some other alliance. Some health maintenance organizations will sell to individuals, as will the Blue Cross/Blue Shield plans. A relatively new option for the self-employed is the medical savings account, or MSA. With an MSA you buy a catastrophic health care policy with a very high deductible (as high as $2,250 for an individual and $4,500 for a family). But you also get to put tax-deductible money equal to 65% of the deductible for individuals and 75% of the deductible for families into a tax-deferred account (reminiscent of an IRA). You use the tax-deferred account to meet any out-of-pocket expenses until the health coverage kicks in. Any tax-deferred dollars you don't use can be rolled over to the next year.

Should you buy long-term-care insurance? We're living longer, and long-term-care insurance offers nursing-home or home-health-care coverage for chronically ill or disabled people. If there is a history of Alzheimer's or other disabling diseases in your family, then long-term-care insurance can be a valuable financial product. The national average for a year in a nursing home is more than $46,000, and home care can easily cost more than $12,000 a year. Yet Medicare and regular health insurance policies don't cover these astronomical costs. The growing demand for long-term-care insurance is translating into coverage at lower prices than before. Still, long-term-care insurance is an expensive investment that should not be done on a whim. It requires serious research and scrutiny. Individual policies without an inflation adjustment feature ranged in cost from $250 annually to more than $3,900, according to the Health Insurance Association of America. Inflation adjustments can add 40% to 140% to the premium.

As you'd expect, long-term-care premiums are based on your age, the benefits you select, and the number of years you want your insurance company to pay those benefits. Another price factor is not so intuitive—the so-called elimination period. Sounds ominous. But it's essentially a deductible that determines when you want your insurance company to start paying your benefits. Now with, say, auto insurance or home insurance, picking a higher deductible saves you money on your premiums. But most experts urge you to choose a shorter elimination period option when buying long-term-care insurance. That's because auto and home insurance deductibles are usually fixed amounts—$250 or $500—so you know what your out-of-pocket expenses will be when you file a claim. But with long-term-care insurance, the elimination period is the number of days, not dollars, before coverage begins. With health care costs rising faster than inflation, your out-of-pocket costs are guaranteed to increase. For example, assume you buy a policy at age 65 that would cover long-term-care costs of up to $100 a day for five years, with a 5% compound-inflation rider so your benefit grows every year. You pick the 20-day elimination period, and your premium payment is $2,036 a year. But if you go for the 100-day elimination period, your premium payment drops to $1,800—saving you $236 a year. But here's what that 80-day difference in the elimination period would really cost you: If you needed care during your first year of coverage, the 100-day elimination period would cost you $8,000 more than the standard 20-day period. It gets even worse. After ten years, your $100-a-day inflation-protected benefit would have risen to $163 a day. Now your 100-day elimination period would cost you just over $13,000 more. After 20 years, the difference would be $21,000.

The point is that shopping for long-term-care insurance should be viewed as an educational process. You can't just pick it out of the Yellow Pages. You'll need an experienced insurance expert or estate planner who can evaluate your needs and then shop around for the best policy to meet those needs. Generally speaking, if your income is under $35,000 a year the premiums are too expensive. At the other end of the earnings spectrum, if you are wealthy, you can probably afford to do without this insurance and just pay the bills. The really tough decision is for middle-class people with savings ranging from $150,000 to $500,000 and a retirement income between $60,000 and $80,000 a year.

When comparing long-term-care policies, also consider other financial options. For instance, do you own your home free and clear? If so, a "reverse mortgage" is a possible alternative. With a reverse mortgage, the lender issues you a loan based on a percentage of your home equity. You receive a lump sum of money or periodic payments, and the loan is retired when you sell the home. Close-knit extended families also offer financial and emotional support to their elder members.

ESTATE PLANNING

Estate planning is for the rich, right? Wrong. Estate planning is all about taxes, yes? Wrong again. Estate planning is about limiting risk and bringing order to your finances.

Now, in year 2000–01 the federal government will levy an estate tax only if your assets are greater than $675,000 ($1.35 million for married couples) after allowable deductions. The exemption climbs to $1 million ($2 million for couples) in 2006. As you can gather from those figures, most families don't pay the estate tax, which can run an onerous 55% for anything above the congressionally mandated limit.

Yet estate planning is for everyone, and it begins with a will. A will is merely written instructions, prepared according to legal rules, directing how a person's property is to be distributed at death. A will is especially important to protect the financial interests of minor children or other dependents. It's critical to think about whom you want to raise your children if both parents die or if you are a single parent. It's increasingly common to designate one person to take care of your children and another person, with better money skills, to manage the finances. If you have written a will, make sure someone knows where to find it when you're gone.

In one episode of *Right on the Money,* I met a very close family, parents Jan and Shawn Dutton and their three children. Shawn was a veterinarian. They had thought about estate planning when they became parents 11 years ago. They drew up an informal document written on a Post-it note that dictates who will raise their children. They keep the Post-it note in their bedroom in a little fireproof box, but they hadn't told anyone it exists. With three kids, they knew they needed a will—and they created one after we talked.

What's more, a will is not a once-in-a-lifetime document. People outgrow their initial wills, and new laws make revisions a necessity. In most cases, I think it pays to hire a lawyer who specializes in wills. Yes, I know about the software and Internet do-it-yourself wills, but this is an area where a mistake or misunderstanding is especially costly.

If you die without a will, the state will essentially draft one for you and will decide who administers it. Most states assume that relatives are your intended heirs. That can be a problem if you're estranged from your relatives. If you don't have any, the state, and the lawyers, will be perfectly happy to keep your money. That could be heartbreaking for the nearly 2 million unmarried couples living together. Most states don't recognize such relationships.

Trusts are an increasingly popular option. A trust is a legal entity created by a property owner that protects and distributes the property according to the owner's wishes. A trust transfers assets to a third party for benefit of a beneficiary. One reason trusts are gaining widespread acceptance is that with a trust your estate avoids probate, and probate has a terrible reputation. A probate court administers a person's will. It's the legal process of settling an estate, and your will becomes a public document. But probate is not as bad as it's often alleged to be. "Actually, as time has gone by, probate proceedings have become easier and easier," says Janet Rau, head of estate planning at the law firm Dorsey & Whitney.

Do you need a trust? There are many different types of trusts, and they can be extremely complex. They're not for everyone—far from it. But if you can answer yes to any of these basic questions, you should look into including a trust as part of your estate planning.

- Are any of your beneficiaries physically or mentally handicapped, or are any of them simply incompetent when it comes to managing money?
- Is there a relative lurking out there somewhere whom you don't want to include as a beneficiary?
- Is there a business, property, or financial portfolio that needs professional management?
- Do you want to maintain control, or do you want your spouse to maintain control, of your assets?
- Do you want to control how your estate is used after your death? Or do you want to restrict access to your estate by your heirs until they reach a certain age?
- Do you have property in several states?
- Do you simply want to keep prying eyes away from your financial affairs?

Trusts have to be done right, and there are a lot of pitfalls for the unwary, the careless, or the confused. So seek competent professional legal advice to see whether a trust, and what kind of trust, makes sense for you. But come armed with lots of questions and a skeptical frame of mind.

You should consider whom you want to carry out your wishes should you become incompetent. The three most common documents are a power of attorney for financial issues, a power of attorney for health care decisions, and a living will, which dictates to your doctor your wishes about life-prolonging health care procedures.

PAT AND TERRI

How did Pat and Terri McKeown do? I felt confident after going over the expert advice we had gathered for them, and addressing some additional questions, that both were more comfortable with the idea of retirement planning. They did review their life insurance and their will. Pat and Terri thought about the trade-off between saving for college and saving for retirement and realized they would do both—but not shortchange retirement. They did decide to move into a bigger home. But the biggest impact on them was in their thinking about long-term investing. Pat realized he had to take a more thoughtful approach toward asset allocation. Even more striking was Terri's change in attitude. Yes, the stock market was risky, but it was even riskier not to invest in equities as part of a retirement portfolio. And the notion of reducing risk by diversifying appealed to her. Indeed, Terri's part-time employer had offered her a 401(k), and she had signed up. "I've learned that you can diversify and make it a little safer for yourself," said Terri.

As for the bigger question of what they wanted to do for retirement, well, that was open for discussion. Which is as it should be. For most of us, the answer won't come about overnight. It will take time and dialogue. "I feel better about retirement in general," says Pat, "because we've been thinking about it a little bit."

What I liked about Pat and Terri's thinking is that nothing dramatic happened. No loud pronouncements or slapping of the forehead. Instead, the response was thoughtful, modest, but more focused. In other words, they are taking concrete steps right now that they can build on and refine as time passes.

THE ECONOMICS OF AGING

Americans are getting older. And we seem gripped with foreboding about aging. Profligate baby boomers aren't saving enough. Social Security will collapse with too few workers supporting far too many retirees. Health care costs will spiral out of control. "Facing old age with less support from children is scary enough even if one is financially flush, but the baby boom generation is looking at a very long period of retirement, reduced Social Security benefits, rising health care costs, decreased health care benefits, and the likelihood of spending a good deal of time in a nursing home," writes economist Lawrence Kotlikoff in his book *Generational Accounting*.

Hold off the apocalypse, please. There are sound reasons for doubting the lurid visions of an aging, decrepit America. The economic and generational picture is far more optimistic. One striking transformation is how companies are using information technologies to raise productivity, which rose in the 1990s at about double the pace of the 1970s and 1980s. And rising productivity, the fundamental building block of higher living standards, will make it easier to fund the future Social Security and health care bills. The Internet holds the promise of even greater efficiencies and wealth creation than many economists thought possible only a few years ago.

What's more, billions of dollars are pouring into retirement savings plans every year as boomers reach those sober ages when savings typically rise. Homeownership is at record levels, and owning a home is another form of savings. Baby boomers also plan on working longer, and, as we have seen, that decision could have a dramatic impact on their future living standards. The population is increasingly well educated.

Some Wall Street analysts fear that stock and bond prices will plummet when boomers try to cash in their savings during their golden years. But the specter of a pension-asset implosion is implausible, largely because of the move toward freer trade and more open borders around the world. The worldwide spread of capitalism is encouraging vast amounts of capital to flow across borders. The current size of the global capital markets is some $78 trillion. By the time boomers need to sell their stock and bond holdings, markets will be far more international than they are now, and there will be plenty of global investors eager to buy U.S. assets in the twenty-first century.

The aging of the population is sure to bring about broad social and economic changes. But there are also many positive forces at work. The nation is more productive than at any previous time since the 1960s. The elderly are more vital than before. Americans can afford to grow old. And they will grow old gracefully.

Resources

Ernst & Young's Retirement Planning Guide, by Ernst & Young (John Wiley & Sons). The title says it all. A good job covering the retirement waterfront.

Making the Most of Your Money, by Jane Bryant Quinn (Simon & Schuster). A section (Step 7) of this massive tome deals with retirement planning. As always, an insightful and comprehensive look at a subject by the best in the business.

Personal Finance for Dummies, by Eric Tyson (IDG Books Worldwide). Tyson covers a lot more than retirement, but this is a good guide for long-term planning and strategic thinking.

You and Your 401(k), by Julie Jason (Simon & Schuster/Fireside). A detailed look at the world of 401(k)s.

A Commonsense Guide to Your 401(k), by Mary Rowland (Bloomberg Press). This slim volume is terrific. Anything and everything you want to know about these retirement savings plans.

IRAs, 401(k)s, and Other Retirement Plans: Taking Your Money Out, by Twila Slesnick and John Suttle (Nolo Press). Hey, you worked hard to save money, but how do you get it out? Since Congress has written and rewritten the rules over the years, it should come as no surprise that it's more complex than you might think—or hope.

The Fountain of Age, by Betty Friedan (Touchstone Books). A sprawling, often frustrating book that has drawn a fair amount of criticism. But I enjoyed carrying on a conversation with Friedan through her book. She has many insights and an unshakable optimism.

Smarter Insurance Solutions, by Janet Bamford (Bloomberg Press). Janet simply writes the clearest, most consumer-friendly guide to insurance.

moneycentral.msn.com. The Microsoft retirement planning site is a source of information, and its calculators are useful for testing various "what if" scenarios. When using financial calculators, do so several times and change your assumptions. That way you get a range of outcomes—always a useful exercise.

tiaa-cref.org. The world's largest retirement system has created a good online curriculum for anyone who has basic questions about investing for retirement.

vanguard.com. The Vanguard mutual fund company offers a wealth of information. A well-organized site with clearly written articles.

troweprice.com. T. Rowe Price is a smart place to go for deciphering the latest wrinkle in IRAs or retirement planning.

fidelity.com. Fidelity Investments is the world's largest mutual fund company.

financialengines.com. William Sharpe, a Nobel laureate in economics, is the main force behind this online company. You answer some simple questions, and Financial Engines uses sophisticated mathematical models to devise an asset allocation for you. The key concept is risk, and everything is in probabilities.

fpanet.org. The Financial Planning Association's web site.

quicken.com. Money management made easy. A rich web site for any money issue. Lots of information on retirement.

aarp.org. When it comes to elder care, a prime stopping place is the web site of the American Association of Retired Persons. AARP covers just about any topic related to getting older, and its information is backed by well-done research.

elderweb.com. ElderWeb bills itself as a research site for both professionals and family members concerned about elder care and long-term care. It lives up to its promise, with thousands of links to information on legal, financial, medical, and housing issues, as well as policy research and statistics.

aoa.dhhs.gov/aoa/NAIC. The government's National Aging Information Center web site offers links to all the government agencies and much more.

ssa.gov. The web site of the Social Security Administration has a wealth of data and calculators. It's an easy site to navigate, too.

insweb.com. An Internet site for insurance quotes and decent articles on insurance.

insure.com. A rich resource for learning more about insurance.

7

Investment Basics

To invest successfully over a lifetime does not require a
stratospheric IQ, unusual business insights, or inside
information. What's needed is a sound intellectual
framework for making decisions and the ability to keep
emotions from corroding that framework.

—Warren Buffett

Two centuries ago, 24 notable New York brokers and merchants met outside 68 Wall Street to sign the "Buttonwood
Agreement." The pact established standard commissions for
trading securities, an agreement that evolved over time into the
New York Stock Exchange. Until the 1980s, most individual
investors were well-heeled businessmen, leading merchants,
financiers, daredevil speculators, and unsavory stock manipula-
tors. Yes, we've all read stories or heard anecdotes about shop-
keepers, cab drivers, housewives, and other ordinary Americans
recklessly pouring their hard-earned cash into the stock market
during the frenzied years leading up to the stock market crash
of 1929. Yet stock market investors in the 1920s were mostly af-
fluent, and historians estimate that at most 15% of the population owned equities. In the 1960s, the newly prosperous middle
class did dabble in mutual funds, but they poured the bulk of

their investment money into homes. Overall, those who owned equities amounted to about one-fifth of the population.

This time is different. Like civic associations at the turn of the twentieth century or homeownership following World War II, investing now has all the characteristics of a mass social movement. Millions of employees are investing in stocks and bonds for their retirement, for their children's college education, and for a financial safety net against a corporate restructuring. Stock market twists are headline news as the Dow Jones Industrial Average more than quadrupled during the 1990s and the NASDAQ Composite Index rose nearly tenfold. The money managed by the mutual fund industry soared from $48 billion in 1970 to more than $7 trillion in 2000. Today, about half of all U.S. households own equities, either through mutual funds or individually.

Thanks to the Internet, you ain't seen nothin' yet. Imagine, in 1994 not one person traded stocks over the Internet. Yet by the turn of the millennium, online trading accounted for nearly 40% of all trades by individual investors. The Internet is a force for democratizing finance at an unprecedented pace. Wall Street has gone middle-class and mass-market.

There is a rub. Like soothsayers of old, working people of all ages are struggling to peer into the future. How, they wonder during conversations at work and around the weekend barbecue, should I invest my money? After all, there are some 4,000 stock mutual funds. Investment styles have proliferated. There are growth funds, value funds, momentum funds, sector funds, and emerging market funds, and that's naming only a few of the better-known investing categories. The more than 2,200 bond mutual funds also offer an astonishingly broad menu of choices, from U.S. government securities to tax-exempt notes to junk bonds. And where should you stash your money? A bank? Credit union? Life insurance company? Brokerage firm? Financial institutions are invading one another's turf to capture more of your money. Yet the investment decisions made today will impact your living standards two to three decades from now—whether you will move into a mobile home or a house by the Jersey shore. The uncertainty is immense. Julia Chivers, a high-powered consultant with a major employee benefits firm, is confused: "The tough thing for me is that there seems to be so many different vehicles out there," she says. "I am not sure really where to start."

Jim Leinfelder shares her frustration. He wants to be a savvy investor, but he doesn't know where to begin. He is a smart guy who is intimidated by the sea of choices. But first Jim needs to become more comfortable with the idea of risk. Because when you invest—whether it's for the short term, say, for your child's college education, or for a retirement date 40 years in the future—you are marrying yourself to some amount of financial risk. Before you invest dollar one, you need to figure out what your goals are, and whether you're comfortable with the amount of risk it's going to take to meet those goals.

Face it—few of us grew up learning to understand and be comfortable with investment risk. To be sure, Warren Buffett, perhaps the most successful investor of the post–World War II era, was charting stock prices when he was in elementary school, and he bought his first stock with earnings from his newspaper route. And Geraldine Laybourne, currently head of the multimedia company Oxygen Media and formerly the driving force behind Nickelodeon, learned how to analyze companies as a kid from her stockbroker father.

Yet investing is surprisingly simple. I'm serious. Of course, grizzled Wall Street veterans shudder at statements like that. It's true that you can spend a lifetime studying the markets and never come close to mastering the art and science of investing. But that is important only if you want to work on Wall Street, labor in a company's finance department, or make a living trading for your own account. And I'm not proposing that all you have to do is buy

stocks and you'll make money. A friend once stunned me when
he said making money in the stock market was easy. All you did
was buy a high-tech stock and watch it go up. That's reminiscent
of comedian Will Rogers, who once quipped, "Buy stocks that are
going up. After they have done that, sell them. If they ain't going
to go up, don't have bought them."

No, what I mean is this: When you invest, you are taking
some of your hard-earned dollars and hoping to get more dollars back at some point in the future. You can invest that money
well as long as you concentrate on understanding a few core
principles, focus on the long haul, and keep your moneymaking
expectations realistic. What's more, you can make savvy financial choices without spending weeks or even months ripping
apart corporate balance sheets, wading through mutual fund
performance statistics, and continuously monitoring every price
twitch in the stock market on television or on the Internet. It's
probably far better for your financial health if you don't.

A commonsense investment framework for individuals has
evolved over the past half century. The basic ideas were developed by such ivory-tower luminaries as Eugene Fama and Harry
Markowitz at the University of Chicago, Paul Samuelson and
Robert Merton of the Massachusetts Institute of Technology,
William Sharpe and Myron Scholes of Stanford University, and
the late Fisher Black of Goldman Sachs. Now, if you try to read
the seminal academic papers in financial economics, you'll notice that they include few words and plenty of equations intelli-
gible only to the quantitative cognoscenti. Economists still
strongly disagree with one another about how the investment
world works, and their understanding of the markets is constantly developing. For instance, two well-known investment
books by two brilliant finance economists are *A Random Walk
Down Wall Street* and *A Non-Random Walk Down Wall Street*. You
get the drift.

Yet strip financial economics of its complexity and contro-

versy, and you'll discover that most economists agree on a relatively simple framework of investing for the mass of Americans.
The framework's centerpiece is the trade-off between risk and
reward. The economic approach to investing is tailor-made for
those who need to invest their savings, but are also busy building a career, raising a family, spending time with friends, caring
for parents, and volunteering time in their local community.
The investment approach I am taking focuses on creating a
household portfolio for all economic seasons. It is also an investment discipline that works for the reality of our busy, messy
lives rather than an idealized version of *Homo investus.*

Let's be clear: In today's world, the biggest mistake you can
make is to not invest. The financial penalty for not participating
in a long-term savings plan is far bigger than the risk of picking
a poorly performing stock or a badly managed mutual fund.
The financial price for procrastinating is more than dollars, dividends, and interest payments. You don't get valuable real-
world lessons about money management by delaying. "You have
to know a little bit. And then you take the plunge. And then you
learn as you go," says Paula Kennedy, a leading financial planner at Ernst & Young LLP. "If we knew everything there was to
know about everything we were attempting to do, we would
never do anything. So you have to take the plunge."

So come on, let's take the plunge.

YOU CAN'T BEAT THE MARKET

Here's a phrase you'll hear a lot when it comes to investing:
"beat the market." Now, the "market" is usually an index, such
as the 30 multinational corporations that make up the Dow
Jones Industrial Average, the 500 large-company stocks that
comprise the Standard & Poor's 500 index, and the small company universe of the Russell 2000.

The Dow is the most famous market index. Charles H. Dow

unveiled the 12-stock industrial index in 1896. He created it as a guide for investors to see how the market was doing. Before the index, it was much harder to answer the question "How is the market doing?" The market was just a bunch of stocks, some going up and others going down, with no readily identifiable benchmark to cut through the confusion. The Dow is a measuring rod to judge the market's direction and for making comparisons. The index is now composed of 30 large, brand-name companies, such as Boeing, General Motors, Microsoft, Intel, Wal-Mart, and McDonald's. Of course, the Dow doesn't capture the entire market. There are thousands of companies not included in the index, such as high-tech behemoths Cisco Systems and Dell Computer. To get a better measure of the market, it's important to look at other, broader-based indexes, such as the Wilshire 5000, a gauge of the entire U.S. stock market. Still, by force of habit, longevity, and custom, the Dow Jones Industrial Average is the world's most recognized index.

Whatever index you use, Wall Street brokers linked to an army of research analysts and computer terminals promise to find you stocks that will "beat the market." Mutual fund managers trumpet their stock-picking prowess and market-beating performance. Investment magazines and newsletters proclaim the ten hottest stocks of the New Year that will, yes, sizzle compared to the overall stock market. Television shows highlight stocks poised to soar. Internet sites offer the hour's hot stock. Taken altogether, Wall Street knows where the market is going next and how you can get a jump on everyone else.

Hold on to your wallet. Trying to beat the market is a loser's game. This is a case where the cliché is right: If it were easy to beat the market, everyone would be rich. For instance, Terrance Odean and Brad Barber, two financial economists at the University of California, Davis, looked at the trading accounts of more than 66,000 households at a large discount brokerage firm from 1991 to 1996. The stock market recorded an annual return of 17.9% during those years, while the return of those who traded the most, after taking commissions into account, was 11.4%. Now you know why they named their paper "Trading Is Hazardous to Your Wealth."

How about those mutual fund ads you see announcing a market-trouncing 400% gain in the first half of the year? What the ads don't tell you is that the fund cratered all of last year. "People who try to tell where the market is going next invariably fail if you watch them long enough," says Meir Statman, a professor of finance at Santa Clara University. "From my studies I know that both individual investors and professionals fail at trying to predict where the market is going next." Harold Evensky, a financial planner based in Coral Gables, Florida, agrees. "If anyone knew how to time the market, he would own the world," he says. "Market timing is consistently—not once, but consistently—predicting not only when to get out of the market but when to get back into the market."

The market is difficult to beat because it's incredibly efficient. Investing may be the most competitive business in the world. The world's stock of equities, bonds, and cash totals some $78 trillion, estimates Lowell Bryan, director at the consulting firm McKinsey & Co. Phenomenal sums change hands every day as millions and millions of very smart people (and many more not so smart ones) try to get an edge on the competition. Markets move at quicksilver speed in a global economy linked by computers, satellites, and fiber-optic cables. There is an additional reason why it is so difficult to beat the market. Thanks to the huge horde of global investors investigating stocks, equity prices often reflect much that is known about a company. What truly moves stock prices in coming days and weeks is new information. But new information is by definition unpredictable—and helps explain why so many investors are always surprised by sudden shifts in market values.

Of course, just as there are great painters, novelists, pianists, and basketball players, so there are investors with un-usual talents and insight. "I don't believe for a second they [the great investors] are just the random winners of the national coin-flipping contest," writes Barton M. Biggs, a longtime ob-server of markets and global investment strategist at Morgan Stanley Dean Witter. "Instead, they must have some special magic with the markets that enables them almost intuitively to do the right thing, buy the right stock, far more often than or-dinary investors. They have what Churchill called the 'seeing eye . . . that deep original instinct which peers through the sur-face of words and things—the vision which sees dimly but surely the other side of the brick wall or which follows the hunt to fields before the throng.' " Yet great investors, like Warren Buf-fett, George Soros, Peter Lynch, Paul Cabot, and a handful of others, are rare. Very few investors have the "seeing eye."

The bottom line is this: Individual investors who trade stocks by the hour or the week, or those who move into and out of mutual funds several times a month or quarter, are wasting their time and money. There is no data that suggests all that ac-tivity is lining your pockets, while there is abundant evidence that a disciplined, long-term approach with minimal trading in-creases the odds that you will reach your long-run financial goals. After all, the point of investing is to reach your lifestyle objectives, not to beat the market. Trading heavily just means you are paying the professionals a lot of fees and commissions. Yes, trading is hazardous to your wealth.

To be sure, picking stocks on your own is fun, and I don't want to be a spoilsport. More people than ever before are matching their wits in the market buying individual stocks, es-pecially now that commission costs are down sharply with online trading. Ringo Starr is investing online. So is Barbra Streisand. And so are many of your colleagues and friends. It's terrific—with this caveat: The money you are investing should be "play" money or "mad" money. Whatever you call it, much like visiting the casinos, going to the movies, or traveling to Disney World, the sums you invest should come out of your entertainment budget. It's money you can afford to lose. I wouldn't make my standard of living in retirement, my children's college education, my emergency savings, and the down payment on a first home dependent on my stock-picking prowess. And resist the advertising pitch of online brokers that you can be rich beyond your wildest dreams if only you trade over the Internet. No, the idea isn't to trade but to invest online. Maintain the discipline of picking companies with good earnings prospects and sound management, and trade very, very infrequently.

THE TRADE-OFF BETWEEN RISK AND RETURN

Does either of these scenarios seem familiar? You're having lunch with a colleague, and he tells you about this high-tech stock he bought and, of course, it doubled in a couple of months. Bam, he sold it at a hefty profit, and now he's into another winner. Or a neighbor has invited several families from the block over for an evening of drinks and conversation, and someone you've exchanged pleasantries with over the years regales you with a savvy moneymaking move she made in the market, such as getting out of high-tech stocks just before they cratered. You feel like a chump, wondering, why didn't I invest in highflyer.com, and why didn't I see that high-tech stocks were poised to plunge? Well, you're not alone. Everyone likes to talk about the money he or she has made. But more than likely you're not getting a true accounting of the braggart's overall investment performance. "We all listen to the guy in the corner who tells us about his winners," says Nobel laureate economist Paul Samuelson. "We don't hear about his losers."

These days, more and more people are embracing the cult of performance. They want their money invested where the ac-

tion is, where the big returns are recorded. Yet the key investment concept isn't return. It's risk or, more accurately, the relationship between risk and return. It is an axiom of modern
finance that the only way to create the opportunity to earn a
higher return is to take greater risks—and the only way to reduce risk is to settle for a lower probable return. All of the major
investment assets—stocks, bonds, money funds, CDs, and real
estate—carry different risks. The trick is to mix and match the
major assets to create a well-diversified portfolio with the highest
probable return for the amount of risk you are comfortable taking. As much as possible, you want to maximize your opportunity to make good money while minimizing the risk of coming
up short. Although there is no ideal portfolio, just a range of
probabilities, it's easier than ever to design a tailor-made investment portfolio thanks to the spread of Internet-based planning
tools. You don't need a Ph.D. in math or a lifelong love affair
with number crunching to do some fairly sophisticated analysis
and to run various "what if" scenarios.

But you still need a grasp of the basic trade-off. Let's start
with some of the basic investment choices.

Equities. Stocks are the riskiest of the major asset classes.
Equities are ownership shares in a company. You are an owner
of Coca-Cola even if you buy only one of its 2,469,980,567
shares outstanding. Similarly, you own a piece of the steel company Nucor if you possess any of its 87.2 million shares. Equities
represent the uncertain earnings returns to entrepreneurship.
The price of a stock is largely driven by the direction of corporate cash flow and earnings. But stocks are volatile because investors are trying to judge future earnings performance—and
that is highly uncertain. Stocks can soar into the stratosphere or
lose half their value with sickening rapidity. Stocks are more
than twice as volatile as bonds. While stocks can diverge from
fundamental value, stock prices tend to move toward value.
Stocks are riskier than bonds, because when a company en-

counters financial trouble, debtholders have first dibs on corporate cash flows while equity holders carry the brunt of any losses. But remember the risk-and-reward trade-off. Stocks leave all other investments far behind when held for the long term. Since 1802, the return on U.S. stocks has been 7% after adjusting for inflation, according to professor Jeremy Siegel of the Wharton School.

Investment equities. We live in a global economy, and investors are increasingly attracted to owning equities of foreign companies. For years, investing internationally meant buying shares in the companies of other major industrial nations, such as Britain, France, Germany, and Japan. Recently there has been greater investor interest in the stock markets of developing nations such as South Korea, China, Poland, Brazil, and Argentina. Another advantage of putting money to work abroad is that some overseas economies will be growing when economic growth flags in the United States, and at other times the United States will be strong when other markets in the global economy are weak. Strength in one region will somewhat offset downturns in other places. Since the early 1920s, the annual return on international equities has been about 7%, after adjusting for inflation, according to William N. Goetzmann, finance economist at Yale University.

Real estate. Two-thirds of Americans own their own homes. But few of us own commercial real estate. It costs big bucks to play that game. That's why REITs—real estate investment trusts—intrigue investors these days. REITs are investment pools that own and run hotels, office buildings, hospitals, warehouses, and other commercial properties. REIT equities trade like any other stock on an exchange. Dividend yields are relatively lush, since by law these trusts pay out most of their income to shareholders. REITs have been around since 1960, but it is only in the past decade that the industry's market value has soared from around $13 billion in 1991 to some $130 billion.

The real return on REITs has been about 6.2% over the past 20 years, according to the National Association of Real Estate Investment Trusts.

Bonds. Long-term fixed-income securities are less risky than stocks. Bonds are loans that typically last more than three years and less than 30 years. A bond is a promise to pay back a set amount of money by a certain date. The bond contract spells out when the borrower must make its interest payments and pay back the loan. The main domestic bond issuers are the U.S. government, corporations, and state and local governments. Interest on state and local government bonds is exempt from federal taxes and often from state taxes. Another major category of bonds is asset-backed securities. These are bonds backed by mortgages, auto loans, credit card loans, and the like. You can also buy the government and corporate bonds of overseas issuers. Although the stock market is more volatile, bonds do have their own risks. A major risk is called credit risk or default risk: A company or a national government can stop interest and principal payments if it runs into financial trouble. The U.S. government is the world's largest borrower, and its debt, backed by the full faith and credit of the federal government, is default-free. But all bonds, including U.S. Treasuries, face interest rate risk. Under certain economic conditions, interest rates can rise and the value of your bond investments will fall. Conversely, when the interest rate falls, your bonds are worth more. The biggest risk facing bond investors is inflation. Rising prices destroy the purchasing power of the money you have lent. Interest rates surge higher when inflation takes off. The inflation-adjusted return on U.S. long-term bonds has been 3.5% over the past two centuries, according to Professor Siegel.

Inflation-protected bonds. In 1997 the U.S. government started issuing a new bond that offers a hedge against inflation. These bonds are called TIPS, meaning Treasury Inflation Protected Securities. With the typical Treasury bond, the interest payment is fixed for the duration of the loan. But with TIPS, the interest rate adjusts to changes in the consumer price index. These bonds are attractive for individuals with a long-term time horizon because of their guarantee that the value of the bond will remain stable.

Cash. The term "cash" on Wall Street actually means short-term loans, such as three-month certificates of deposit, three-month, six-month, and one-year Treasury bills, and money market mutual funds. The financial world calls these securities "cash" because the loans are outstanding for such a short period of time. These loans carry very little risk since investors get their money back quickly. The long-term real return on short-term government securities is 2.9%, calculates professor Siegel.

THINKING ABOUT RISK

How much risk are you willing to take? What does risk suggest to you? "Risk" is a rich word with many shades of meaning. It hints at dangers to be avoided, such as smoking cigarettes or dashing across a busy eight-lane highway. But the word also prompts stirring images of entrepreneurs starting their own company, immigrants moving to the United States to begin a new life, and snowboarders flying down the ski slopes with reckless abandon. Risk means different things to different people.

Similarly, there is no one definition of risk in the capital markets. As I mentioned above, the risk that inflation or rising prices will erode the value of a dollar haunts all investors. Credit risk is the danger that a borrower or a company will go bankrupt. Liquidity risk is a fancy Wall Street term for the possibility that you won't be able to find a buyer when you'd like to sell a stock or a bond—or you will have to sell the security at a steep loss. But the most common meaning of risk to finance professionals is volatility—the swings in asset prices. Stocks are far more volatile than bonds, and bonds are more volatile than cash. The annualized volatility of stocks is about 20% compared to 8% for bonds and 1% for cash. The close relationship between risk and volatility is reasonable. High volatility increases the odds that you'll suffer a loss if you need to sell an asset to raise money, and the returns on very volatile assets are uncertain. Still, risk and volatility aren't the same. Conservative investors often seek to keep their money safe by investing in Treasury bills or bank certificates of deposit. Stocks, they say, are too risky. Yet today, many people have rightly decided that the risks associated with volatile stock and bond markets are less than the risk of not having enough money during their twilight years. In this instance, the risk isn't volatility. It's not having the money you need to live as well in your 80s as you did in your 50s.

Time figures prominently into any investment risk equation. If you plan on buying a $15,000 car next year or would like to make a down payment of $25,000 on a home three years from now, putting that money into the stock market is a mistake. Equities are too volatile for such a short-term time horizon. The same goes for long-term bonds. The odds are too high that the value of your investment will be down sharply just when you need the money. A money market mutual fund, short-term certificates of deposit, or Treasury bills are suitable, though. These are investments where the value of your principal is stable, the money is easily accessible, and you earn a decent rate of interest.

Yet the risk of investing in the stock market shrinks— although it does not disappear—with time. And the reward for holding stocks increases. "Stocks are relatively predictable over long periods of time and very unpredictable over short periods of time," says Ross Levin. "So if we look at stock returns and say we have 20, 25 years, it allows us to be much more growth-oriented than if we have 20 or 25 months."

Time also allows for tapping into the power of compound interest. For instance, if you invest $1,000 a year in an Individual Retirement Account—about $19 a week—and you earn 8% on your money, you will have almost $16,000 in 10 years; in 20 years you will have $49,000; and in 30 years you will have more than $122,000. Now you know why Albert Einstein called compound interest one of man's greatest inventions. For those intrigued by the long pull, $1,000 at 8% will grow to $2,550,749 in 100 years and into $42 quadrillion in 400 years, calculate Sidney Homer and Martin L. Leibowitz in *Inside the Yield Book.* "Evidently the first hundred years are the hardest," they dryly note.

Obviously, the key investment question is how much investment risk can you tolerate? You can get an idea by taking one of the risk tolerance tests offered by many mutual fund companies on the web. Here's a sample question from Fidelity Investments, the world's largest mutual fund company: "If you could increase your chances of living more comfortably after you retire by taking more risks, would you (1) be willing to take a lot more risk with all your money? (2) be willing to take a little more risk with all your money? (3) be willing to take a little more risk with some of your money? (4) be unlikely to take much more risk?"

Although there is nothing wrong with these tests, and they can get you thinking in the right direction, I am not a big fan of risk tolerance quizzes. The results tend to be bland and not especially informative. They don't seem to get at this critical scenario: You've run through various portfolio options on the web, thought seriously about your goals, talked with some knowledgeable friends about their investment approach, read a number of books and articles on risk and reward, and settled on your portfolio. Now bad times hit, and the value of your wealth sinks. Gloom sets in over Wall Street, and investors despair. Books are rushed to print predicting a stock market crash rivaling 1929. Suddenly, that $50,000 portfolio that you forecast would reach $886,000 in 30 years, assuming a 7% rate of return and an annual contribution of $5,000, is now worth only

$30,000. How will you react? Will you stay the course? Make a few minor adjustments? Or bail out of the market? Risk, in other words, is the fear of losing money.

Of course, none of us really knows until we're caught up in tough times. But by taking a broad perspective on risk in our lives, we can get an idea. If your income is secure, you might be able to deal with a higher-risk portfolio. Alternatively, if your earnings vary significantly every year, you might need the anchor of a more conservative overall portfolio. The stock market periodically is roiled by a 10% to 15% decline. Ask yourself, how troubled were you when the market went lower week after week? How did you react when you had the opportunity to leave a good job at a stable company for a smaller, more entrepreneurial outfit? Did you decide the switch was too risky? Or did you jump at the chance?

The questions don't end there. If you are young and starting out on your career, you definitely should lean toward a riskier overall portfolio, since you have time on your side— time to allow your money to compound and time to make up for any financial mistakes. In sharp contrast, the typical person in his or her 70s should create a more conservative portfolio because he or she will need to live off the income generated by the investments. Then again, some people in their 70s have a secure pension, and they are investing for their grandchildren currently in diapers. In that case, their investment time horizon could be anywhere from 20 to 60 years. Peter Bernstein, a philosopher of risk and author of *Against the Gods: The Remarkable Story of Risk,* put it this way: "The problem does not end there. Few people feel the same about risk every day of their lives. As we grow older, wiser, richer, or poorer, our perception of what risk is and our aversion to taking risk will shift, sometimes in one direction, sometimes in the other. Investors as a group also alter their views about risk, causing significant changes in how they value the future streams of earnings that they expect stocks and long-term bonds to provide."

Take a very broad perspective on risk in your life, and then incorporate your investment strategy into your risk preferences. It pays to spend a lot of time thinking about risk, learning about what risks we are willing to embrace and what risks we're desperate to eliminate or at least minimize.

ASSET ALLOCATION AND DIVERSIFICATION

When most people think of investing, they imagine picking a stock or a mutual fund. Is General Electric a good buy? Should I invest with Fidelity's Magellan Fund? How do you choose from the nearly 8,000 mutual fund options out there?

You don't. Instead, focus on the one investment decision that truly matters: how you allocate your money among the major investment assets. Economic research suggests that for all the time that people spend trying to pick the right mutual fund or stock, how you divide your portfolio among stocks, bonds, cash, real estate, and other assets is the main determinant of your portfolio's long-term performance.

The essence of asset allocation is the balance between risk and expected return. But investors are rewarded only for taking on certain risks and not others. A key distinction is the difference between idiosyncratic risk and structural risk, an idea introduced by economist William Sharpe in the early 1960s. Let's start with idiosyncratic risk. A major auto company plans to come out with a brand-new line of cars. If the new models catch on with consumers, General Motors will pocket enormous profits, and stockholders will benefit from the future lush earnings stream. But if consumers turn a cold shoulder to the cars, the auto company's multibillion dollar investment will be exposed as a huge waste of money and investors will abandon the company's stock in disgust. That's an idiosyncratic risk. So is the risk that Merck will not get FDA approval for a new drug. Or that Walt Disney's next animated feature movie won't be a hit with moviegoers. Idiosyncratic risk can be eliminated through diversification. In other words, by owning a lot of stocks, including automakers, drug companies, and entertainment companies, you essentially eliminate the risk that bad corporate bets will take your portfolio down; any losses will be offset by other companies with savvy managements and better-than-expected profit results.

Structural risk is a different matter altogether. The stock market is vulnerable to major market crashes, such as those of 1929 and 1987. When the economy slumps, it takes the stock market with it. Similarly, a sustained surge in inflation will hammer the value of bonds. For example, in the 1970s bond investors saw the value of their investments plummet as inflation soared into double-digit territory. Structural risk is very difficult to shed. All you can do with structural risk is reduce your exposure to it and, therefore, your potential return. "Investors are rewarded with higher returns for taking structural risks, but they are not rewarded for taking idiosyncratic risk," says Michael Mandel in his book, *The High-Risk Society*.

The name of the investment game is to diversify away your idiosyncratic risks and then decide how much structural risk you are willing to take. Diversification, the notion of not putting all your eggs in one basket, is among the most celebrated concepts in modern finance. Economist Harry Markowitz even got a Nobel Prize for turning your parents' oft-repeated advice into mathematical equations. Diversification both reduces investment risk and increases the odds that you'll earn a decent return over time. Spreading your investment funds among different assets—and they don't usually march in lockstep—cushions the volatility of your portfolio while still providing growth potential. The main asset classes are the ones we've discussed—stocks, bonds, cash, real estate, and overseas investments. By mixing some of each asset class into a portfolio, you give up some performance, but you will lessen the risk of having your savings all go down the drain at once. But diversification is more than simply creating a margin of safety and adjusting the risk level of your portfolio. Since no one really knows which markets will soar or sink in the future, investing in all the major asset classes creates an opportunity to catch the next big market upturn.

A warning: Don't fall into an all-too-common mistake committed by people participating in a retirement savings plan at work. A paper by Ben Shlomo Benartzi, a professor at UCLA, and Richard Thaler of the University of Chicago shows that the funds offered in a 401(k) plan can have an enormous effect on asset allocation. Case in point is a comparison of the retirement savings plan offered to TWA pilots with that offered to University of California employees. The TWA plan offered five core stock funds and one core bond fund. The participants in this plan had invested 75% of their money in stocks—well above the then national average of 57%. In sharp contrast, the University of California plan had only one core stock fund and four core bond funds. The employees had put 34% of their money in stocks, well below the national average. The two economists have found that this pattern exists across a wide variety of companies with retirement savings plans.

Unfortunately, in recent years diversification has been increasingly considered a quaint idea. The reason is simple: Since 1995, the best investment move by far would have been to put all your money into brand-name high-tech stocks and dot-com high fliers. Diversification only dragged down performance. But how much does that matter when you are investing over a lifetime? And are you really willing to risk your savings in a single-minded pursuit of market-beating performance? You can't escape uncertainty and surprise in the financial markets. Even legendary investors such as Warren Buffett, George Soros, and Leon Cooperman, armed with unusual insights and access to the best information available, are wrong some—much?—of the time. Economists, despite their large-scale econometric models and sophisticated quantitative techniques, don't have an edge on the future. The financial markets are highly susceptible to mass enthusiasms that embrace good ideas and over time transform them into money-losing delusions. Trees don't grow to the sky, and markets are always changing.

Diversification pays.

THE EQUITY RISK PREMIUM

Equities should form the foundation of any long-term investment portfolio. But don't get carried away by the stock market's recent performance.

That's a recipe for dashed expectations. I once gave a talk before a conference room full of financial planners. I noted that the average annual return on stocks from 1982 to 1999 was some 16%, after adjusting for inflation. But the real return on stocks since 1946 was 7.5%. My forecast was that returns on stocks over the next 16 years—from 1999 to 2015—were likely to be closer to 7.5% than 16%. One planner waved his hand, upset with me. How, he wondered, could he persuade anyone to buy his products (with hefty fees attached, I think it's safe to guess) with such a low return forecast? Turns out he was using a 12%-plus figure for his long-range return projections. It was reminiscent of financial types who sold products based on long-term projections of 14% long-term government bond yields in the early 1980s, just about the time bond yields started their long march down to well below the 7% level.

What's next for the stock market? 36,000? Don't laugh. *Dow 36,000* is the title of a book published in 1999 by James Glassman and Kevin Hassett. Now, on one level that's a conservative forecast. Professor Roger Ibbotson of Yale University, a leading authority on markets, is forecasting that the Dow Jones Industrial Average will pass the 120,000 mark in 2025, assuming an average annual return of 11.6% in stocks not adjusted for inflation. It's not an unreasonable assumption.

But the essence of Glassman and Hassett's argument has implications for our discussion of risk. They argue that two centuries of U.S. stock market history show that equities are no more risky than bonds over the long haul. Yet investors demand a higher return on stocks to compensate for the greater perceived risk of owning equities over bonds. That higher return is the so-called equity risk premium. For instance, since 1946 stocks have returned about 6 percentage points more than bonds, after taking inflation into account. They believe that once investors realize that stocks are no riskier than bonds, money will pour into the equity markets and drive stock prices higher until the equity risk premium disappears—which will occur, according to their calculations, when the Dow is at the 36,000 level.

It is true that the equity risk premium has come down sharply over the past two decades. There are good reasons for believing that the equity risk premium over bonds will stay down. For one thing, millions of workers setting money aside in retirement savings plans have gotten the message that equities are the best-performing long-term investment. For another thing, corporate earnings are less volatile than before as swings in the business cycle have moderated over time. In addition, with most nations embracing market capitalism, it's hardly unreasonable for investors to anticipate higher growth rates at home and abroad. The recent halving of the equity premium also reflects a strong bond market. History also shows that bonds do well when inflation is low and investors are confident they will get their money back. Stock and bond returns run neck and neck when prices are stable. One such period was 1870 to 1900, when prices declined at a −1.5% pace. Stocks returned a real 8.5% and bonds 6.6%.

Yet stocks still represent the uncertain returns to entrepreneurship (Internet stocks, anyone?), while bonds are contracts that spell out when borrowers must make principal and interest payments. What's more, when the economy does turn down—and recessions are inevitable in a freewheeling capitalist system—bondholders will still have first dibs on corporate cash flows while equity holders will carry the brunt of any losses. Economist Laurence Siegel of the Ford Foundation put it this way: "If the bondholders have arranged to be paid first, they must have agreed to be paid less!"

Indeed, many economists agree that no amount of statistical archaeology or economic modeling satisfactorily explains America's huge equity premium over the past half century. But one theory is that a time-honored financial rhythm was at work: Bold pioneers earned unusually lush rewards. After World War II, Wall Street was stuck in the doldrums even as the U.S. economy stirred and American business dominated world markets in autos, steel, and other mass-production businesses. Memories of the devastating 1929 stock market crash lingered with the public, and professional investors constantly fretted about "another '29." Stock dividends yielded some 7%, but the wealthy sought safety in bonds paying 3%, while the new middle class preferred putting its money into banks and thrifts offering depositors about 1.5%. It was not obvious at the time that the United States would enjoy half a century of growth never before experienced in human history, says John Cochrane, professor of finance at the University of Chicago. Stock investors were truly intrepid back then—and their judgment was amply rewarded. Today, an equity risk premium of about 2% to 3% is more reasonable. Stocks are still riskier than bonds, but the return gap has narrowed. I would own a diversified portfolio that included both stocks and bonds.

Resources

Against the Gods: The Remarkable Story of Risk, by Peter Bernstein (John Wiley & Sons). Perhaps the most important finance book of recent years. "What is it that distinguishes the thousands of years of history from what we think are modern times? The answer goes way beyond the progress of science, technology, capitalism, and democracy. The revolutionary idea that defines the boundary between modern times and the past is the mastery of risk: the notion that the future is more than the whim of the gods and that men and women are not passive before nature." An engrossing history of risk, gambling, probability, and financial markets.

Capital Ideas: The Improbable Origins of Modern Wall Street, by Peter Bernstein (Free Press). Ideas do matter. A superb introduction to the revolution in finance that has transformed the world over the past half century. A revolution fomented in the halls, offices, and computers of academia. A nice mix of character profiles and intellectual history.

Reminiscences of a Stock Operator, by Edwin Lefevre (John Wiley & Sons). First published in 1923, this is a fictionalized biography of Jesse Livermore, a great nineteenth-century speculator. A wonderful discourse on the art and discipline of speculation.

Manias, Panics, and Crashes, by Charles Kindleberger (John Wiley & Sons). The classic work on financial crisis and speculative disasters. Opens with a quote from the nineteenth-century British thinker Walter Bagehot that nicely captures Kindleberger's subject: "Much has been written about panics and manias, much more than with the most outstretched intellect we are able to follow or conceive; but one thing is certain, that at particular times a great deal of stupid people have a great deal of stupid money. . . . At intervals, from causes which are not to the present purpose, the money of these people—the blind capital, as we call it, of the country—is particularly large and craving; it seeks for someone to devour it, and there is a 'plethora'; it finds someone, and there is 'speculation'; it is devoured, and there is 'panic.' "

A Short History of Financial Euphoria, by John Kenneth Galbraith (Viking Penguin). Galbraith is a truly gifted writer and wry observer, and his short excursion through the madness of financial crowds is a delight.

A History of Interest Rates, by Sidney Homer and Richard Sylla (Rutgers University Press). The late Sidney Homer was a Wall Street pioneer in bond market research. Richard Sylla is an economic historian at New York University. By design, the book is relatively light on economic analysis, but it is incredibly detailed and rich in recording interest rate trends through the ages. How can you not like a book with a first chapter that begins like this: "In historical times credit preceded the coining of money by over two thousand years. Coinage is dated from the first millennium B.C., but old Sumerian documents, circa 3000 B.C., reveal a systematic use of credit based on loans of grain by volume and loans of metal by weight. Often these loans carried interest."

"The Hedgehog and the Fox" in *Russian Thinkers,* by Sir Isaiah Berlin (Viking Penguin). In this essay, the recently deceased British philosopher beautifully spins out an argument based on a line by the Greek poet Archilochus, "The fox knows many things, but the hedgehog one big thing." It is a sentence that Berlin believes marks one of the great divides in intellectual life. "For there exists a great chasm between those, on the one side," he writes, "who relate everything to a single central vision, one system less or more coherent or articulate . . . and, on the other side, those who pursue many ends often unrelated and even contradictory, connected, if at all, only in some de facto way. . . . The first kind of intellectual and artistic personality belongs to the hedgehogs, the second to the foxes." Well, investing is a world that attracts a lot of hedgehogs—and they typically charge a hefty fee. Yet investing is an activity for philosophical relativists.

A Random Walk Down Wall Street, by Burton Malkiel (Norton). Well written. Good history. Memorable anecdotes. Malkiel has done a superb job translating into layman's language an enormous body of academic and historic research into investing. The best single guide to investing.

The Intelligent Investor, by Benjamin Graham (HarperCollins). A classic on investing with discipline and your head, rather than haphazardly and with emotion.

Stocks for the Long Run, by Jeremy Siegal (McGraw-Hill). This book by a finance professor at Wharton illuminates for the new retirement savings crowd the superior long-term returns investors have earned on stocks. Over the long haul, stock returns are so stable that equities are actually "safer" than government bonds or Treasury bills.

Irrational Exuberance, by Robert J. Shiller (Princeton University Press). A powerful indictment of the stock market and a gloomy prognosis of the stock market's prospects.

It Was a Very Good Year, by Martin S. Fridson (John Wiley & Sons). A readable history of extraordinary moments in the stock market, starting in 1908.

Ibbotson.com. A leading investment consulting firm. The articles in their library are heavy going, but worth studying.

russell.com. The pension consultant offers up some market basics for individual investors struggling to make sense of their self-directed retirement savings plans.

8

Money in the Market

Time is Archimedes' lever of investing.
—Charles D. Ellis

You've come to grips with risk, and now it's time to decide who gets your hard-earned money. Suddenly all that abstract thinking about goals, risk, and return seems like kid stuff. But don't worry. I'm going to expand on the basic principles in the previous chapter and give you the tools you need to make your decision. Strip away the hype and jargon, and any financial product boils down to risk versus return. You know best what you need for your retirement years or for that college education, and it takes only a little homework to figure out which balance of stock, bonds, and cash will lead to your definition of success.

Let's start with a few helpful tactics for the long-term investor. To answer the question "How are you doing with your investments?" the measure you want to use is the "total return." For stocks, the total return comes from the sum of dividend payments plus any price appreciation or loss. With bonds, the total return is based on interest payments plus price changes. In addition, you want any return figures adjusted for inflation, especially for long-term investments.

You should periodically rebalance your portfolio. Here's the issue: Let's say you settled on a portfolio that was 60% domestic stocks, 25% international equities, and 15% bonds. But market prices are changing all the time. Twelve months later, thanks to a surging U.S. stock market, anemic overseas equities, and lackluster bonds, domestic stocks now make up 75% of your portfolio. Should you accept the market's judgment or rebalance your portfolio to get back to your original risk profile? Most financial planners like the idea of rebalancing your portfolio, although they differ somewhat on the technique. For instance, financial planner Harold Evensky looks closely at his clients' portfolios every quarter. He allows for a 7% drift away from the original asset allocation before adjusting the portfolio. Barbara Raasch, a financial planner at Ernst & Young, thinks once a year is enough.

Another tactic that makes for savvy long-term investing is dollar cost averaging. It is a realistic discipline for investing in good and bad markets. Technically, dollar cost averaging means putting the same amount of money into an investment on a regular basis over a long period of time. The real benefit of dollar cost averaging is that it takes emotion—fear, greed, and panic—out of investing. You are automatically dollar cost averaging in retirement savings plans like 401(k)s and 403(b)s when your employer regularly sends a portion of your paycheck into the markets. "Over time you are not worried about the price of a particular stock or a mutual fund or any other kind of investment," says Jesse Brown, an independent financial planner based in Chicago. "You are investing on a systematic basis."

MUTUAL FUND BASICS

For many people, the easiest, most convenient, and most sensible way to invest is through mutual funds. The mutual fund industry is one of the great entrepreneurial success stories of the post–World War II era. Over the past 30 years the industry's assets have swelled from $48 billion to more than $6 trillion.

Here's how a mutual fund works. It takes small amounts of money from thousands of individuals, pools that money, and invests it on their behalf in stocks, bonds, cash (that is, short-term financial obligations such as Treasury bills), or some combination of assets. In most cases, a professional money manager runs the mutual fund portfolio, backed by a small army of researchers and analysts. These days, many people invest in mutual funds through their 401(k), 403(b), or other type of retirement savings plan.

Mutual funds offer investors a number of advantages. For one thing, for an initial investment that can be as little as $100, you own a diversified portfolio containing anywhere from dozens to hundreds of stocks. The same goes for bonds and bills. You can easily buy and sell mutual fund shares over the phone or over the Internet. Mutual fund companies offer many services, typically educational material, check-writing privileges, Internet access, 24-hour telephone service, and easy switching between funds.

How do you make money in mutual funds? You buy shares in a mutual fund portfolio, let's say an equity portfolio. The fund gets the dividend income from its investments and distributes that to you as dividend income. Fund managers also buy and sell securities throughout the year, and any gains from sales are distributed to you as profit. Finally, you can sell your mutual fund shares at a profit, assuming they have appreciated in value—or at a loss if the money manager has made some bad bets.

When it comes to fees, the mutual fund universe divides into two: load funds and no-load funds. Load funds typically charge a sales levy of 2% to 6% of your investment. The load is the commission paid to the broker who advised you to get into a particular fund. The load is usually paid when you buy the fund, but some mutual fund companies impose the fee when you sell (a so-called back-end load). Others may offer a combination of the two. Here's how the numbers work. Let's use the example of a front-end load. You invest $1,000 in an equity mutual fund with a 5% load. So $50 goes to the broker or the professional adviser who steered you to this fund. And $950 goes into your investment.

As a general rule, loads are a bad deal for investors and a terrific source of income for mutual fund companies. There are only two good reasons for paying a load. The first is if the fund is managed by a professional whom you really want to manage your money and paying a load is the price of admission. The other reason is you need professional help choosing a fund.

A no-load fund doesn't impose a sales charge when you invest in it or get out of it. In most cases, you can find a no-load fund that meets your needs, and all of your investment money gets to work right away—all $1,000 of your hypothetical investment. But no one will guide you toward the fund. You have to do your own research and invest your own time.

With either a load fund or a no-load fund you pay an operating fee. And that fee can vary significantly, from 0.20% to 3%. Again, common sense says that low fees are better than high fees. One fee to avoid is a 12b-1. It's a charge mutual fund companies impose on their owners annually, largely to meet marketing and distribution expenses. Yet there is no benefit to shareholders from paying the 12b-1. It simply cuts into the shareholders' return—and pads the professionals' pockets.

It's critical to figure out the total cost of ownership of mutual funds. Once you know the total cost of ownership, you can start comparing funds. The good news is that mutual fund cost comparison has never been easier. For example, the Securities and Exchange Commission has a "Mutual Fund Cost Calculator" on its web site. It's a free, Internet-based tool that lets investors easily compare the total cost of owning a mutual fund. The calculator's estimate of mutual fund ownership costs includes everything from sales charges to the annual operating expenses paid by investors. Better yet, the calculator also figures out any forgone earnings—money that could have been earned had those fees been invested instead. There is no reason to pay high fees. Wall Street loves to talk about performance and gloss over fees. But high fees reduce your long-term return. It does look as if the Internet and online trading are putting downward pressure on mutual fund fees. That's good news for consumers.

THE PROSPECTUS

When you want to open a mutual fund account, you will be sent a prospectus. It's required. The prospectus is a legal document that contains valuable information for the investor. Now, everyone involved in the markets likes to make fun of prospectuses. They are boring, and yes, reading one is a cure for insomnia. But the prospectus of a fund you're considering investing in is definitely worth a close look. It's really worth going through the whole prospectus. Here are a couple of items I especially like to focus on.

Expense table. All mutual funds have to lay out in a standardized format all the fees associated with owning shares in the fund. If there are fees to buy and sell a fund, it's there. Plus all the ongoing charges imposed by the fund.

Financial highlights. It's a lot of numbers. But these figures give you a good indication of how the fund has done over time. I particularly like the total investment return figure—so you can see how shareholders have done under different market conditions (assuming it's not a brand-new fund).

Investment objectives. Is this fund run with an eye toward generating a dividend income? Or is the money manager striving for long-term capital appreciation? Is the money manager charged with picking high-flying tech stocks or more stable electric and telephone companies? This section discusses the goals of the fund.

Investment strategy. A detailed discussion of how the fund has done over the years. This is where a lot of the numbers are explained to you.

Investment risk. We love to talk about return and how the fund has done over time. Don't forget risk. This section lays out all sensitivities of the fund to general movements in the market, and any peculiar economic or market risks that may sway the portfolio one way or another.

Management page. You can find out whether the fund is run by an individual or a committee. Many investors prefer a single portfolio manager to be in charge. It makes the investment style more apparent—and concentrates responsibility for performance in the money manager's hands.

PICKING AN EQUITY MUTUAL FUND

The simplest and cheapest way to invest in mutual funds is also the best option for long-term investors: Create a core portfolio out of "index" funds.

An index fund duplicates the performance of a particular market index. The most famous index mutual fund is the Standard & Poor's 500 equity index. It is made up of the largest U.S. companies. But there are many other indexes, such as the Wilshire 5000, which captures the U.S. stock market; the Russell 3000, a way to invest in smaller companies; and the Europe Asia Far East (EAFE) index for investing overseas. Indexing is called passive investing because there is no professional money manager trying to beat the market. If you invest with index funds there's no reason to watch CNBC or CNN for hot tips, worry about nosebleed valuations on Internet stocks, or struggle to pick the next top-performing mutual fund. Yet a majority of professional money managers fail to do better than index funds. For example, since 1976 the Wiltshire 5000 has done better than two out of three money managers. Says finance professor Meir Statman, "You can do everything you need to do in a portfolio with index funds."

A huge advantage of index funds is their low cost. The annual fee for investing in the Standard & Poor's 500 index is some .20% versus an average of 1.5% for actively managed mutual funds. Index funds can charge such low fees because there are no research costs and no multimillion-dollar salary for a money manager. Index funds are also tax-efficient since there is very little trading, except when a stock gets added to or dropped from an index.

If you add together the average equity mutual fund fee and the cost impact of active trading (which is substantial), the effect on performance is substantial. John Bogle, the legendary founder of the Vanguard Group, the mutual fund behemoth, gives this example. A $10,000 investment in the Wilshire 5000 equity index with an expense ratio of .20% would have compounded at a 16.2% average annual rate between 1984 and 1999. The same investment in an actively managed mutual fund with an annual expense ratio of 1.3% and transaction costs of .8% would have grown by 13.6%. That's a big difference. And if the mutual fund is held in a taxable account, the index fund investor would have earned $83,300, while the investor in the actively managed fund would have only $45,300. Index funds are cheap and tax efficient. They are superb investments for both tax-deferred retirement savings plans and taxable accounts.

Perhaps most important, index funds concentrate the mind on asset allocation and diversification. By definition, with an index fund you are making a commitment to a market rather than to a money manager who may or may not remain true to an advertised goal of sticking to growth, value, or big- or small-company stocks. Indexing works not just for equities (and I would buy the broadest stock market index available, such as the Wilshire 5000 or the Russell 3000). Indexing is a good strategy with bonds and international equities.

What's more, if poring over balance sheets and studying company managements is not your passion, index funds are the best way to invest. Even Omaha-based Warren Buffett, the legendary stock-picker, concedes that point. "By periodically investing in an index fund . . . the know-nothing investor can actually outperform most investment professionals," Buffett wrote in 1993 in the Berkshire Hathaway annual report. Allocating your assets carefully and investing them in index funds may not make you the next Sage of Omaha. But it's a strategy that has worked well for many people.

Still, if you want a professional money manager, it's easier than ever to compare mutual funds, especially if you have access to the web. The major business magazines and newspapers, such as *Business Week* and *The Wall Street Journal,* publish annual and semiannual mutual fund report cards that offer a wealth of information and commentary. Mutual fund rating services, such as Morningstar, Lipper, and Value Line, have enormous databases for examining mutual funds from all kinds of angles.

Avoid hopping onto the performance sweepstakes derby. Some funds do really well one year—and collapse the next. "A real hazard in investing is to look in the rearview mirror, because when you're looking at performance, you're looking at history," says Mary K. Sterne, president of the SIT mutual funds. "What you need to do is really look at how the performance was attained."

Although there are some 4,000 equity mutual funds, you can cut through the list fairly quickly. Start with your goals. If this is a long-term investment and you are starting out, you'll want an equity mutual fund that invests in a broad swath of the economy. You can ignore for now narrow-sector funds, option funds, mutual funds that invest only in dot-com companies, and other fringe investments. You'll want to look at long-term performance figures compared to the fund's peers. In other words, you don't want to compare a growth-and-income fund to a small-cap aggressive growth fund, but to other growth-and-income funds. You will then want to scrutinize fees.

This is a good point to deal with two important divides in the mutual fund universe. The first is the difference between growth and value funds. Growth funds invest in glamour stocks, fast-growing companies with a good story that suggests huge earning increases. For example, high-tech companies such as software, Internet, and biotechnology are growth stocks. The gains in growth stocks largely come from capital appreciation—actual increases in the stock price. Growth stocks pay little or no dividend income. When you are investing in growth, you are investing in the future.

Value stocks are more of a contrarian play. Value funds invest in out-of-favor companies, old-line firms with hefty dividend payments, and companies whose stock price has been beaten down. The basic idea is to buy a good company with a cheap stock price. Value buyers are bargain hunters.

Another major divide is between large-capitalization and small-capitalization stocks—big versus small. Large-cap stocks are brand-name companies such as Coca-Cola, IBM, Nike, and Microsoft. Large-cap companies typically sport a market value of $5 billion or more. (Market value is calculated by taking a company's share price and multiplying it by the number of shares outstanding.) Small-cap stocks are often those of less seasoned companies with fewer financial resources. Small-cap stocks typically have a market cap of under $2 billion. In recent years, investors have favored large-cap stocks for their global reach, ample financial resources, and strong earnings performance.

As we saw from the Bogle example, investors should pay close attention to taxes. You don't have to worry about taxes if your mutual fund investments are in a tax-deferred retirement or state-sponsored college savings account. But if you own a mutual fund in a taxable account, you will quickly realize that mutual fund owners get hit on taxes in several ways. You'll pay income tax on dividend income, capital gains tax on any profit earned by the fund from selling securities, and capital gains tax again when you sell the fund shares (assuming you make a profit). With a few exceptions, mutual fund companies ignore the tax consequences of their portfolios even though many investors own mutual funds in their taxable accounts. Every year, mutual fund companies mail their investors a Form 1099 detailing their tax liability on income and capital gains distributions. The fund company has no choice, and you have to pay the tax bill. In a study published in the *Journal of Investing*, analyst James Garland calculated that federal taxes absorbed some 44% of the average stock fund's performance from 1970 to 1995.

Check out the fund's trading activity or "turnover" rate. For example, the average equity mutual fund has a turnover rate of 90%, meaning a $1 billion fund does some $900 million in trades every year. Frequent trading will boost your tax bill. Indeed, some mutual funds that rank high on the return sweepstakes fall toward the bottom of the list once the tax consequences of frequent trading are taken into account. Index funds are tax-efficient because the only trading activity that takes place is when a stock falls out of the index or is added to the index. Similarly, some mutual fund companies are marketing "tax-efficient" funds whose managers take the tax consequences of their actions on shareholders' taxable returns into account.

INVESTING IN INDIVIDUAL STOCKS

Buying stocks on your own is growing in popularity. One reason is the advent of online trading and low commission costs. Another reason is taxes. When you own individual shares, you control when you sell the stock and, therefore, accept the gain or loss for tax purposes. If the company pays a dividend you will owe tax on that income, though.

There are many techniques for investing in stocks. In all cases, it pays to develop a discipline, to spend time researching a company, and to buy stocks you want to own for the long haul. I would stick with quality companies. The technique I prefer for picking stocks is called fundamental analysis. It's an approach followed by Wall Street research analysts, Warren Buffett acolytes, and leveraged buyout financiers. The foundation of fundamental analysis is forecasting corporate earnings. Fundamental analysts carefully study economic conditions, industry trends, management and workers, dividend payouts, and other basic data in order to get a sense of a company's earnings prospects and whether the stock market is undervaluing or overvaluing its growth potential. Some investors focus on finding companies with fast-growth prospects, while others prefer to toil in the rubble of the securities market, seeking out unloved, underappreciated, undervalued stocks. But the basic philosophy is rooted in understanding and divining corporate earnings, in the belief that the stock market will eventually recognize a company's true earning power.

The other traditional approach toward buying stocks is too expensive for individual investors. The idea is to discern and ride the market's rhythm. Earnings aren't important. Dividends don't matter. Market psychology is what counts. In a famous passage in *The General Theory of Employment, Interest, and Money,* economist John Maynard Keynes uses the example of the newspaper beauty contests that were popular entertainment in the 1930s—the trick was not to pick the most beautiful woman, but to figure out what average opinion would think was the most beautiful contestant. Investors, he wrote, "are concerned, not with what an investment is really worth to a man who buys it 'for keeps,' but with what the market will value it at, under the influence of mass psychology, three months or a year hence."

Technical analysts divine the market's mood by creating charts and graphs that show when a stock is poised to rise above its recent trading range, or fall below it. There are plenty of techniques for reading the mood of the market. Problem is, they all add to commission costs, and are short-term in orientation.

There is another method popularized by Peter Lynch, the famed money manager. Lynch champions the idea of owning companies you encounter in your everyday life. Your family discovers a new restaurant, and you think it's terrific. Well, is it a publicly traded company? If so, check it out. Or you find out that you and your neighbors are all shopping at a particular store for much of your household needs. Go on the Internet and start researching the company. It may not be the most lucrative technique, but it's the most fun.

<u>BONDS</u>

Bonds are the Rodney Dangerfields of the investment world: They get no respect. For many people, bonds are synonymous with dull. "Bonds I look at as being for my parents," said one young man on the street. He added, "I would buy them if I were 80 years old." Others find bonds confusing. "I don't know enough about bonds to participate in them," said another man. "In all honesty, I don't truly understand bonds." With stocks sizzling in recent years and bonds lagging behind, many investors consider stocks investment diamonds and bonds zircon. Yet bonds deserve a prominent place in a well-diversified portfolio.

A bond is an IOU. The amount borrowed is the principal or face value of the loan. The IOU is outstanding until its maturity date. A bond pays the investor a rate of interest for the use of his or her money. Technically the rate of interest is called a coupon or yield. So if you buy a three-year U.S. government bond for $1,000 with an annual coupon of 7%, you get three yearly interest payments of $70, and you get your $1,000 back at the end of three years. Similarly, if you lend the government $1,000 for 10 years at an annual 7% rate of interest, you get 10 annual payments of $70 plus your $1,000 back after 10 years.

Bonds can be bought and sold on the open market. But interest rates change all the time. Inflation may be higher or lower. The economy may be strong or weak. Whatever the reason, think of interest rates and bond prices as two ends of a seesaw. When interest rates are up, bond prices are down. As interest rates go down, bond prices go up. Let's go back to the ten-year bond yielding 7% that you bought for $1,000. If interest rates soar to 10%, and you want to sell your bond, its price will fall until it offers a buyer a competitive yield. Now, let's say interest rates come down. The government is selling bonds with a yield of 6%. Well, your bond with a 7% yield is much more valuable and the bond price goes up. Of course, if you just hold on to your bond you won't care so much about the market's gyrations.

Bonds offer investors a lot of flexibility for financial planning. For instance, let's say in two years you have to buy a new car or meet your freshman's college tuition bill. You can buy a two-year note, earn a decent rate of interest on your investment, and the money is there when you need it. But bonds carry several risks. The biggest problem is inflation, which erodes the value of fixed-income securities because higher prices mean those future interest payments won't buy as many goods and services as today. With U.S. Treasury securities, there is no risk of default. But default risk is very real with many other types of bonds, especially companies laden with lots of debt. Credit rating agencies monitor the default risk of corporations and municipalities and rank them according to their financial strength. Repayment risk is the chance that a company or municipality will pay off its bonds early. If you have a ten-year bond yielding 10% and three years later interest rates drop to 8%, the issuer can, if the bond contract permits it, retire the debt early. The income generated by that 10% rate of interest is gone.

The bond world is incredibly complex. Wall Street rocket scientists have devised all kinds of exotic securities. I would keep my bond investing simple and deal only with U.S. Treasury securities, creditworthy corporate bonds, and financially sound tax-exempt securities. If you stay in the blue-chip sector of the bond universe, the major risk you will face is changes in interest rates. Municipal bonds are often attractive investments for anyone in a high tax bracket.

Should you buy individual bonds or bond mutual funds? The advantage of buying individual bonds is that you know the rate of interest you will receive and when the bond matures. If you buy a three-year bond at 5.5%, you will be paid 5.5% until the three years are over. In sharp contrast, a short-to-intermediate-term bond fund is always adjusting its portfolio to stay in the designated two-to-five-year range (or whatever limits the fund puts on itself). The bond fund never matures, and the interest rate is always changing. You'll also pay a higher fee to own a bond fund than a new-issue U.S. Treasury security you buy directly from the government. Bond funds do have some advantages. You can dribble small amounts of money into the fund and reinvest your interest income. If you need to sell, it's much easier with a bond fund than an individual bond. And with the exception of U.S. Treasuries, commission costs on bonds are too high for all but those with big bucks. In other words, unless you are buying U.S. Treasury securities directly from the government and holding them until maturity, it makes financial sense to buy a bond mutual fund until you have a lot of money to invest. Bond index funds are a very attractive, low-fee option.

A good fixed-income strategy is to create a bond "ladder." The idea is to invest in U.S. Treasuries with different maturities. For example, you plunk down $10,000 each to buy one-year

Treasuries at 5%, two-year at 5.25%, three-year at 5.50%, four-year at 5.75%, and five-year at 6%. Now, let's say interest rates fall. Well, you have some five-year bonds yielding an attractive 6% in the new lower-interest-rate environment. Alternatively, if interest rates rise, you have some one-year Treasuries coming due that you can reinvest at the higher rate. A bond ladder combines the benefits of a higher average yield and peace of mind.

LEARN ABOUT TIPS

Investors should check out inflation-indexed bonds from the U.S. Treasury. An inflation-indexed bond offers a fixed interest rate above inflation as measured by the consumer price index. The bond's principal is adjusted as the CPI changes. The idea of a fixed-income security whose value cannot be eroded by inflation has been around since at least the late eighteenth century. Israel, Canada, Sweden, New Zealand, Britain, and other countries have long issued inflation-protected bonds. In 1997, the U.S. government unveiled its version, called Treasury Inflation Protection Securities, or TIPS.

Still, TIPS haven't caught on with investors. After all, inflation is a fading force in recent years. Yet these securities have a number of appealing features for long-term investors who are building a well-diversified portfolio. By design, TIPS protect the value of an investment dollar. And default risk is nonexistent, since these are obligations of the U.S. government. These securities add to diversification, since the correlation between movements in TIPS and other fixed-income securities is relatively low. TIPS can stabilize a portfolio.

Here's an important caveat for any individual investor contemplating these bonds: taxes. In essence, you have to pay taxes on your inflation-adjusted gains before you ever get any of your inflation-adjusted money at maturity. That's why these bonds

work best in a tax-deferred retirement savings account, such as
an Individual Retirement Account. That way, you won't have
to worry about paying taxes until after you retire. Another
alternative is the current I bond. These are the inflation-
protected U.S. savings bonds. Your money compounds tax-
deferred, you pay no commission costs, and your investment is
protected against a rise in the consumer price index. If slow
and steady is your ticket, TIPS or the I bond is a good place to
look.

SOCIALLY CONSCIOUS INVESTING

Investing with your conscience, the so-called socially responsible investing movement, has long raised hackles on Wall Street.
One reason may be terminology. The phrase "ethical investing"
or "socially conscious investing" implies that everyone else is
amoral or unethical with his or her money. Another reason is
the sense that the only acceptable values in the socially responsible investing universe are those shared by tree-huggers and
aging hippies—everyone else need not apply. Still, the biggest
rap against the movement has been the belief that marrying
personal values to an investment portfolio, while perhaps a
noble idea, inevitably cuts into returns. In other words, doing
well and making money don't mix.

Not necessarily. Recent studies suggest that there is little difference between pooling money to make money and pooling
money to make money and express values. Professor Meir Statman of Santa Clara University analyzed the performance of the
Domini Social Equity Index fund and actively managed socially
responsible mutual funds for the period 1990 to 1998. His con-
clusion: The risk-adjusted returns on socially conscious equity
index funds are roughly comparable to those of the Standard &
Poor's 500 index. The performance of actively managed socially
responsible mutual funds is about equal to their conventional ac-

tively managed mutual fund peers. Indeed, Statman notes that the real investment danger is active mutual fund management. The socially conscious index fund and the S & P 500 index fund left all active managers—socially conscious or not—far behind in the performance sweepstakes. One way to fall short when it comes to stock market returns is to pick an actively managed mutual fund, socially conscious or not, over a broad-based index fund.

What's more, his research suggests that the conventional divide between socially conscious investing and conventional mutual fund ownership is much smaller than either the proponents or opponents of value investing believe. Statman is a leading researcher in the emerging field of behavioral finance. It's a broad area of study that brings together economists, psychologists, sociologists, and others fascinated by how culture, fads, emotions, and other human elements influence markets. For example, these scholars are probing into the impact of fear, regret, and overconfidence on investment decisions. Why not values? Our values enter into many of our money decisions. The notion of investing with values is much more powerful and broad-based than the narrowly defined universe of socially conscious mutual funds.

WOMEN AND INVESTING

Profit and loss don't recognize gender. But there are important money and investing differences between men and women. Traditionally, women have tended to handle the checkbook and not the investment portfolio. Women are also more dependent on Social Security for income in their later years. The reason lies in the interaction of demographics, culture, and social change with the Social Security system. Social Security is the main lifetime income benefit for many people. Women tend to live longer than men. Women are the nation's primary caregivers, taking time out from market-based work to care for children, aging parents, relatives, and disabled husbands, and

those years with little or no earnings can cut into their Social Security benefits. What's more, women are increasingly likely to
be unmarried. For instance, the percentage of women currently divorced has risen from 2.54 in 1970 to 8.16 in 1997. The
nation's primary safety net for the elderly hasn't adjusted to a
world of two-income couples, let alone a large population of elderly divorced and never-married women.

Still, there are heartening signs that the income and investing gap is narrowing fast. Women are doing better than ever in
the job market. In the new economy, employers are eager for
skilled workers, and women earn a majority of associates, bachelor's, and master's degrees, as well as 42% of doctorates.
Women also make up about two-fifths of business, medical, and
law school graduates. Their labor force participation rate is at a
record 60%, up from 33.9% in 1950. The wage gap between
men and women is narrowing, especially after adjusting for education.

The ranks of women investors are swelling, too. According
to the 1998 Investment Company Institute survey of mutual
fund shareholders, the typical female mutual fund shareholder
today with sole responsibility for household investments is 44
years old, has a median household income of $38,000, and has
financial assets of $60,000. The survey also showed that most
couples jointly decide on the household's investment strategy.
Perhaps most striking, the percentage of all women who will receive Social Security benefits based on their own earnings will
jump from 37% in the year 2000 to 56% in 2030, according to
Social Security Administration calculations.

Women tend to be better investors than men. A body of psychological research suggests that men are more confident than
women, at least in the aggregate. Boys, in other words, will be
boys. This difference in attitude can lead to two investment
predictions, according to two economists at the University of
California at Davis, Brad Barber and Terrance Odean. The first

is that women will trade less than men, and the second is that their stock portfolios will do better than those of their male peers. Guess what? After studying data on more than 35,000 households from a large discount brokerage firm, the researchers found that men trade 45% more than women and earn an annual risk-adjusted net return of 1.4% less than women. (Still, both groups performed poorly relative to the market or an index fund. Neither gender, their data showed, was much good at timing the market or selecting securities.)

Take Julia Chivers. She lives in a small town outside Boulder, Colorado. Her husband left her with two young kids when she was around 20 years old. She worked for a while at low-paying jobs and decided that wasn't for her. She got a college education and an MBA, and now she's a benefits consultant. One of her daughters is a sophomore in high school and the other is in seventh grade. She feels she needs to be doing more with her money. Her questions to me revolved around affording college for her two girls and making smart investments for retirement. Her money was invested very conservatively. "The real irony here is that she is taking the biggest risk of all," said Ruth Hayden. "A savings account is not even going to keep up with inflation, much less the tax ramifications."

Julia was a risk taker, except when it came to her money. But her attitude is changing. "In the back of my mind I always thought, what if I make the wrong decision?" she said. "And now I am beginning to realize the wrong decision is doing nothing. And doing something and getting started and taking risks in that area is more beneficial than doing nothing."

In a sense, that's the point of this whole chapter.

INVESTMENT CLUBS

Investment clubs are a good way to learn about investing. An investment club is much like a book club, except that individuals get together to talk about stocks. The investment club is also a legal partnership.

I met with the Ebony Investment Club for a *Right on the Money* episode. It has a long and successful history; the club exemplified the principles that should guide any investment club. The 14-member Ebony Investment Club meets one Saturday a month. The club's main objective, as its name suggests, is providing a vehicle for African-Americans to grow wealth through investment. The Ebony Investment Club gets together to learn about the stock market, make some money, and have fun. Says club member Maria-Renee Grigby, "There were two reasons that I joined the Ebony Investment Club. One, there is no way that I could gain the knowledge on my own that I learned from the other members. The second reason is to be a member of an African-American investment club. To be with other African-Americans controlling our money and deciding what we're going to do with our money, and not having somebody else from the corporate world come in and do it for us, is a wonderful experience."

Investment clubs stress research, education, and investing for the long haul. You won't beat the market, however. For instance, the Beardstown Ladies, an investment club made up of elderly women, made headline news with their market-trouncing average annual returns of 23.4% in the ten years ending in 1993. But it turned out they had made a mistake in their calculations. Their actual return was a measly 9.1%, far less than the 14.9% gain in the Standard & Poor's 500 over that same time period. Similarly, economists have found that investment clubs on average underperform the market by a considerable amount. "I think the step of joining an investment club, if you don't know anything about the market, is a really good idea because you will have a lot of friendly people to teach you who aren't interested in making a buck off of you. They are interested in making a buck with you," says Robert Barker, a *Busi-*

ness Week investment columnist. "But if your goal is to beat the market, a club isn't the place to do it."

A LONG-TERM FORECAST

The stock market put on an incredible performance in recent years. But the gains in the stock market were so remarkable that many fear it was a bubble. "Bubble" is an ominous term in finance. The disastrous cycle of prosperity leading to investment delusion and ending in economic hardship when the bubble bursts has a long history. The Dutch bid up prices of tulip bulbs into the stratosphere in the seventeenth century—only to watch them crash later on. The same goes for the U.S. stock market in 1929 and the Japanese stock market in 1989. In other words, if the stock market is a bubble, then the economic fundamentals haven't changed significantly. Instead, what we have been witnessing is a time-honored mass delusion and speculative bubble. Yes, the economy has done well, but much of that better-than-expected performance relates to coincidence, luck, and long work hours.

Certainly, all of us can tell tales of appalling investor ignorance and Wall Street excess. The market, as always, is vulnerable to an abrupt shift in market sentiment or an unexpected political or economic jolt. Still, I don't think this is a tulip bulb market.

In 1980, the value of the U.S. stock market was some $1.4 trillion. The total market value of corporate America now exceeds $14 trillion. Yet hindsight tells us that this huge surge in the market has largely been within the realm of reason. Thanks to the spread of the microprocessor, heightened international competition, and the widening deregulation of the economy's commanding sectors, corporate profits are strong and U.S. companies are among the most competitive in the world. The United States is investing heavily in both physical and human capital, with real investments per worker, including outlays on education, running about a third higher in the United States than in other major industrial nations. The Internet is a deflationary force revolutionizing the spread of information and the terms of trade between consumers and providers worldwide.

The payoff: Productivity growth, the fundamental building block for higher living standards, is running around a 2% pace—double the rate of the business cycle upturn of the 1970s and 1980s. It's strong productivity growth that allows business to produce more products and raise workers' wages while keeping a tight lid on prices. This economic performance suggests the economy can grow much faster without generating inflation than most economists assume.

There is another troubling aspect to the talk about the U.S. bubble economy: It focuses too much on the level of the stock market—whether stock market values are too high or too low—and not enough on the impact of the stock market itself on allocating resources away from the more stagnant sectors of the economy to the sectors with greater growth opportunities.

In any discussion of the economy, the impact of the financial markets is often slighted. Yet the wellspring of economic growth isn't just technology, globalization, investment, or even productivity. It's also risk taking, what the great British economist John Maynard Keynes called "the animal spirits of capitalism." Everything else pales in comparison to the entrepreneur risking all on a new way of doing business, from retail superstores to the Internet. Without risk taking, even the most promising technology would gather dust in the university lab. Today, it's the mass movement toward investing that is fueling the entrepreneurship, the risk taking, and the innovation propelling the economy forward and living standards higher.

Put it this way: The move toward the markets is shifting

power away from the commanding heights of government, corporate giants, and other established institutions and toward millions of employees, investors, and entrepreneurs. In 1956, William Whyte's *The Organization Man,* an extraordinary work, captured and analyzed the society and culture of an economy dominated by employees who labored in gigantic bureaucracies. Mass production ruled. Work was fragmented. Tasks were highly specialized. Management was extremely hierarchical. Power was centralized and stock ownership was concentrated. Today, in an era of global competition, high-speed communications, and quicksilver finance, growth seems to depend more than before on "creative destruction," economist Joseph Schumpeter's evocative metaphor for the unsettling, tumultuous process by which new technologies, new markets, and new organizations supplant the old. That's why executives are relinquishing control, organizing work teams, and struggling to break down bureaucratic barriers. It's not because they're generous but because they need to generate more moneymaking ideas and innovations throughout the organization.

They'd better, too. Hordes of enterprising people, many of them lured by the achievements of Michael Dell of Dell Computer and Steve Case of AOL, are creating and taking over companies in all kinds of industries and businesses. Immigrants are flocking to our labor market, accounting for a fifth of all U.S. chemical engineers and computer scientists. Women are starting businesses at twice the rate of men, and the number of women-owned businesses has doubled over the past decade.

Perhaps most intriguing, the more pervasive the stock market, the quicker investors allocate resources toward growth industries and entrepreneurial management. Take the emergence of the U.S. economy in the nineteenth century. Historians often attribute the American economy's rapid growth back then to new technologies, transportation innovations, and the opening of the West. But these same growth drivers were also found in Canada, Mexico, Brazil, Argentina, and other parts of the New World, notes Richard Sylla, an economic historian at New York University. Only the United States had a vibrant stock market and an intensely competitive banking system at the time. That financial system paved the way for a huge flow of investment capital from Europe to America. The U.S. financial system was so good that the assets it generated appealed to foreigners, and the United States was the most successful emerging market ever, says Sylla.

No, what's going on today is reminiscent of railroad building in the late 1800s and the investment in automobiles of the early twentieth century. Railroads went bankrupt and auto companies merged, but in the meantime, a new economy was built. Today, globalization, technological innovation, and the democratization of finance are transforming the way Americans work and live. Along the way, fortunes will be made and lost. Stock prices will get out of whack with fundamentals. Companies will fail and products will vanish. But what's going on is real, and we can feel the effects every day.

However, I do think the public's love affair with stocks will cool somewhat. I like stocks. Smart long-term investing is built on an equity base. But the stock market has put on a remarkable, perhaps a once-in-a-lifetime, performance. The stock market has posted average annual returns of around 16% since 1982, after adjusting for inflation. Yet the stock market's long-run inflation-adjusted return since 1802 is 7%, and, since 1946, 7.5%.

While the case for U.S. equities is often oversold, the case for bonds may be undersold. Stocks beat out bonds by thinner margins when inflation is muted and lenders are confident of earning decent inflation-adjusted returns. For an intriguing historical analogy, look at the period between 1870 and 1920. As now, it was a time of surging international trade and capital flows. The economy grew fivefold and real incomes nearly tripled. Intense competition and rapid technological change—coupled with a tight-money policy linked to the gold standard—kept prices down. Inflation rose at an 0.7% yearly rate during that half century, and stocks returned 5.5% and bonds 3.4% annually.

Diversification is still the best strategy for the long run.

Resources

Investing for Dummies, by Eric Tyson (IDG Books Worldwide). This book is a real gem.

Bogle on Mutual Funds, by John Bogle (Dell). By the founder of the giant Vanguard mutual fund company. Bogle brought equity and bond indexing to the masses. A certified curmudgeon with a passion for helping investors understand markets and make money.

Everything You've Heard About Investing Is Wrong, by William H. Gross (Times Business). Gross is a legendary bond investor, and an astute observer of the markets. This book makes you think.

Global Bargain Hunting: The Investor's Guide to Profits in Emerging Markets, by Burton G. Malkiel and J. P. Mei (Touchstone Books). The authors make a strong intellectual case for investing in the world's developing nations, and supplement their insights with practical investment advice.

The Only Investment Guide You'll Ever Need, by Andrew Tobias (Harcourt Brace). The author often uses himself as a financial guinea pig. Brash, funny, good stories—and sound advice as well.

The Warren Buffett Way, by Robert Hagstrom (John Wiley & Sons). Although this is a gray, rather boring book, it does give a systematic overview of the investment techniques of Warren Buffett, the great stock-picker.

Buffett: The Making of an American Capitalist, by Roger Lowenstein (Doubleday). This biography of Warren Buffett is a solid, immensely readable look at the Wizard of Omaha.

25 Myths You've Got to Avoid—If You Want to Manage Your Money Right, by Jonathan Clements (Simon & Schuster). Clements is a clear writer with good insights.

ms.com. Every morning I check into this web site to get the latest reading on the global economy from Morgan Stanley Dean Witter. Lots of good information and analysis.

yardeni.com. Edward Yardeni is the chief global economist of Deutsche Bank Securities in New York. Yardeni is always bold and a good read. Among Wall Street economists he has done an especially stellar job grappling with the economic implications of the end of the Cold War and the spread of information technologies.

vanguard.com. The Vanguard mutual fund company offers a wealth of information, especially about mutual fund investing, retirement, and indexing. Well-organized site with clearly written articles. Best of all, though, is reading Vanguard chief John Bogle's insightful and strongly held views on the mutual fund industry.

woodrow.mpls.frb.fed.us. Maybe it's a regional bias, but I frequently find myself using the Federal Reserve Bank of Minneapolis for economic research and commentary. It is also my link to the Federal Reserve Board and the 11 other Federal Reserve banks around the country. The Fed system as a whole is a rich source to mine for economic information, data, analysis, and research.

berkshirehathaway.com. Warren Buffett runs Berkshire Hathaway, essentially a holding company for a wide range of businesses. His witty annual letter to shareholders is a terrific read—and a genuine education in investing.

better-investing.org. The National Association of Investment Clubs has everything you want to know about setting up your own club.

dismal.com. A place to go for economic numbers, economic analysis, and a handy stock market valuation calendar.

morningstar.com. The main mutual fund rating service.

socialinvest.org. A giant clearinghouse of information about socially responsible investing.

9

Credit Cards

Beautiful credit! The foundation of modern society. Who
shall say that this is not the golden age of mutual trust, of
unlimited reliance upon human promises? That is a
peculiar condition of society which enables a whole
nation to instantly recognize point and meaning in the
familiar newspaper anecdote, which puts into the mouth
of a distinguished speculator in lands and mines this
remark: "I wasn't worth a cent two years ago, and now I
owe two millions of dollars."

—Mark Twain, *The Gilded Age*

What's the most ridiculous thing you've ever charged?

"The silliest thing I ever did with a credit card is I got a cash advance to pay on my other credit card."

"Silliest? Oh, chocolates, emery boards, something really silly."

"A soda. For a dollar."

"Graduate school tuition."

"Just about everything I charge is ridiculous."

How about $5,500 for a used red-and-black Jeep Wrangler? Add in a high-tech mountain bike, some furniture, a computer, and other miscellaneous expenses, and Greg Rettich is carrying $10,000 in credit card debt.

I met Greg at his rental apartment on a tree-lined street in a quiet neighborhood in West Hartford, Connecticut. He's renting out the bottom floor of a two-story home, and his bright red Jeep with a black top was parked in front. A soft-spoken, regular guy, 28-year-old Greg is a former pilot, a dog lover, and an enthusiastic sportsman. He does like his toys. "I was looking to buy a Jeep that was older but in good shape," said Greg. "It was a little on the expensive side, but I thought it was well worth it."

Greg makes about $30,000 a year working as an insurance adjuster in Hartford—so his credit card debt equals a third of his annual income. What's more, his commute to work is only three miles, and he drives an Acura. Greg is single, rents, yet he owns two cars. Now, that is extravagant. Still, he makes enough money to cover his bills, but thanks to his credit card debt he is living paycheck to paycheck. He looks forward to the day he can stop paying for the past and start building more of a financial future. "Right now I'm trying to put a certain amount of money toward the debt to erase it," he told me. "We have a year-end bonus that comes around in February where I work. That's going toward the debt itself. But, of course, it would be nice not to use that money toward reducing debt. It would be nice to go on a vacation or what-have-you with it."

I guessed that Greg's budgeting habits weren't the best. So when I was at his house, I asked him to show me where he keeps his bills. The newest bills were tacked on a bulletin board above the stove—convenient if he needed to burn them. He kept the rest of his bills and money-related papers filed neatly away in a crate. Greg had tried to track his spending on the computer, but he found it tedious and stopped doing it after a while. He just tried to make do with a ballpark estimate of his spending—a system that wasn't working too well.

We talked for a long time, and Greg's basic question was the classic "How can I reduce my debt quickly—very, very quickly—

and not have it hanging over my head anymore?" For far too many people, personal finance means getting out from under credit card bills. Sadly, there is no magic bullet, no quick short-cut, for accomplishing that goal. Usually, it takes years to build up a big debt burden, and it may well take a long time to work it off. There are many sources of help for those deep in debt, from nonprofit counseling agencies to bankruptcy court. But most people can pay off their debt on their own. You can kick the debt habit with a budget and imagination.

PLASTIC PRAISE

The credit card industry is huge. I don't know about you, but it seems everyone I know gets credit card solicitations all the time. Americans use plastic for almost everything, from ordering on-line to dinner at a restaurant to a late-night snack at the corner deli. In 1998, some 68% of American families had a bank-type credit card, and 44% of families had some credit card debt. For families carrying credit card debt, the median total balance was $1,700, according to the Federal Reserve Board. The median credit card limit was $10,000. The typical interest rate was 15%. Credit, debit, and business card use is at an all-time high, with about a quarter of every $1 in discretionary consumer spending on plastic, according to Cardweb.com. Credit cards were a major culprit behind the record filings for personal bankruptcy in the 1990s. In 1998 some 1.4 million Americans declared bankruptcy, about double the 1990 figure and five times the number of personal bankruptcies in 1980.

Indeed, the spread of plastic horrifies many commentators. Once, after we had finished a *Sound Money* radio broadcast live at the Minnesota State Fair, an older man collared me to de-mand my help in preventing young men and women from get-ting or using credit cards. No plastic, period. It was for their own good, he said. Similarly, Robert Heady, founder of Bank Rate

Monitor, an ardent consumer advocate, a street-smart, wonderful man, gets practically apoplectic when it comes to credit cards. "America is sick, addicted to plastic," he told me. "We are slaves to credit cards."

Credit cards are risky. Credit cards make it easy to spend more than you should. The credit card companies continually amaze me with their dubious business practices, from teaser rates to credit insurance. The credit card giveaway on the nation's college campuses is especially disturbing. ("Have we got a deal for you! Sign up for our credit card and you get a free T-shirt!") About 60% of college undergraduates have credit cards, while 21% have four or more cards, according to Nellie Mae, a student loan company. Little wonder growing numbers of college students are getting in credit card trouble.

But hold off the credit card apocalypse. Credit cards have made life better for the mass of Americans. Plastic is convenient. You can use it at practically any retail store, including most neighborhood grocery stores and corner dry cleaners. Credit cards make record keeping easy. They're an electronic store of emergency savings. For some transactions, such as renting a car or booking a long family vacation, a credit card is practically a necessity. The credit card is a financial and technological advance that helped open up money management to the middle and working classes. Journalist Joseph Nocera captured the largely beneficial force of the money revolution in *A Piece of the Action: How the Middle Class Joined the Money Class:* "The financial markets were once the province of the wealthy, and they're not anymore; they belong to all of us. We've finally gotten a piece of the action. If we have to pay attention now, if we have to come to grips with our own tolerance for risk, if we're forced to spend a little time learning about which financial instruments make sense for us and which don't, that seems to me an acceptable price to pay. Democracy always comes at some price. Even financial democracy."

From an economic point of view, the rewards from the spread of plastic outweigh the risks. But that is cold comfort for those who fall behind on their credit card payments and watch in horror as their balance mounts month after month. You've heard—and probably cringed at—the admonition "Borrow wisely." It's glib. It's easier said than done. But it is true. In today's economy, "Borrow wisely" largely means don't run up credit card debt. No matter how powerful the temptation, and sometimes the lure is strong, credit cards shouldn't be used to spend more than you make. Basically, you already know what to do when it comes to credit cards. The tough part is following through on your knowledge. The goal of this chapter is to get you moving in the right direction. The bill should be paid off monthly.

CREDIT CARD BASICS

How many credit cards do you have? One? Three? Five? How many should you have? Greg has two credit cards, one charging a 13% interest rate and the other 16%.

Why not just one? I can't really think of a good reason why anyone would want more than one, unless one is for personal use and the other for business expenses. I can see why the credit card companies want you to have more than one card— it means more fees and potential interest charges for them— but not you. If you do have several credit cards, why not get rid of all but one?

What kind of credit card should you have? If you pay off your entire bill every month, you're not affected by the interest rate charged by your credit card company. You never pay any interest. (I would still try to get as low a rate as possible, though.) What really matters to you is finding a credit card with no annual fee or at least a very low fee. You also want a 25-day grace period during which no interest is charged to your account. By the way, you get the benefit of a grace period only if you pay off your bill completely by its due date.

The interest rate matters a lot if you don't pay off your bill in full. Obviously, the lower the rate the better off you are financially. The only problem for some people carrying a heavy debt burden is that the really low rates are reserved for people with solid credit records.

Most credit card issuers charge a variable rate. In other words, the interest rate you pay is pegged to an underlying interest rate, such as the banks' prime rate. The prime rate used to be the interest rate banks would charge their best corporate customers for a loan. Companies now borrow at a far cheaper rate in the capital markets; the prime rate has evolved into a rate set by the banks for their consumer loans. Anyway, the rate you are charged on your credit card changes depending on some sort of defined formula. For instance, if your credit card rate floats 5 percentage points above the prime rate and the prime rate is 8%, your credit card rate is 13%.

There are fixed-rate credit cards. But the term "fixed" is somewhat misleading. The fixed interest on a credit card is not the same as that on a fixed-rate mortgage. The interest rate on the latter never changes. Credit card issuers can change their "fixed" rate with as little as 15 days' notice, although it can be longer depending on the state or the credit card's contract terms.

What about those very low "teaser" rate offers of 3.9% or so that many of us get in the mail? I usually toss them away. Typically, the very low rate is offered for only a brief period of time, somewhere between three and six months, and then the rate can move up and down, depending on the credit card's interest rate formula and the economic environment. Usually, that credit card formula seems designed to give you a very high rate overall. If interest rates soar, your "low-rate" card could hit the stratosphere. However, if you have taken on too big a debt burden and you are working down your debt, and you can get one of these very low introductory rates—take it. You can transfer your debt burden to the new card, and the low interest charge could save you a few dollars in interest payments.

It pays to read the fine print before accepting any credit card solicitation. Luckily, comparison shopping has been made easier thanks to the "Schumer box," named after then congressman and now senator Charles Schumer. (Although I do wish someone would do something about the fine print; you need a magnifying glass to read much of the information.) The Schumer box tells you how much the credit card costs. Among the important information included in the Schumer box is the annual percentage rate; the grace period for purchases; the minimum finance charge; the balance calculation method; annual fees; transaction fees for cash advances; and late payment fees.

Here are some brief definitions:

Annual percentage rate: The APR is the amount of interest you will pay on a yearly basis. You can compare one credit card rate to another by looking at the APR.

Annual fee: These typically range from zero to $100.

Grace period: When does the clock start ticking on interest charges? A 25-day grace period is typical, although a number of credit card issuers are instituting shorter time frames, such as 22 days.

Balance calculation method: Even consumer credit card advocates mutter over this calculation. It's the method the credit card issuer uses to figure out what you owe, and the formula has a big impact on how much you will pay. One of the better methods for consumers is the average daily balance, excluding new purchases. Each day, the bank totals up what you owe it, excluding new purchases. That sum is divided by the number of days in the billing cycle to calculate your average daily balance, and then a finance charge is imposed. Most credit card issuers include new purchases in the calculation. Consumers should avoid the two-cycle average daily balance method, which calculates the average daily balance for two billing cycles, the current one and the previous one, including new purchases. The best way to avoid credit card charges is to pay the bill off in full every month.

Other fees: Special fees include late fees, over-your-credit-limit fees, and lost-card-replacement fees. Cash advances can be costly, too.

It pays to shop around, especially now. The reason is that many credit card owners are becoming smarter consumers and are getting much better at paying their bills on time. Credit card industry profits are pinched, so issuers are coming up with all kinds of creative ways buried in the fine print to earn more money. For instance, many credit card companies are sharply raising their special fees, such as late-payment charges. Still, the industry is competitive, and you can find good deals. Now, if you do find a better credit card, before shifting your account to another company, call your current issuer. Explain that you are thinking of moving your account to take advantage of a competitor's cheaper interest rate, lower annual fee, or better overall product. Your current company probably doesn't want to lose you as a customer, so it may at least match the offer. It's well worth the price of a phone call.

PAYING OFF CREDIT CARD BILLS

If all goes well, you'll never carry a balance. But almost all of us run up credit card debt at some point. Typically, it's when we face a pressing financial circumstance, such as a job loss or a major illness in the family. Sometimes, people just get carried away at the mall or take a vacation that adds up to big bucks. Or, like Greg, they impulsively fund an extravagance. No matter what the reason, it's easy to do. When it happens, the first thing to do is confront the bill. Don't hide it. Don't tuck the bill away in a drawer well out of sight. Put the credit card away.

Here's how to pay off your credit card bill. If your debt isn't too extravagant, the simplest thing to do is figure out the total amount you owe. Divide that sum by 6 or 12. This will give you a rough idea of how much you need to send monthly to your credit card issuer to pay off that bill in six months or a year—or quicker if possible. If you have savings, tap into the money to pay down the debt. More likely, you'll have to cut back on spending by, yes, making and sticking to a budget. Whether you draw down savings or slash spending, increasing your monthly payments by even relatively modest sums can make a huge difference. For example, say you have a credit card bill of $2,000, with an 18% rate of interest. If you make the minimum required $40 monthly payment, it will take you nearly eight years, and interest charges of more than $1,700, to get rid of the debt. If you can eke out another $60, so that you are sending $100 a month to the credit card company, you'll be done with the bill in two years and incur interest charges of only $396. So send in more than the minimum.

It's important to take a hard, realistic look at your finances. As we saw in Chapter 2, a budget is not the same as bookkeeping. Greg did try to create a budget on the computer. But he found it tiresome and eventually stopped. Budgeting is bringing your goals, your expectations, and your finances into accord. "All of a sudden we wake up one morning and there's $10,000 in debt, and we never meant it to happen," says Grace Weinstein, a longtime financial writer. "So one of the things that I always tell people is to really think about their goals. Where do you want to be a year from now, five years from now, ten years from now? And then map out a way to get there. And if it means cutting back on some spending that isn't that important to you, then do that."

Of course, it's psychologically and financially painful to cut spending and pay down debt. That's why looking at a budget as a way of achieving your goals and values rather than simply a cash-flow statement is so important. To further bolster your resolve to get out from under credit card debt, you could keep with you a reminder of a tangible reward when you are finally through with credit card bills. One woman I know who spent several years eliminating her credit card burden always carried in her purse a picture of a house she liked. A place to call her own was her reward, and when I met her she was well on her way toward achieving her goal.

If you have more than one credit card debt, which one should you pay off first? It's financially savvy to pay off the credit card with the highest interest rate first and then work your way down. However, some people need the psychological boost of successfully eliminating a bill. In that case, attack your smallest bill first, get rid of it, and bolster your determination to get out of debt.

THE SIGNS OF TROUBLE

Here are some very common warning signs that you may be carrying way too much debt: Are your credit card balances mounting despite your best efforts to pay down your debt? Do you find yourself making the minimum payment on this month's bill, last month's bill, and so on? Have you taken on new credit cards to increase your borrowing power? Are you using your credit cards to pay for food, utilities, and other essentials even as your old bills pile up? Greg had reached another worrisome sign: His debt amounted to a third of his annual income.

What do you do when you find yourself truly unable to pay off your credit card bills, even with a budget? You need to take charge of the situation and negotiate for some financial relief. One approach is to call someone in the collection department, explain your circumstances, and ask for a reduction in payments as a temporary measure to bridge your current situation. Those who find it difficult or intimidating to talk with lenders should get professional help by visiting a nonprofit debt-counseling organization. The best known is the Consumer Credit Counseling Service, with offices around the country. Other organizations, such as Debt Counselors of America, also offer financial guidance. Many universities and local colleges have credit-counseling classes. Nonprofit debt-counseling agencies will help you develop a budget and negotiate better payment terms with your creditors. One important caveat: Be aware that credit card issuers fund many of these nonprofit services, so they are not likely to recommend bankruptcy, even if that is your best alternative.

On *Sound Money,* the public radio show I cohost, I had a heartening interview with a woman who had tumbled deep into debt three or four years after graduating from college with a degree in a low-paying profession. Reality struck when she got a note from one of her credit card companies suggesting that she get help from a debt-counseling service. Like many people, she was in fear of being told that she was a bad person for being there. "But the people were really gracious and welcoming," she said. "They built me up rather than tore me down." And by helping her create a budget, they enabled her to make a change in her life. Her debts were paid off, she got a better job, and she began participating in a 401(k). Yet she remained careful to stay within her budget. "I still enjoy my life, and maybe I enjoy my life even more, because I'm a little more thoughtful about what I'm actually spending my money on."

Bankruptcy makes economic sense for some people. Most households that do file for bankruptcy are living through a financial catastrophe, such as divorce or illness. Many filers are from low- to middle-income households with few assets and uncertain incomes. Still, declaring bankruptcy is a drastic step, so make sure you have done everything you can to get your financial house in order. Bankruptcy is a last resort. True, it no longer carries the same personal or financial stigma as before, but it is far from a painless process. Despite the anecdotes you hear about people blithely filing for bankruptcy, in most cases it takes a huge emotional toll. "I would say that the time to consider it, if at all, is when you really have gotten in over your head and maybe through illness or loss of job or some major catastrophe you just haven't been able to pull yourself out," says Grace Weinstein.

There are two basic kinds of bankruptcy for individuals. The first, Chapter 7 bankruptcy, lets you get rid of all debts with some important exceptions, such as alimony, child support, and student loans. With Chapter 7 bankruptcy you turn over designated assets to a trustee. The trustee sells the assets and uses the money to discharge your debts.

The other form of bankruptcy is Chapter 13, what used to be called "wage earners' bankruptcy." You get to keep your assets, rearrange your finances, and set up a debt repayment plan over a maximum of five years. No matter what, if you are contemplating bankruptcy, get the professional advice of an attorney and make sure you understand all the ramifications before filing.

STAYING OUT OF CREDIT TROUBLE

Clearly, getting out of debt is only part of the story. The real issue is not going back into debt. Eric Tyson, the author of several of the "Dummy" books on finance, suggests that many people should get rid of their credit cards altogether. Sarah Rose, a reporter at *Money* magazine, had some unconventional advice on how Greg could cool his spending if getting rid of his credit cards was not an option. "If he is finding that for some reason he is just having a very hard time saying no to mountain bikes and Jeeps," she said, "he might consider the very old trick of freezing his credit cards"—actually putting them in a glass of water and freezing them. "If he has the urge to go to buy something compulsive, then he has to think about it while it's thawing." About a year after our conversation I met a women who did freeze her credit card and swore it was a great discipline.

Everyone should check out his or her credit report. There are three main credit bureaus, Experian, Trans Union, and Equifax. You should periodically review your credit report to make sure the information is accurate. You can't change the past, but you can dispute in writing any inaccurate or outdated information. If there is a mistake in your report, fill out the dispute form offered by the credit bureau and ask that the mistake be corrected. If there is a dispute, you have the right to make a brief written statement explaining your side of the story. You should also get any positive information added to your credit history. Your credit report will cost you no more than $8, and in some states you can get it for less, or get one copy a year for free. If you have been denied credit or a job because of something on your credit report, you are entitled to a free copy.

There are services that will get you your credit report for $39, $100, or some other hefty charge. Forget it. And steer clear of the outfits that guarantee they'll repair your credit, again often for a substantial fee.

In our society, bad credit is a genuine problem. It can make it difficult to rent an apartment, qualify for a job, get a mortgage or a car loan (at least at a decent interest rate), and do many other things we take for granted. It takes time, but you can repair your credit. Focus on the future, and pay off your bills on time. Remember, creditors will pay more attention to your more recent transactions than to some older ones. So if your recent credit history is good but there were some problems with late or missed payments several years ago, it's not as important.

One way many people repair their credit record is to take out a "secured" credit card. In essence, you open a savings account with a bank that issues you a card. Your credit is equal to or somewhat less than the amount you deposit. You will make some interest off your security deposit. Eventually, after showing a pattern of paying off your bills on time, you can usually switch to a traditional unsecured credit card.

A debit card is an alternative to credit cards. In essence, a debit card is an electronic check that looks like a credit card. Most businesses accept debit cards. Many banks are replacing their ATM cards with debit cards carrying the Visa or Master-Card logo. Consumers are embracing debit cards because you don't run up any debt. With a debit card you can't spend more than you have in your checking account. "You are not going to be able to spend beyond your means because the money gets deducted from your checking account," says Eric Tyson. Tyson is a strong advocate of debit cards.

Not everyone is enamored with debit cards. They do have several drawbacks. First, if you pay your credit card bills on time, you can do better using a no-fee, low-interest-charge card. After all, you enjoy an interest-free loan until you pay your bill, and credit card holders often get frequent-flier miles or other perks from their credit card. Credit cards also offer greater consumer protections. If you lose a credit card and someone runs up a $2,000 bill, federal law limits your liability to $50. But if you lose a debit card, the $2,000 could disappear from your checking account. There could be bounced checks and overdraft charges. You'll eventually get your money back, but it's a hassle. Technically, your debit card liability is limited to $50 if you notify the bank within two days of uncovering the loss or fraud. If you notify the bank later than that, your liability could be $500, and after 60 days your liability is technically unlimited. Yet both Visa and MasterCard offer consumers greater financial safety than required by law, essentially treating debit cards and credit cards the same when it comes to consumer protection. Check out your bank's policy if you opt for a debit card.

I think debit cards are a terrific discipline for anyone who is at risk of running up a credit card bill.

WHAT ABOUT THAT JEEP?

I met up with Greg again at an indoor driving range. He could swing a mean golf club. He was reducing his debt. "I think what I'm doing now is saying, if I don't need it, why buy it?" he said. "Do I really need it now?"

And how about that Jeep Greg loves so much? Everyone I talked to agreed that Greg had to get rid of the Jeep or his Acura. He could get rid of a big chunk of his debt by selling one set of wheels. "I'm not going to tell him which vehicle to get rid of, but he clearly has too many," said Eric Tyson. "If he had a family of four kids and a wife, maybe he might justify having two vehicles. But that's an awful lot of money to spend on transportation at his age and his income level." Bob Heady put it this way: "Greg, I hate to tell you this, but that Jeep has got to go. Kiss it good-bye, sayonara, gone." Greg agreed he should get rid of it, and he agreed that was the sensible thing to do. But first he wants to take a cross-country adventure. He promises to sell it—just as soon as he gets back. I liked Greg. But will he ever get his credit card habit completely under control? I am somewhat dubious. "I believe most people are always looking to further buy things. You know, no what matter what people say, no matter what people do, they'll always have some sort of debt," he said. "So I think it's more or less as long as the credit card is there and it's easy access, people will most likely use it." As far as I am concerned, that's a recipe for trouble—all risk and no reward. And if you agree with Greg, I advise you to get rid of your credit cards right now.

Resources

The Ultimate Credit Handbook, by Gerri Detweiler (Penguin USA). A strong consumer advocate. I like Detweiler's stuff because she is willing to offer down-to-earth advice for getting out of debt and staying out of debt.

Slash Your Debt: Save Money and Secure Your Future, by Gerri Detweiler, Marc Eisenson, and Nancy Castleman. Another helpful guide to managing your finances well.

bankrate.com. A gold mine of information and a genuine commitment to the consumer's welfare.

abiworld.org. Want to know how many people declared bankruptcy in the latest quarter? The data are here at the web site of the American Bankruptcy Institute.

cardweb.com. A good source for consumer and industry information about credit and debit cards.

Visa.com. A wealth of product and consumer information from the credit, debit, and business card giant.

Mastercard.com. This behemoth has plenty of consumer-friendly information.

Nolo.com. It publishes a number of comprehensive consumer self-help books, including *Money Troubles: Legal Strategies to Cope with Your Debts* and *Credit Repair,* both by Robin Leonard. Nolo's web site is a terrific source of information for consumers.

The main credit bureaus:

Experian at 1-800-520-1221 or www.experian.com.

Trans Union at 1-800-916-8800 or www.transunion.com.

Equifax at 1-800-685-1111 or www.equifax.com.

myvesta.org. Formerly Debt Counselors of America, Myvesta.org is an Internet-based nonprofit organization that offers all kinds of savvy debt information. It also has debt management programs and a crisis team of professionals that can swing in if you are in over your head. An intriguing use of the Internet to offer debt management services rather than relying on a bricks-and-mortar network.

cccssf.org. The Consumer Credit Counseling Service of San Francisco will work with you in person, on the telephone, or online. If you are in a tight credit spot, they'll come up with a debt management plan for you, negotiate with your creditors, and perform other standard credit counseling services.

Consumer Credit Counseling Service. Call 1-800-388-2227 for the office nearest you. It's a nonprofit community organization with a good reputation.

10

Kids and Money

Yes, having a child is surely the most beautifully irrational
act that two people in love can commit.

—Bill Cosby

I love being a parent. This is one of those rare instances when
almost all the clichés, from the joys to the heartaches, ring true.

Now, when it comes to a discussion of kids and money, I've
never understood the never-ending stream of articles proclaim-
ing how much that bundle of joy is going to cost you. The dollar figures are often shocking—from hundreds of thousands of
dollars to millions—once you add up all the expenses for diapers, clothing, food, and college, while also taking into account
any lost job and income opportunities as one or both parents
take time away from work for family.

So what? Millions of children are born every year. Obviously,
many people believe the financial trade-off is well worth making.
Have you ever heard someone sadly remark, "If only I had spent
more time working"? But I have heard people regretfully admit
that they didn't spend enough time at home with their kids
when they were growing up. I can't think of anything better to
spend money on than raising and educating your kids. What's
more, you still have to live within your means whether or not you
have children. That's why we create budgets.

No, when it comes to money and kids, the vital topic is teaching children to manage money well. Educating kids about personal finance is good for them and an investment by parents in their children's future. Parents are increasingly anxious to teach their kids about money. The desire to instruct kids about the value of money starts when they are little and they want "more than anything" that Sesame Street figure or the Kid's Meal at McDonald's. Teenagers still covet toys, they're just more expensive, such as a high-tech MP3 portable music player or leather basketball shoes. Madison Avenue and its corporate clients love kids, too—with good reason: Kids under 14 spend about $20 billion a year, and they influence another $200 billion in spending by parents. Many cartoons are nothing more than half-hour-long commercials for licensed toys, while music videos send teens off to the nearest music store. Parents are understandably concerned that the money lesson their kids are absorbing is to spend with abandon.

Another reason parents feel an intense pressure to raise financially literate children is the increasing money responsibility faced by young adults. When I went to college—and no, that wasn't in the dark ages—no one offered me a credit card. I did get a pension plan at my first several jobs. But they were the old-fashioned kind. You automatically joined the plan as an employee, but you got nothing unless you worked at the company for more than ten years. Today, when Jane and John go off to college, they'll be offered a credit card as soon as they register for classes—and if they are 18 or over they don't need your permission to get a credit card. Their first employer after college will likely ask them if they'd like to participate in the company's retirement savings plan and, if they say yes, how much of their salary will they contribute and how do they want to invest the money. They will probably be paying off a hefty student loan bill, too.

A cottage industry has sprung up in recent years offering all kinds of learning aids about money for kids, from videos to worksheets to web sites. I've spent a fair amount of time as a reporter and parent exploring many of these products, and many—although not all—are hardly worth the trouble and expense. Far better are the lessons that can be learned at home on the cheap from your daily interaction with your child or children. Remember, what you do with your money every day, your values and your habits, will be the biggest influence on how your kids deal with money when they grow up. The risk of not educating your kids about money through example and conscious effort is that they will absorb the wrong lessons early in life and end up in money trouble when they go off on their own. The reward of instilling financial literacy at a young age is to watch them take their earnings and pursue their dreams and values.

LEARNING THE VALUE OF MONEY

Wayne and Teresa Lomax wanted to know how they could send the right signals to their two sons about money. Wayne is the pastor of a church with some 500 parishioners in Timber Pines, Florida. Teresa is a head nurse at giant Jackson Memorial Hospital in downtown Miami. Christopher is 15 and Marcus is 11.

I met with the Lomaxes at their home on the outskirts of Fort Lauderdale one fall evening. While the adults sat around and talked jobs, sports, and finance, the kids were busy giving their dog, Licorice, a bath and doing their homework. It was readily apparent that this was a very loving family and that the children were responsible. Still, like many parents, the Lomaxes were concerned about the values their children were developing about money in our shopping mall society. "We are trying to instill in them the principles of saving, budgeting, and prioritizing," said Wayne.

Teresa and Wayne wondered how they should handle allowances. What is the best way to instill the work ethic? Is it a good idea to involve the kids in the family's finances? What can they do to combat the powerful influences of advertising and peers to own the latest fashion? "What are some techniques that parents can use to communicate to the kids that you don't always have to have the expensive thing, and yet provide for their needs?" asked Teresa.

Christopher and Marcus joined us, and they had their own queries. Christopher works hard at school, he plays in the county jazz band, and he is a guard on his high school basketball team (as I learned to my chagrin when we shot hoops). But many of his friends earned money working nights and on the weekends. He wondered if he should get a job and a paycheck. Christopher also wanted to know about investing. "Where should I put my money so that I can benefit from it a lot later in life?" he asked. Marcus had a very different issue. He was still learning how to save—and stay out of debt. "Well, I'm just getting out of a very bad habit of borrowing from about everyone," he admitted somewhat sheepishly. "So I'm trying as hard as I can not to borrow and to save up my money so I can buy stuff on my own."

EARLY MONEY MANAGEMENT

Many families start teaching their children about money with an allowance. Yet opinions about allowance are all over the lot. It's fascinating to explore some of the family-oriented web sites and read the vociferous discussions about allowances. Parents and experts alike disagree on whether to give an allowance and how much to give.

Perhaps there are so many different approaches to allowances because we all bring different experiences to the issue. For instance, Wayne's father served in the Army for some 25 years, and the family lived all over the United States and overseas. When Wayne was growing up, he and his two sisters used to get a dollar each once a month from their dad. "It was always a challenge to use that dollar wisely," he said. "I remember trying to save the dollar for one month so that I could have $2. That was quite an experience for 30 days. I managed to do it." In sharp contrast, Teresa remembers getting an allowance of $20 in high school. But the allowance was irregular. "That was just a couple of times, a few times that my mom would give it to me," she said.

An allowance is a good way to teach saving and spending skills. Christopher and Marcus get an allowance, and I like their parents' system. Christopher gets $40 a month, and Marcus gets $30. But there are responsibilities that come with the money. Both are expected to do chores around the house, take care of the dog, and pay for their haircuts. Christopher also gets all of his lunch money at the beginning of each semester.

A monthly allowance teaches money management skills, but it is too much to ask of most kids before the age of 11 or 12. I would start out with a weekly allowance until a child is ten years old or so. You could then shift to a biweekly system for a couple of years and then go monthly after that. For example, a monthly allowance is probably too much for Marcus. It might be easier for him to operate on a weekly allowance until he is a bit older.

Kids are barraged by message after message that if they just own this they will be so cool or have so much fun. To counteract some of these pressures, should you insist that your children save some of their allowance? Saving is a vital lifelong skill, but delayed gratification is difficult—even for adults. So try to turn saving into something that is fun, with the reward of saving readily apparent. For example, if they get weekly allowances, maybe they could set aside 10% to 30% of their allowance every week for a month. At the end of the month, they could take their accumulated savings and spend it on whatever they want (subject to your family restrictions on purchases). You can create the same deal with a fixed amount. Once they get to $10, $20, $30, or whatever sum you choose within reason, you'll take them to Target, Wal-Mart, or some other favored store. Another popular idea is to match all or part of their savings. For every dollar they set aside, you'll add another dollar or 50 cents.

When your children are very young, each one can have a piggy bank, a jar, or some other storage place at home. This way they can see their savings and count it, and you can talk about it. But when they get older, say ten or so, open a savings account at a bank so they can start learning about depositing money, watch their money grow, and understand how they can get it out later on.

You should also spend time teaching your children to be savvy spenders. One way to do that is to take advantage of everyday shopping experiences and turn them into learning moments. For instance, when you shop for food at the grocery store, do you pick out a brand-name cereal or a generic? How did you go about choosing an Internet service provider or a sweater? Why did you purchase a used car instead of a new car, or a BMW instead of a Ford Focus? There are no right answers. But financial decisions like these offer an opportunity for you to discuss with your child your approach to spending. Here's another possible money moment: If you use a check or a credit card to pay for an item, you could take the transaction as an opportunity to explain how to balance a checkbook or why it is financially savvy to pay off credit card bills in full and on time. You can use the Sunday classified ads to talk about the cost of renting or different jobs and salaries. Of course, these exercises will force you to confront your own spending habits. If you preach austerity and practice profligacy, all your kids will learn is that there is a double standard in your household. Teaching moments are valuable for parents as well as kids.

Here's another tactic that teaches both savings and investing lessons. You are going to clothe your child for school and play. But let's say your budget limit is $50 for sneakers and $35 for a sweatshirt. Your child desperately wants a pair of sneakers that cost $70 and a sweatshirt with a football logo that costs $45. Tell them that you'll fork out $50 for the sneakers and $35 for the sweatshirt, and if they really want the brand-name, high-priced product, they'll have to come up with the extra $20 for the sneakers and $10 for the sweatshirt. "Kids will spend unlimited amounts of money as long as it's yours," says Janet Bodnar, better known as Dr. Tightwad, who writes a column on kids and money for *Kiplinger's* magazine. "Once it's theirs, they have this responsibility, and it's a whole new ball game."

Indeed, as kids get older, they often want a job so that they have their own money to spend. I think I am a bit out of step with the times when it comes to teenagers working. Kids become adults all too quickly. Summer jobs are good, but working throughout the school year makes me nervous.

Christopher was interested in earning his own paycheck. His parents didn't want him to take a job, but they were concerned that he wasn't gaining valuable work experience. Yet Christopher is working. His job is to get good grades and to participate in extracurricular activities. That's his job, and he demonstrated at school, on the basketball court, and in the county jazz band an admirable work ethic. Too many kids worry about earning and spending money and not enough about their studies. Some young people have no choice but to work to help out their family. But for many others, the job just isn't worth all the time and effort. "The part-time job that they have when they are 16 is not going to be their career," says Janet Bodnar. "So as long as they are thinking ahead to what their real job is going to be after they graduate, what their real career might be, and the work ethic that you learn by having to organize your time, show up at events on time, work with a group, maybe be responsible for a group, which you would do in extracurricular activities, that is just as critical as anything that you would learn on a paid job at that level."

FINANCIAL LITERACY

Money management in the early years means learning how to handle an allowance. Marcus had already learned a valuable lesson in money management. He had spent beyond his means, borrowed money from his brother and friends, and then struggled to get out from under his debt burden. He did, to his credit. Jesse Brown, a Chicago-based financial planner, identified with Marcus. He recalled when his parents had given him a small monthly allowance. He would blow much of it in the first week or so, and then he would start borrowing to get through the month. "What happened in my household is we would get little promissory notes," he said. "I knew after a couple of months that I'd better budget money because I couldn't afford the usury rate that my father was going to give me."

About age 16 or so, with college looming in a few years, many youngsters should get a checking account. A student in college will end up spending $2,000 to $3,000 more than tuition, room, and board during the school year on entertainment, clothing, laundry, and assorted other necessities and wants. A valuable skill is learning how to write checks, balance a checkbook, and cope with bigger financial responsibilities. Of course, young people will make mistakes, and you should give them room to make errors without getting into serious financial trouble. That's how they will learn. You might want to consider a debit card, too, which is essentially an electronic checking account. But unlike checks, a debit card is accepted by almost all businesses that welcome credit cards. Wayne liked the idea of a checking account for Christopher. "I do think the checking account experience, learning to manage your own money in that manner, is really good," he said.

What about a credit card? I'm skeptical. Yes, the moment students walk on campus, credit card companies are soliciting their business. They're seducing students to sign up with everything from free T-shirts to Frisbees. And note that as long as they're over 18, students don't need their parents' permission to get a credit card. Yet most young people don't need a credit card on campus. Cash, a checking account, and a debit card are more than enough. "I think it's really important for them to learn how to manage cash," says Janet Bodnar. "It's like learning to walk before you run."

If you do want your youngsters to learn how to live with plastic, talk to them about responsible credit card use. You might want to steer them toward a "secured" credit card. In essence, they open a savings account with a bank that will then issue them a card that looks like any other credit card. But their credit will be the amount you deposited—say, around $250. With a secured credit card, there is a limit to how much debt trouble a youngster can take on.

Here's a test for any parents thinking about their teenager and money. Would you trust your child with a month's or even a semester's worth of college allowance? If you can say yes, then you've taught your child good money management skills. If you break out in a cold sweat at the thought, then you need to work some more on your child's money management skills.

Parents are also eager to teach their kids about investing these days. Parents would like their kids to be well prepared for retirement savings and other long-term savings goals.

The stock market also opens up to youngsters a whole new way of looking at the world, from learning about product development to the economic bridges linking the globe. Along the way, you and your youngster exploring the world of investing might find another activity and conversation to share. And that is what really counts anyway.

If the goal of getting your child interested in investing is to make money, then an equity mutual fund is probably the best route. For not much money, say between $250 and $500, you can get professional money management, a well-diversified portfolio, and the automatic reinvestment of dividend income. There are mutual funds that cater to kids, too. These mutual funds tend to invest in companies that youngsters know about, like fast-food restaurants and entertainment companies. They will also send a newsletter to your child, a good way to pick up some investment literacy.

Although mutual funds have their advantages, I think it's a much richer learning experience to buy individual stocks. The reason is that picking stocks is fun, far more fascinating than putting quarters into a piggy bank or dollars into a savings account. Your child can find stocks to investigate just by noticing what shoes their friends are wearing—and then looking into the company that makes them. Is McDonald's the place to be, or is there a fast-food challenger to research? Who's going to win the video game wars? Sony? Sega? Nintendo? Concerned about the environment? There are companies with a strong record of protecting the environment. Whatever your child's passion or interest, there are public companies to research and follow on the Internet and in the newspaper. I have no clue whether your child will make much money, although he or she will probably do okay. But your child will have the excitement of identifying with a product, researching the company, watching the stock fluctuate, and reading articles about the company. And online trading has truly cut down on the costs of buying and selling stocks. "A young person who is interested in investing at a young age is really assuring his success," says Jesse Brown. Adds Arva Rice, formerly director of the economic literacy program for Girls Inc., a nonprofit organization: "I think that investing is important because we want to teach our children that money can work for them."

You will need to open a custodial account for your child. (Custodial accounts are governed by the Uniform Gifts to Minors Act, or UGMA.) Any investment firm, discount brokerage, e-trading firm, or bank with a retail trading division will set one up for you. You control the account, since your child can't trade. But it is the child's money. Once your child becomes an adult, age 18 to 21 depending on the state, the account is theirs.

FAMILY FINANCES

How involved should your children get in your finances? They will absorb more than you think. While I don't think they need to know exactly how much you earn—unless you want everyone in the neighborhood to know—it is a good idea to keep them informed about family finances. They should know about taxes, how hard you work to pay the bills, and why you are saving for your retirement. "I advocate that there should be a family budget and that the young people in the family become aware of the budgetary items such as housing, transportation, and food," says Jesse Brown.

You can also involve your kids in your charitable giving and explain why sharing is important to you. Nathan Dungan knows a man who gives each of his kids two gifts of money during the holiday season. One check is money the child can spend on himself or herself. But the other check—a blank check made out for an identical amount—has to go to a cause, a community group, a religious organization, or some other type of charitable organization. The idea of giving money away made an impression on both Marcus and Christopher. "Yesterday, my brother gave me a lot of money for no reason. I was happy," said Marcus. "So if I gave something to them, I guess they will be happy too." Christopher added: "It feels good when I give people money—it just makes you feel good."

Sometimes your finances will take a turn for the worse. Let's say you lose your job. Money is going to be tight. Your kids will pick up on the tension and the worry. While it would be wrong to burden them with all the financial risks you face, they should understand what is going on.

Money is a touchy subject. But chances are if you are talking to your kids at all about money, you are probably doing something right. The goal is to consciously work the saving, spending, and giving choices you make all the time into the ongoing dialogue you have with your kids. Here's Janet Bodnar: "You are trying to give your kids a healthy attitude toward money and the ability to manage it." Jesse Brown says that the earlier in a child's life he "understands the value of money, the better he is going to be able to manage it as he becomes a teenager and a young adult and actually goes out into the work world."

Sounds good to me.

Resources

Street Wise: A Guide for Teen Investors, by Janet Bamford (Bloomburg Press). Teens can learn a lot and make money by investing in the stock market.

Kids and Money, by Jayne A. Pearl (Bloomberg Press). A good resource for parents. Deals with all the critical issues, from preschool to college.

kiplinger.com. Go right to the articles by Dr. Tightwad, a.k.a. Janet Bodnar. She helped us out on our show, and she is great when it comes to kids and money. She's also the author of *Dollars & Sense for Kids* and *Mom, Can I Have That? Dr. Tightwad Answers Your Kid's Questions About Money* (Kiplinger Books).

investorguide.com. This web site's "kids and money" section has a number of useful links to other sites devoted to helping kids learn about investing.

moneyopolis.org. This game, geared toward grades six through eight, was created by the accounting firm Ernst & Young to teach kids about math by tapping into real-life issues involving money. There are seven "Learning Centers" at the site: Personal Financial Planning Center, Job Center, Education Center, City Hall, Banking Center, Shopping Center, and Community Center.

collegeparents.org. In partnership with MasterCard International, this nonprofit has created a Money Talk series to help parents and college-age youngsters talk about and deal with money matters.

younginvestor.com. A good web site for kids eager to learn more about investing.

11

Love and Money

The course of true love never did run smooth.
—William Shakespeare,
A Midsummer Night's Dream

You're a match made in heaven. You both enjoy reading. You like eating out, visiting friends, going to the movies, and arguing over politics. Sure, you occasionally fight—who doesn't?—but the anger fades as quickly as tempers flared. But when it comes to the financial side of your partnership, you've learned you're polar opposites. And in this case, the difference isn't charming. No, it's a festering source of stress, anxiety, and resentment. Contrary money management styles are corroding trust in your relationship. Suddenly you understand why money is a leading cause of marital discord and divorce.

Take Mike and Brenda Polis. They are a typical American family with their money struggles. Mike is an accountant. Brenda used to work at a large marketing and travel company. About a year ago they decided that Brenda would leave her private-sector job and become a stay-at-home mom for their two daughters, ages three and one. For the first time in their seven-year marriage, Mike is the family's sole breadwinner.

Naturally, money is tighter now that they are living on one income, and they have a lot of bills to meet. Mike and Brenda are juggling a monthly mortgage, credit card debt, and living expenses while trying to invest in their daughters' futures, pay off student loans, find some money to stash away for retirement, and still attempt to accelerate their mortgage payments. Brenda has also set herself up as an independent contractor with a photographic scrapbook supply company. She goes into people's homes and educates them on putting together a family scrapbook. But the Polises took on additional debt to get her started.

Mike and Brenda have a lot to manage, and lately the pressure has put more than a financial strain on their union. They aren't used to living paycheck to paycheck. Neither likes it, and sometimes toward the end of the month they don't even know how they are going to pay all the bills. Those are tough evenings. The joint decision for Brenda to take care of their kids full-time has brought them face to face with their mismatched money styles.

For instance, Mike is an accountant and, in this case, it is both a professional designation and an apt description. He keeps track of their cash flow on their home computer, and he has created an extremely detailed system for monitoring their spending and expenses. Every time there is a "disbursement," he categorizes and records it. Mike has gone so far as to put together an annual budget based on their month-to-month expenditures. But Brenda sometimes loses the receipts for diapers, formula, shoes, and other household items. The receipts get misplaced or thrown away, which isn't surprising considering all the running around any stay-at-home parent with two kids does. Problem is, a computer-based budgeting tool is only as good as your data. "I keep asking Brenda to be more conscious and to keep track of the spending, even if it's just taking the receipt and throwing it in her purse so that we can keep track of it," says Mike. "It seems like it's a conversation we have every month."

In addition, Mike's carefully constructed monitoring system seems designed more for managing a corporation's cash flow than running a household budget. It is complicated enough that Brenda gets frustrated struggling to put the data in the right category. Mike's correcting her data entries also offends her.

"I don't think I looked over your shoulder," protests Mike.

"Yeah, you did," says Brenda. "The thing is, you have so many categories. And I'm so petrified that I look at 'gas,' and is it 'auto gas' or is it 'fuel gas'? It's not a very simple thing. As we have said before, maybe it's my teaching background, but you get frustrated quickly when I ask questions."

"Well, I disagree," replies Mike. "I think whenever you have had questions, I have been patient and more than willing to answer them."

"That's your perception," she says, a playful challenge in her voice.

"That's my perception," he says stiffly.

Get the picture? Mike and Brenda are smoldering over their money differences. Mike is aggrieved at Brenda for forcing him to act like the "money Gestapo." He feels she has put him in the difficult position of always being the one to monitor their spending and say no. Brenda, in turn, feels pressured to be frugal all the time and count every penny. She craves some spontaneity in their lives and wishes Mike would lighten up. "I wish life would be more *carpe diem*, seize the day, and less worry about money," said Brenda. "Again, I'm not a big shopaholic, but I would like to see us go do more family things. Just on a whim, let's go out for dinner and see a movie and not be worried that we have to go before five o'clock because the movies are cheaper then."

It isn't just money that is dividing them. Brenda is wrestling with a loss of independence now that she isn't earning a paycheck. Mike is sensitive to her concern, and both recognize the value in everything she does at home. Nevertheless, no longer bringing home steady earnings bothers Brenda. "I think my issue is having gone from being independent and having my own money and working full-time and now staying home on one income," she says.

As Brenda and Mike have learned, there is a significant psychological element to any financial issue, and that is especially true when it comes to a major lifestyle change, such as the stay-at-home option. But Mike and Brenda are remarkably open about their money gap, and they are determined to surmount the problems created by their divergent money management styles. That desire to work together is critical, and they can build on that base by returning to the financial fundamentals. Sometimes the best answers are the simplest. Think about your shared values and goals; order your priorities using a risk-and-reward framework; keep your money management approach simple; expect change will come with time rather than overnight; and, above all, communicate with each other about money on a regular basis. The rewards of your relationship will grow from it, and the risk of pulling apart will shrink.

MONEY AND VALUES

How many of you had a long talk about money with your partner before you started living together or got married? My wife and I didn't. Most couples don't, unless there is a glaringly apparent money problem, such as one partner carrying a huge credit card bill into the relationship. Otherwise, we're vaguely aware that one of us is frugal and the other easygoing when it comes to money, that one of us keeps close tabs on where the money is going and the other doesn't really care. Instead, we're focusing on romance, fun, sharing ideas, becoming comfortable with each other, and creating a life together. Money is essentially something we spend to do things together. What's more, money is a difficult subject to broach between couples, and you have enough going on without adding a frank financial discussion to the mix. "When couples start being a couple, they often don't talk about money because it's such a loaded subject," says Eric Tyson. "It's not surprising that these problems don't come out until later. And the differences can be pretty significant."

Why do we have different approaches to money? There are many reasons. For one thing, we often find a partner, consciously or unconsciously, who has some strengths or weaknesses we don't. But the disparity only becomes obvious during a major life event, such as having kids. "It is a threatening thing when that happens, and that does cause tension if you haven't thought it through or thought about the joint values that you have," says Cicily Carson Maton, a Chicago-based financial planner.

For another, our parents often exert a large influence on our money personalities. Some parents are indulgent with their children, reaching into their pocket for a soda or a small toy without much protest or thought. Other parents strongly enforce an allowance system. The soda or toy is bought with allowance money, and if there isn't enough money in the piggy bank, that's tough luck. And there are many other shades of money-raising styles. Parents also influence our attitude toward money in subtle ways. Perhaps your father was always losing his job and your mother had to pinch pennies for months on end. Now that you are an adult, you prize financial security above all. Maybe your parents lived in hock but always had the latest gadget for the home and the hottest car on the block and gave frequent parties for friends and neighbors. You find yourself always taking out the credit card and buying what you want.

For instance, both Mike and Brenda grew up middle-class. Yet their experiences with money were very different. Brenda's family took some trips, she got an allowance, and her family wasn't afraid to spend money. They'd go out to restaurants and stay at a Holiday Inn every once in a while. "That's the kind of money values that were passed on to me," she said. "You work hard and you spend your money and play with it." Mike grew up in a family of five kids. His father was a teacher and sole bread-winner. They had to be frugal and very conscientious about money. "I think a lot of those habits were passed on to me," said Mike.

The key toward a solution is focusing on shared values. In-deed, far too much of the "love and money" literature seems to thrive on emphasizing the money differences in a relationship. The trick seems to be coming up with clever typologies for cap-turing one extreme or the other and then asking where you fit into these pigeonholes. What's lost is that most people probably agree about money much more than they disagree. The idea is to bring the shared values out into the open and then start re-newing the money relationship on that foundation. For exam-ple, Mike and Brenda share a strong commitment to family. It was a huge step for Brenda to give up her career to stay at home with the kids, and for Mike to take on the burden of becoming the family's sole earner. Education is another jointly held value. Mike is a CPA, Brenda has a master's degree, and they have started college funds for their two young children. When I was with them, they also laughed easily at each other's jokes.

The financial gulf between Mike and Brenda is not that wide when the focus shifts to their shared values. Now it's time to start prioritizing goals and making some financial trade-offs. In other words, it's time for conversation and compromise.

THERE IS A SEASON

The Byrds were one of America's first superbands in the 1960s. One of their most famous songs is "Turn! Turn! Turn!" It was written by folksinger legend Pete Seeger, with the words from the Book of Ecclesiastes. The chorus starts:

To everything (turn, turn, turn)
There is a season (turn, turn, turn)

Reminding ourselves that there is a season, a rhythm to life, is a sensible way to begin bringing some order to a troubled money relationship. Let's return to Mike and Brenda. Like many parents today, they are well aware of the value of saving and investing for long-term goals. They are putting aside $100 a month for their daughters' college education. They're funding their retirement savings plans. They're also paying extra on their mortgage every month to reduce the principal quickly. Mike has run the numbers, and the interest savings are enormous from shortening the life of their mortgage loan. Yet Mike and Brenda are also struggling to get out from under debts—student loans, credit card bills, and business start-up costs. Simply put, they are trying to do too much all at once. Yes, there is a season, a time for making priorities and trade-offs, when it comes to money.

Mike and Brenda could decide that they are working with a four-to-five-year time frame. Their primary investment is in their family and children. For now, their money focus should be on stabilizing their finances and improving their cash flow so that they can enjoy the family situation they have created. These could be the best years of their lives. They have financial options, too. Sure, it's great to set some money aside for their daughters' college education, but now is not the time. Five years from now, when their daughters are in school, Brenda may decide to re-enter the professional workforce full-time. Their college savings fund could be replenished at that point. They should certainly stop paying extra on their mortgage. "To put additional stress on the household by trying to pay off the mortgage more quickly now doesn't make sense," says Eric Tyson. "It especially doesn't make sense with the consumer debt they have." In a sense, this love-and-money issue boils down to acceptance: We make this much; we spend this much; we can probably save this much; and we are not going to be millionaires by the end of next month. Says financial educator Ruth Hayden: "Goals have to be prioritized. Investments have to be prioritized."

BRIDGING THE GAP

It's time to take some concrete steps to bring about greater money harmony. Mike mentioned that he no longer wanted to be the money police. He wishes that Brenda would take more of a leadership role. For another couple, the issue may be managing the investment portfolio or taking charge of the daily living expenses like grocery shopping. Whatever the issue, there is genuine resentment and anger over an ongoing financial imbalance in the relationship.

Here's one tactic for creating greater financial equity. A couple can swap monitoring the budget and paying the bills, perhaps every three or six months. Mike couldn't look over Brenda's shoulder and say, no, that's the wrong category. Instead, he would go for a walk or play with the kids. Mike has to be willing to give up control for three to six months, and Brenda has to be the responsible money partner during that period of time. What's more, if Brenda wants to go out to dinner or a late-night movie, it would be up to her to figure out how to find the money in their budget. Mike would then take over the bill paying when Brenda's turn is done. This is a good tactic for rebuilding trust in a relationship. "They have to trust that it's going to work," says Cicily Carson Maton.

Now, I've gone into the philosophy and mechanics of bringing financial order into a household in the chapter on budgeting, and you may want to refresh your memory by reviewing Chapter 2. But I do want to comment on Mike's budgeting system, because it has a serious flaw that dooms far too many budgets: Mike's detailed cash-flow accounting system would work fine for a small business but doesn't make sense in the home. For one thing, a household budget is supposed to make it easy to track the money flow. Instead, his system has added a whole new layer of complexity. Plus, do they really need all that information? It's critical to gather as much information as possible in the first month or two of putting together a budget. But after a while, the budget should evolve into a spending and investing pattern that reflects your priorities and habits.

Put it this way: If you are saving a reasonable percentage of your salary and you're not carrying any credit card debt, does it really matter whether last month you spent more on food and wine entertaining friends and less on lunch at work, while this month very little of your money went toward going out and more was spent on movie rentals and books? Once your system is in place, it's the broad categories of saving and spending that matter most, and the fine distinctions fade in importance. "I would encourage them to think through do they really need to be tracking all of their spending on a monthly basis, because if they set a specific savings goal, like we are going to save 10 percent of our income or 8 percent of our income each month, and they are able to do that, then my feeling is, well, who cares where it goes after you have accomplished that savings?" says Eric Tyson. "Maybe if the two of them together can decide on their goals and figure out a way to save that amount of money each month, it would be okay if she didn't keep all the credit card receipts."

Creating a budget, and swapping financial responsibility for the budget, is a good start. But it's only a beginning. To encourage an ongoing money conversation without waiting for a money blow-up, it's important to set up a weekly meeting. The meeting should be short and focused. The idea is to institute a regular discussion about money so that problems don't fester for months, allowing resentment to build and tempers to explode. The meeting is also a place for compromise, for brain-storming and figuring out where you and your partner want to be in coming months and years.

Ruth Hayden has another suggestion for easing money tension in a relationship. Regularly go out on a date, perhaps as a reward after the weekly money meeting. The rule is that you can't talk about money, children, the in-laws, or upgrading the home during your evening out. After all, you didn't talk about those things when you were first attracted to each other (okay, maybe the in-laws). And when you're at home, it's hard to get away from all the mundane daily chores and everyday pressures.

The big word is "compromise." Each partner in the relationship needs to understand where the other is coming from. And there are some things you are just going to have to let go of and other aspects of your partner's money personality you are just going to have to understand. Sometimes, you have to go into a closet and scream or go for a long walk. But there has to be some give-and-take. Fact is, two people at opposite ends of the money pole can get along so long as each respects the other and tries to find a middle ground. It's possible to do.

MINGLE THE MONEY OR KEEP IT SEPARATE?

Most people agree it's not a good idea for couples to mingle their finances until they have settled into a long-term relationship, like marriage. It's prudent to keep finances separate and to write checks or pay cash for shared expenses. There are plenty of different ways of doing this, and the only question is what system works for you. For instance, some couples will split the bills they have in common, such as rent or utilities, no matter what each earns. Other couples will prorate the bills based on income. And some people will keep track of everything and each is responsible only for what he or she spends. Whatever you do, don't lend out your credit card or get yourself into a situation where you could be liable for someone else's credit card debt. "Once you start mingling finances, and putting your names on each other's credit cards, you are obligated," says Michelle Singletary, a personal finance columnist at *The Washington Post*. "And a lot of couples don't take that last step and get married. And then you've got the debt of somebody you no longer see."

What about when you get married? Should you mingle funds or keep them separate? Again, people develop all kinds of different systems, but my bias is toward mingling finances, especially if kids enter the picture. It takes too much time to figure out who is responsible for what when you are exhausted from late-night feedings, driving the kids to sporting events, getting dinner on the table, and reading every evening to your children. Anyway, mingling finances is a concrete expression that you are in the family together and both of you carry equal responsibility. In a sense, merging your money is a defining difference between a relationship and a long-term commitment. Still, there are plenty of good reasons for each partner to keep his or her own checking account, ranging from independence to the practical. For example, any freelancer will need a separate account.

When money gets tight in a relationship, it's natural to wonder if the stay-at-home partner should get a job. Or, if one partner earns less than the other, perhaps it's time to get a better-paying job. I don't think there is a right or wrong answer here, since so much goes into the decision of what job to take (let alone whether a higher-paying job is available) and whether or not to stay home with the kids. The real answer is what fits with your values and priorities. But homing in on the topic of divergent money management styles, people fight over money no matter what their income. More money is not the solution to the problem. Without discipline and understanding, spending will always rise to income.

For instance, in Mike and Brenda's case, they have made it a priority for her to stay at home with the kids. The decision for her to go back to work full-time would come with a financial as well as emotional price. It costs money to be a working parent, and you need to deduct some or all of these costs when figuring out whether it is worthwhile or not. Child care, wardrobe expenses (including dry cleaning), the cost of commuting, unreimbursed business expenses, the extra costs of take-out meals, any additional income taxes you may pay because that second income pushes you into a higher tax bracket (check the IRS's rate web page to make this calculation), and paying for things you could do by yourself if only you had the time, such as housecleaning and minor home repairs—it all adds up. "Brenda could go back to work and earn more money and that would solve some of their problems, but maybe that wouldn't make them happy," says Eric Tyson. "They should recognize what their priorities are and then work toward them and not be upset or feel they are not doing everything that they could be if they can't accomplish every one of their financial goals."

GETTING PAST THE BLAME GAME

Mike and Brenda have started making some realistic compromises. They realize what's true for any couple: Shared values and a commitment to each other make long-term relationships work. If you're battling the money issue, keep in mind that each partner's contribution is equal, no matter how much money he or she makes. For instance, Mike has developed a greater awareness of just how much not earning a paycheck has chipped away at Brenda's sense of self-worth. "You are contributing to the family," said Mike. "You always said that, but I didn't believe it in my heart because I didn't have the paycheck," she replied.

Mike and Brenda have decided to hold weekly money meetings and to trade off handling the family finances every three or four months. Yes, they once tried something similar, with disastrous results. But this time Brenda is determined to use a system that works for her. Mike has agreed to the trade-off. "You have to feel like I'm going to be responsible," said Brenda. "I think that's going to be a stretch for you." Mike replied, "You might be right. I am not completely close-minded. I'm willing to try."

Brenda has gone back to work part-time at her old company for 10 to 15 hours a week at a decent wage. Her mom is helping out with the day care, so her costs are staying under control, and her earnings are targeted toward paying off the credit cards. They also jumped on the idea of a date. It would be too difficult to do every week with two kids, but both like the idea of going out together and not talking about money.

The bottom line: "We're making progress," said Brenda. "We are making definite progress here," Mike agreed.

Remember, the key word is "compromise." You are a team. A union. And you're much more likely to achieve your financial goals together than apart.

Resources

How to Turn Your Money Life Around: The Money Book for Women, by Ruth L. Hayden (Health Communications). I can't rave about Ruth enough. Her book is well worth reading cover to cover—a rarity among personal finance books.

For Richer, Not Poorer: The Money Book for Couples, by Ruth Hayden (Health Communications). Ruth Hayden teaches a class for couples—and it's always oversubscribed. This book distills her wisdom from years of teaching and working with couples.

You Just Don't Understand, by Deborah Tannen (Random House). It's not a money book. But sociologist Tannen offers some intriguing insights into why men and women can talk past each other—even with the best of intentions.

moneyminded.com. A Hearst Corporation web site for women. Some good articles and useful ideas.

ivillage.com. This web site has a number of straightforward articles on making money work in your relationship.

msmoney.com. An excellent web site devoted to women's financial and investment needs.

12

Taxes

The tax which each individual is bound to pay ought
to be certain, and not arbitrary. The time of payment,
the manner of payment, the quantity to be paid, ought
all to be clear and plain to the contributor, and to
every other person.

—Adam Smith, *The Wealth of Nations*

The Scottish philosopher and economist Adam Smith had the right idea. Unfortunately, the authors of the U.S. tax code have not heeded his admonition. No, doing your taxes is a lot like going to the dentist. As much as we all would like to avoid it, we all have to do it. But unlike a dentist appointment, a date with the tax man can't be put off. And if you miss it, you won't just get a friendly reminder in the mail. It's against the law not to file your taxes.

The government hasn't made the annual rite of filling out tax forms easy. The federal tax laws and regulations take up nearly 47,000 pages, and the codebooks keep getting longer, not shorter. Imagine, the instructions for the 1040EZ form, the easiest one, consist of over 30 pages. The tax code is riddled with far too many deductions, credits, exemptions, exclusions, phase-outs, and enhancements. The number of taxpayers who turned to a paid preparer jumped from 42% to 52% from 1981 to 1997. Economists estimate that the annual cost of filing for individuals and businesses, taking into account time and the money spent on expert advice, ranges between $75 billion and $130 billion. Meanwhile, the administration and Congress are proposing new tax breaks and tax law changes all the time. The mind reels.

Certainly, Ann and Scott Alger are frustrated and intimidated by taxes. The mother of an active two-year-old, Ann also runs a licensed day care center in her home. Like any small business owner, Ann has to keep track of her income and expenses. She spends much of her time running after kids and chasing down lost receipts. Her husband, Scott, is an eighth-grade science teacher, a coach, and a part-time referee. Like many families, the Algers are apprehensive as April 15 approaches. "We have a lot of anxiety when it comes to tax time," Ann said.

When I met with the Algers, the questions about taxes poured out. Among them: What records should they keep? What about a Roth IRA? What are the tax benefits associated with the home? Can they deduct the interest on student loans? What about education expenses? What is the difference between a deduction and a credit? How do they keep track of all the changing rules? "Where do average people who are not familiar with the tax code find the answers that can help them?" asked Scott.

Their nervousness over the tax code went beyond confusion over its complexity. The Algers worried about an audit, one of the most ominous words in the English language. Would taking legitimate deductions and credits trigger an Internal Revenue Service audit? Ann recalled her parents dealing with an IRS audit when she was young. She remembers receipts spread out all over the whole house and her parents rummaging through shoe boxes full of papers. The family was miserable during the audit, and the term still haunts her.

NAVIGATING THE TAX CODE

Still, it's not all that difficult for most working-class and middle-class people to gain a reasonable grasp of the tax code. It's also a smart move to bring tax planning into your overall financial blueprint. After all, we'll spend more money per capita on taxes ($10,298) than on food ($2,693), clothing ($1,404), and shelter ($5,833) combined, according to the Tax Foundation. Indeed, we're spending more on federal taxes alone ($7,026) than on any other major household budget item.

My goal is not to impart all the twists and turns in the tax code. That is another book, or rather books. Instead, check out the resources listed at the end of this chapter for detailed guides to doing your taxes. Besides, the tax code is always changing, sometimes with major consequences, as in the 1997 tax act, and occasionally with only minor policy shifts. Nevertheless, even in a quiet year new tax rules are significant to you and me. A good way to stay on top of the most important changes and refresh your knowledge of the tax basics is to read the broad tax review articles published from late November through March in business magazines and major newspapers and on the tax-related Internet sites. The information is written in plain English and well reported.

This chapter will cover the main points anyone should know about taxes. It will provide a framework for savvy tax planning. You shouldn't be afraid of taxes. Take full advantage of the all the credits, deductions, and exemptions you qualify for. For example, the best tax shelter around is a retirement savings plan. It reduces your taxes, and you build up a nest egg so you won't have to work for the rest of your life.

A vital caveat: An old saying in finance is "Don't let taxes drive any investment." Evaluate any investment on its economic merits, and only then look at the tax incentives. For instance, in the 1980s many investors embraced limited partnerships because of their huge tax write-offs. But the underlying investments in real estate, oil and gas, containers, and other properties were overpriced and poorly managed. When the tax laws were tightened, the limited partners lost a fortune. These days, I get nervous when it's recommended for anyone paying credit card interest charges, which are not tax-deductible, to take out a home equity loan and pay off the credit card bill. Home equity interest payments are deductible. Still, why put your home at risk to pay off credit card debt? If you miss your home equity payments, your lenders can start foreclosure proceedings against you. If you miss your credit card payments, you'll have to deal with your creditors eventually, but no one can seize your home. Yes, swapping credit card debt for a home equity loan may be a smart tax move, but it's questionable finance.

Finally, it bears repeating: Steer clear of tax write-offs that are too good to be true and tax maneuvers too complex to grasp. Keep your taxes simple and straightforward.

A COMPUTER OR A CPA?

At some point in their work life, most people wrestle with whether to do their taxes on their own or hire a professional tax preparer. It's easier than ever to do your own taxes. There are a number of excellent tax preparation software packages and web-based programs. The electronic tax preparers are well designed, offer plenty of supporting tax information and definitions, do the math for you, and allow for electronic filing with the IRS. These programs are getting better every year, and they adjust well to tax law changes. Some people should do their own taxes because there isn't much to report, such as college students with limited incomes, young people earning their first steady paycheck, low-income folks who don't qualify for any of the major deductions, and middle-income families with very simple finances. The biggest advantage from filling in your own tax forms is that you get an intimate, detailed snapshot of your finances every year.

Who should use a CPA? The more complex your financial life, the smarter it is to hire a professional. Certified public accountants—CPAs—know the most about the intricacies of the tax code. For instance, if you have capital gains, income from partnerships, and property in several states, you are a likely candidate for turning to an accountant. Anyone going through a major life change, such as a divorce, should also consider a professional tax preparer. The self-employed typically confront a number of difficult tax questions, such as the home office deduction, as does anyone participating in a corporate stock option plan. "If you are just doing your home mortgage, just itemizing a typical return, you probably could do it yourself or use a tax program," says Deatrice Russell-Tyner, an accountant based in Washington, D.C. "Once you start getting into a business, you really do need to have professional help." Adds Ed Slott, a leading tax expert: "Once you are a home owner, and you have kids, and you have a self-employed business, you don't won't to be spending your valuable time doing all this paperwork and maybe missing out on thousands of dollars of deductions."

The decision whether to do your own taxes or go with a CPA lies along a spectrum from simple to complex. But time is another factor to consider. Many of us lead busy lives, and it may actually save money to hand the tax work over to someone else. No matter what, you will have to keep good records during the year and stay on top of your tax picture. Otherwise, you are asking for trouble.

These days, you can file your tax return electronically whether you figure out your tax liability on the computer or a professional does it for you. E-filing is easy and cheap for most taxpayers. Among its biggest advantages: You'll get your refund about twice as fast as paper filers will. And if you owe the government money, you can have the sum automatically debited from your bank account. You have to pay it, so why not make the process relatively painless? The IRS will contact you within 24 hours confirming that it got your return. And since your return goes right into the agency's computers, there is less chance for human error. According to the IRS, over 20% of returns prepared on paper have errors versus 1% of returns prepared electronically. Many tax preparers, software programs, and web sites will do the transaction for a small fee. Those filing the classic 1040EZ form (the very simple form) can do it for free. Don't have a computer? If you come under certain income limits, you can still file electronically over the telephone through the IRS's Tele-File system.

There are some drawbacks to e-filing, not the least of which is that most people have to pay for the privilege. Also, e-filing doesn't work for anyone with a complicated tax form, and many states lag well behind the federal government when it comes to cyberreturns.

YOUR TAX BITE

Have you heard this one?

A businessman on his deathbed called his friend and said, "Bill, I want you to promise me that when I die you will have my remains cremated."

"And what," his friend asked, "do you want me to do with your ashes?"

The businessman said, "Just put them in an envelope and mail them to the Internal Revenue Service and write on the envelope, 'Now you have everything.' "

Comedians love the IRS, accountants, and the tax system.

They're fodder for their jokes. Unfortunately, there is nothing fun about doing your taxes.

There are a lot of taxes. Many of us learn about taxes when we fill out a W-4 form at work. Our first paycheck is a startling lesson in the difference between gross income and after-tax income. Companies withhold from our paychecks federal, state, and local income taxes, as well as payroll taxes for Social Security and Medicare. Most state and local governments also levy their own taxes, from property taxes to retail sales taxes. Investors pay ordinary income taxes on dividends and interest payments and capital gains taxes on the sale of assets held for longer than a year. When someone dies, the federal government imposes an estate tax if the assets are greater than $675,000 in year 2000–01, after allowable deductions ($1.35 million for married couples). The exemption climbs to $1 million ($2 million for couples) in 2006.

You can file earlier, but you must send off your income tax return on April 15. You can file for an extension, but an extension only gives you several more months to pull together your tax forms. It doesn't allow you to hold off paying any money you owe the government. If you don't have the money on April 15, apply for an installment payment plan with the IRS. You attach a form to your return and ask if you can pay in monthly installments. The IRS generally approves the request.

The U.S. tax code is a progressive income tax system. Despite many loopholes and instances of bad tax law, it's still true that the more you make the more you'll pay in taxes. What matters is your marginal tax rate, which is the rate you pay on the last dollars you earn. For example, in 2000, a married couple filing jointly and earning $150,000 a year will pay a 15% tax on the first $43,850, a 28% tax on the next $62,000, and a 31% rate on the remaining $44,050. The married couple's marginal tax rate is 31%.

DEDUCTIONS AND CREDITS

Every year, you will gather together all your sources of income, such as wages, salary, interest, and dividends. You'll then look at the 1040 form and make some adjustments to come up with your adjusted gross income, or AGI. For instance, your contributions into a retirement savings plan, such as an Individual Retirement Account or 401(k) plan, are not considered part of your taxable income. Alimony payments and half the self-employment tax are also excluded. Taxpayers also get an automatic personal exemption that reduces taxable income. The amount you can claim for your personal exemption in 2000 was $2,800. If you're married, your spouse can claim a similar exemption, and you can claim for your kids. However, the exemption is reduced if your adjusted gross income is greater than $193,400 in 2000. Your adjusted gross income is the key figure when it comes to figuring out credits and deductions.

Now, everyone qualifies for the standard deduction, but the amount of the deduction depends on your marital status. In 2000 the standard deduction for single filers is $4,400, and for married filers filing jointly it is $7,350. Taxpayers can decide to itemize their deductions if their value is greater than the standard deduction. Some people must itemize their deductions. A deduction is an expense you subtract from your income before you calculate the tax you owe. In other words, deductions reduce your taxable income. For example, interest payments on a home mortgage are deductible. If you paid $10,000 in mortgage interest, and you were in the 36% bracket, you could reduce your actual tax by $3,600.

The major deductions are mortgage interest expense, state and local taxes, charitable contributions, medical and dental expenses, and casualty and theft losses. Interest is deductible on mortgage loans of $1 million or less, and on home equity loans of $100,000 or less. Interest on student loans is now deductible, but you can't deduct more than $2,000 in 2000. The allowable deduction will rise to $2,500 in 2001. Credit card interest, interest on auto loans, and interest on other personal loans are not deductible.

Charitable contributions are another popular deduction. You can deduct charitable contributions of up to 50% of your adjusted gross income. You can carry forward into the next tax year any contributions over the limit. Doing good is tax-savvy.

Medical expenses are also deductible, but the hurdle is steep. The rule is that you can deduct only the amount of medical costs you paid that is greater than 7.5% of your income. In other words, if your income was $60,000, you can deduct medical expenses that exceeded $4,500. State and local taxes are also deductible from your federal taxes. There is a grab bag of other deductions, ranging from job-hunting costs to the fee you pay to a tax preparer to do your returns to the home office deduction.

A tax credit is even more valuable than a deduction. Credits are subtracted directly from your tax and therefore reduce your taxes dollar for dollar. For example, if you're in the 28% tax bracket, a deduction of $1,000 saves you $280 in taxes. But a credit of $1,000 saves you $1,000 in taxes. For example, the Lifetime Learning Credit allows you to subtract education fees from your actual tax. A percentage of qualified tuition payments and fees comes right off the bottom line. The tax credit equals 20% of up to $5,000 in tuition and fees, with a maximum benefit of $1,000. The credit will increase to 20% of $10,000 after 2002. The credit phases out for joint filers with an adjusted gross income between $80,000 and $100,000 and for single filers between $40,000 and $50,000. Another credit is the $500 tax credit for dependent children. Parents adopting a child can claim a credit for qualified adoption expenses of up to $5,000 per child. The credit is a maximum of $6,000 for special needs adoptions. Qualified adoption expenses include adoption fees, court costs, and attorney's fees.

SMART TAX MOVES

You should always start doing your taxes by reviewing last year's return. You never know what mistakes you might catch, and it gets you in the right frame of mind. Here are several tax moves that work for just about anyone.

We all work hard and we're all expected to pay taxes on the fruits of that labor, but whether you work for a corporation or you work for yourself, one of the best ways to trim taxes on your income is to start a retirement plan. You'll hear terms like SEP-IRA, 401(k), 403(b), Keogh, and SIMPLE thrown around. These are all pretax retirement plans. That means the money you put into them won't be part of your taxable income. And that decreases your taxes. The Roth IRA offers a slightly different twist. You fund a Roth with after-tax dollars, but you can withdraw the money during retirement tax-free.

The American Dream is synonymous with owning your own home. A home is also a tax-favored investment. Homeowners get to deduct their mortgage and home equity loan interest payments. Homeowners also get a great deal when they sell. Gains are untaxed up to $250,000 for singles and $500,000 for married couples. For instance, let's say you buy your home for $100,000 and you sell it for $150,000—that's $50,000 in your pocket, tax-free. There are some restrictions. You must have owned and used the home as your primary residence for at least two years. But there is no lifetime limit on how much profit from your home sales you can pocket tax-free.

Investors have several savvy tax moves to explore. If you are in a high tax bracket, you should see if you come out ahead on an after-tax basis by owning municipal bonds. The interest you earn on tax-exempt bonds issued by state and local governments is free of federal taxes and often state taxes, too.

Take advantage of the capital gains tax rates. Investors get hit with two kinds of taxes, ordinary income and capital gains. Interest and dividend payments are taxed at your tax rate. You have a capital gain if you sell an asset like a stock for a profit, and if you owned that stock for more than a year, you are taxed under the long-term capital gains rules. The top capital gains tax rate is 20%, versus a top rate of 39.6% on ordinary income. The capital gains tax rate can drop to 10% if you are in the 15% bracket. What's more, you don't control when companies or banks make their interest and principal payments. But it's your choice to sell an asset and trigger capital gains. If you bought a stock for $10 a share and it has soared to $300 a share over the past three years, you haven't paid any tax on the appreciation—and won't until you sell.

Of course, markets go down as well as up, and you may show a capital loss. You can use capital losses to offset capital gains. Plus, if you have capital losses that exceed your capital gains, you can use the difference to offset ordinary income taxes up to $3,000. And if you still have unused capital losses, you can carry them over to the next year. No investor likes to lose money, but Uncle Sam does cushion the blow.

Donating to charity is a wonderful way to do good and save money. Make sure you get receipts for the value of everything you donate, from clothes to used cars to cash. Consider giving appreciated stock to your favorite charity. You get the deduction, and the nonprofit can sell the stock without triggering any tax consequences.

AVOIDING AN AUDIT

Taxpayers dread audits, and with good reason. The good news is that most people don't get audited. About 2% of all taxpayer returns get audited each year. Tax specialists note that the group at the greatest risk of an audit is self-employed businesses with more than $100,000 a year in income. For instance, in fiscal 1998, the IRS audited 1.13% of filers with incomes of $100,000 or more, but of the self-employed filers with that income, the audit rate was 2.85%. If you've been especially aggressive with deductions compared to your peer group, your return could warrant another look. Bad math and unintelligible tax returns don't automatically trigger an audit, but they highlight your return. And why would you want to do that? "I see this all the time," says Ed Slott. "The returns can't be scanned. You can't read the writing. Somebody at the IRS actually has to stop the presses—'What is that? Get this guy in here!' So sloppy returns with mistakes tend to get audited because they can't be read."

If you are self-employed, don't commingle your personal and business money. Keep a separate set of records, a separate checkbook, and a separate business expense log. The reason is that the IRS is suspicious that you might be commingling expenses and income and trying to pull a fast one. Don't go there. It's much easier to maintain a financial firewall between personal affairs and business.

I recommend you keep your actual tax returns forever. Even if you work for 60 years, that's only 60 tax returns stored in a box in a closet or basement. Ed Slott tells this story to illustrate why saving tax returns is a good idea. His father applied for Social Security when he turned 65 in 1990. He had worked all his adult life, but the Social Security Administration said he hadn't worked in 1977. Ed's father knew he hadn't taken a year off, and to prove it he showed the Social Security Administration his 1977 tax return. "You never know when you are going to need something like that," says Ed Slott. The backup information, like receipts for expenses you claim, should be kept for at least three years.

What if you have "forgotten" to file a return over the past several years, and now you want to straighten out the mess? Gather your information, hire a CPA who has worked closely with the IRS in tax disputes, and make up your returns. If the government owes you a refund, you'll get your money back, assuming you file within the three-year statute. If you owe the government money, you'll have to pay the bill plus penalties.

ORGANIZATION COUNTS

When it comes to taxes, the most important part of the process isn't knowing all about deductions, credits, and exclusions. It's having good, well-organized records. Sound record-keeping habits will make it much easier for you or a professional to do your taxes and make sure you get all the benefits Uncle Sam has sprinkled throughout the tax code. Another thing to keep in mind is that the IRS is not out to get you. Only a small fraction of taxpayers get audited each year. And hey, there are even tax perks that encourage us to do things like buying and selling homes, save for our retirement, and invest for the long haul.

So breathe easy, and do your taxes with a little less stress.

Resources

Your Tax Questions Answered: A CPA with Over Twenty Years of Experience Answers the Most Commonly Asked Tax Questions, by Ed Slott (Plymouth Press). Ed is amusing and irrepressible, and he is an encyclopedia when it comes to taxes. In addition, if you have any IRA questions, especially when it comes to estate planning, check out his web site, IRAHELP.com.

Taxes for Dummies, by Eric Tyson and David J. Silverman (IDG Books Worldwide). A clear guide to the U.S. tax code that deals with the basic issues well.

Kiplinger Cut Your Taxes, edited by Kevin McCormally (Kiplinger Books). I like this book. For example, it has a very clear discussion of retirement plan options for small businesses and independent contractors.

The Ernst & Young Tax Saver's Guide, edited by Peter W. Bernstein (John Wiley & Sons). A handy perennial. Every financial reporter I know has one of these on his or her bookshelf.

J. K. Lasser's Your Income Tax, by J. K. Lasser (MacMillan). A detailed, well-known guide to taxes.

irs.gov. For all the griping about the Internal Revenue Service, it is sometimes helpful to go right to the source. A user-friendly site.

turbotax.com; macintax.com. What kind of a computer do you use—a PC or a Mac? Both of these programs are tops. Their web sites also have a helpful tax center, tax calendar, and other information. By Quicken.

taxcut.com. The competing program from *Kiplinger's* and H. R. Block.

moneycentral.msn.com. Good information about tax law changes, and helpful articles such as "Unlucky Seven: The Top Taxpayer Mistakes and Tax Strategies That Definitely Don't Work."

About the Author

CHRIS FARRELL is host and managing editor of *Right on the Money*, the personal finance show produced by Twin Cities Public Television. He is also cohost of *Sound Money*, a weekly one-hour personal finance call-in show produced by Minnesota Public Radio and heard on public radio stations across the country. He is contributing economics editor for *Business Week* and has been associated with the magazine since 1986. He lives in Minneapolis.